"Sarthak gives you a comprehensive, step-by-step playbook on acing the startup journey. Extremely well-written and highly recommended."

Varun Alagh

Co-founder & CEO - Mamaearth| Angel Investor

"In his first book, Sarthak provides value that will last for decades. I am so happy that such a comprehensive, honest and practical guide is now available to entrepreneurs. If you intend to raise capital at any stage, miss this book at your own peril."

Ankur Warikoo

Co-founder - Nearbuy| Educator & Content Creator| Angel Investor

"Sarthak has provided a succinct and systematic explanation of what it takes to ensure your business makes financial sense and creates opportunities for serious growth. I've seen his content grow leaps and bounds, and I'm happy to see the culmination in this excellent book."

Aman Arora

Co-founder & CMO - Keventers| Angel Investor

"Every Indian dad dreams of having a son like Sarthak. He has more degrees than I knew existed. Don't let his humble bald persona fool you because he is not your typical investment banker. This guy is also an influencer who talks about his learnings from the startup world. I have personally learned several nuggets of startup wisdom from him both through his content and through live discussions for my own venture. As India is heading towards a $5 Tn economy, Indian startups will play a crucial role in determining our world dominance. Sarthak's book will be the perfect lifelong aid for everyone who aspires to dream the impossible and make it a reality."

Sharan Hegde

Personal Finance Content Creator (@financewithsharan)| Angel Investor

"An avalanche of books are available on fundraising in the context of the Silicon valley, however, none like this enables us to decode the nuances of fundraising in the Indian context. This book is indeed a first mover in the right direction. It becomes hard to resist this meticulously crafted manual on fundraising, especially in the context wherein Indians are shunning their reluctance towards entrepreneurship."

Pratham Mittal

Founder - Masters' Union| Partner - 606 Ventures

"Simple is the hardest. But, Sarthak has done it beautifully well. It's not very often you come across books that will explain complicated topics with such ease and with examples that you're familiar with. Would recommend it to all the startup enthusiasts."

Ayush Wadhwa

Founder - Owled Media| Content Creator

"Simplified, Scientific and Specific - These are 3 words that describe this book best. Sarthak has poured all his heart and wisdom into this book and created a holistic how-to guide for anyone who is serious about building a meaningful startup. Daily Coffee & Startup Fundraising cuts straight to the chase on what you need to do through the journey of building your startup."

Rajiv Talreja

Business Coach| Bestselling Author - Lead or Bleed

"Sarthak has been a great consultant and a trusted advisor. His knowledge of startups and fundraising makes him an asset to our team. He takes a 360-degree approach and looks at the opportunity from all perspectives, whether from the founders or investors. An expert in his domain, I have no doubt that this book will bring value to new entrepreneurs across India and beyond."

Ankit Gupta

Co-founder - Burma Burma

Daily Coffee & Startup Fundraising

A comprehensive guide to starting up and raising funds in India

Sarthak Ahuja

Published by Wyzr Content Pvt. Ltd.

Author's note: Data with respect to a few companies provided in the book is compiled and derived from Ministry of Corporate Affairs (MCA) filings by private enterprises and news reports. The inferences made from such limited data may be based on extrapolations and may not be accurate. Such data is meant to be read as a means to assist the reader in understanding the concepts, and not to form any financial or other opinions on any of the companies named. The examples used are of businesses that have created immense value, with founders and teams that the author and publisher have immense respect for.

ISBN: 978-81-958168-0-4 (Paperback)

Editors: Yashraj Sharma, Ankita Prakash, Amlan Chakravarty
Typeset in Adobe InDesign by Kajal Ahuja
Marketing Strategy by Aditi Randev
Cover by Syed Rizvi

Printed and bound by Gopsons Papers Private Limited., Noida
First printing edition 2022

To the Indian Entrepreneurial Spirit

Also by Sarthak Ahuja:

Founder's Office
150+ Impactful Lessons to Drive Better Business Results

Contents

Part II : Starting the Fundraising Journey

Before you start

Starting up has almost become synonymous with fundraising today. As a vociferous cheerleader of all founders, funded and bootstrapped alike, I must begin by stating that I don't consider raising funds alone as a hallmark of success. It's a means through which driven entrepreneurs can reach their goals more efficiently, but it's not the goal post itself.

While I do offer an investor's perspective on different aspects of business and fundraising, I don't prescribe fundraising as the key to building a thriving business. Great businesses are built by exceptional people, and they'll succeed with or without VC funding.

Capital can be a great catalyst to speed up and achieve things that would otherwise take much longer. But capital is often not the only catalyst. So till the time you get to it, don't lose sight of the other markers that contribute to a startup's health.

This book is in the service of all such driven entrepreneurs who are out there building, and the aspiring ones who dream to build well.

Preface

It's not easy being a founder. The odds, when you start out, are heavily stacked against you. It's said that only one in ten startups succeed, but that depends on how you define 'success'. My guess is that the actual number is much lesser. Yet, so many in our country have chosen to become entrepreneurs, and they deserve to be applauded and supported.

Having worked with over a hundred startups, I find it fair to say that no degree or background really prepares you to be one. Founders are built less by education and more by character. But what are these characteristic traits, you might ask?

Avnish Bajaj, Founder & Managing Partner, Matrix Partners India, mentioned 9 of them in a post: Curiosity, Grit, Hunger, Self Control, Zest, Social Intelligence, Optimism, Gratitude, and Hustle[1].

Further, he suggested that you could rate yourself and your co-founders on these traits as 0, 0.5, or 1, with 0 indicating low and 1 high. A score of 6 and above is considered great when you sum your scores across all 9 traits.

Is this foolproof? Certainly not. But it gives you an idea of what a successful founder is characterized by.

If I had to add one more, it would be the *ability* to learn.

All the founders I have worked with or have known closely have this innate ability and desire to learn new things and implement them fast. Some of them are naturally good at it, but most develop this trait out of a necessity to survive and thrive.

An ability to learn and implement fast also gives one the *courage* to do things that an average person would consider risky and pass. And without courage, ideas just remain ideas.

Founders and startups fascinate me in equal measure. They bring a much-needed speed and glamour to what I believe is a Chartered Accountant's otherwise mundane life. In 2017, on graduating from the Indian School of Business, I took a conscious decision to spend more time working with startup founders while letting the rest of my family continue serving our other, more traditional clients. While I still work with them and love them, you know by now where my heart truly lies.

When I started actively working with startups, helping them raise funds and set up right, I myself would need to speak with other CAs, lawyers, and Company Secretaries to understand specific issues that I hadn't encountered. I realized that there was a lot of information scattered across different professional pockets, and no one had really managed to compile them all in one place. Since I was advising startups across financial, legal, fundraising as well as business aspects, I could also comprehend the founders' challenges better than those who were probably exposed in a more limited capacity.

Further, the information gap for founders between what they think needs to be done and what actually needs to be done, on matters pertaining to fundraising, legalities, compliances, and sometimes different aspects of business, is quite large. I help bridge this gap for the startups and founders I advise individually. But I also believe that such information should not be unavailable to other founders and startup professionals, and I try to address that in a small way through my Instagram handle (@casarthakahuja). I create short video content where I try to simplify one complex (and sometimes not so complex) startup-related topic daily.

While Instagram reels are great to deliver small nuggets of information, it's not the best medium to deliver anything in depth. This is corroborated by the countless direct messages I receive seeking one simple recommendation - "Can you recommend a book on how to start up right?" While I do recommend them something based on what they need, most of those books have a heavy American context that fails to assist Indian founders meaningfully. I have not yet come across any book that addresses the information gap well enough in the Indian context. With this one, I aim to fulfill that.

The title of the book suggests it's about fundraising, and it indeed is. 2021 was, in many ways, a milestone year for the Indian startup ecosystem. VCs infused the largest amount of capital to date, and more startups turned into unicorns than in all the previous years combined. However, just as the Indian ecosystem seemed to be coming of age, the ensuing 'funding winter' of 2022 saw several startups being ground to dust and many more shedding excess baggage in the form of employees. VC funding, it turned out, didn't guarantee success. 2021, in today's context, seems more an aberration than a sign of things to come. While funding can be a positive signal, the long-term success of a startup is determined more by the tenacity and leadership of its founders, and the efficiency of its business model. So even though the title of the book suggests it's solely on fundraising, I consider it more a book about addressing problems that every Indian founder today deals with, regardless of whether they raise funds or not. My endeavour is to equip every startup founder with the right tools and guidance to make their journey easier.

If you are looking to raise funds, this book will help you understand the nuances of the process, save you from pitfalls, and make the journey efficient for you. If you're not looking to go that route or are undecided, this book will help you understand the various pros and cons of external funding.

The book is divided into three parts to clearly demarcate the topics essential to understanding business metrics in general, fundraising, and compliances and legalities.

Part 1 of the book covers business concepts relevant to startups, where the objective is to make you understand clearly the metrics one should track and how investors perceive them. For the more experienced entrepreneurs, those sections will serve as a ready reference to ensure comprehensive readiness. For the less experienced, these chapters will equip them with the appropriate business understanding necessary to start up.

Part 2 covers the fundraising process. We understand who the stakeholders are, their objectives and motivations, the pros and cons of fundraising, and the vehicles that enable the process.

Part 3 is on compliances and legalities that every startup founder, bootstrapped or funded, experienced or young, must know and understand.

In this book, I have poured in everything I have learned that I think will make a founder's job easier. If, by the end, you do find it useful, then do *share it with someone who may need it!*

Part I
Getting the House in Order (Startups 101)

1. Taking the Idea to MVP Through a GTM

All successful startups exist because they solve a problem experienced by a sufficiently large number of people. As simple as it sounds, the reality only unfolds when one starts executing. In the initial stages, aspiring founders often get one of the two wrong - the problem or the number of people experiencing it - and only discover their mistakes much later after months, and sometimes years, of anguish.

However, learning the hard way isn't the only option. Hundreds of thousands of successful businesses have been built, and some of their founders have graciously documented their learnings to make your (and my) life easier. Being prudent in the early days can save you redundant effort and set you up for a successful long haul. Doing that partly means being aware of the challenges and opportunities starting up presents. This chapter and the subsequent ones in Part I throw light on concepts employed by successful startups around the globe.

The journey of a startup always begins with an idea. But this often begs a question.

How do you find an idea?

"Sir, I want to run my own startup but I don't know how to find the idea to work on. I don't seem to find anything", complained a student at Delhi University. He was pursuing a Bachelors in Management Studies from my alma mater, Shaheed Sukhdev College of Business Studies. I was there to adjudge a B-plan competition and impart *gyaan* to youngsters who might give entrepreneurship a go at some stage in their lives. I remember telling this boy to observe the world around him and spot problems. Find things that are broken that he could possibly mend. I don't know if it helped, but I have thought and researched since about finding ideas to work on.

A startup idea, in other words, **is about offering a unique or disruptive solution to a problem experienced by a large number of people. A problem can be classified into either of the two: an unmet demand or a latent need.**

Unmet demand is one where a market already exists for the problem, but a better solution is needed. The new solution adds more convenience, is better and faster, and is easy to use among other things. Did we not hail cabs before Ola and Uber existed? We did, but the process was arduous. Uber used technology to remarkably ease the mechanism of hailing taxis.

But today, in cities like Bangalore, the driver-rider dynamics have evolved so much that, paradoxically, booking a cab itself has become a cumbersome process. People rarely get their rides accepted instantly, and it often takes at least 3-4 hits and misses to finally book. With the rising congestion and increased demand, the average commuter reliant on cabs is today placed precariously. There's clearly an unmet demand for a quick, comfortable, and reliable mode of transportation. Can you think about a solution for this? One of them, ironically, could be going back to the old ways of manually finding a ride to get into. I know enough people who wouldn't mind doing that.

A latent need, as opposed to unmet demand, is not conspicuous. People don't realize a need for a solution until they experience it, but when they do it potentially alters their behaviour for good. Everyone understands that fitness is important, but Fitbit made it measurable. A Fitbit smartwatch tracks one's daily physical activities and basic health indicators. It has simplified the process of tracking one's physical well-being to a great extent. Before it launched, no one really felt the need to own such a device to track their daily fitness metrics. Only the most ardent enthusiasts probably felt that daily activity needed tracking. But as of August 2022, Fitbit in itself has a market cap of over USD 1.8 billion[1]. Moreover, at least in India, it has almost become a status symbol to wear a Fitbit smartwatch.

Building a solution for a latent need requires deep customer insight. One way to start is to look out for emerging technologies and brainstorm possible use cases. For example, can you use blockchain for smart contracts in travel insurance? Or can you use it to make visa processing faster and more efficient? There are so many formal documentation and processes that take painfully and unpredictably long times. Can you use any of the emerging technologies to address such inefficiencies?

A startup idea can come from anywhere if your mind is constantly open. You need to break your echo chambers and have conversations with different people, more experienced and better exposed than you. Participate in insightful conversations about ongoing challenges in business and the world in general, and what requires change. Read more and build your perspective on the issues being raised. Maintain proximity to smart people with problem-solving mindsets and a futuristic outlook. Design your environment and your own approach to spot problems and develop insights, and you will surely discover plenty of ideas to work on.

Is your idea really worth it? - Idea Validation

Any start-up, as discussed before, exists because it solves a problem for a sufficiently large number of people. As an aspiring founder, when you stumble upon an idea, the right thing to do is to validate it first.

Understand if it's really a problem that needs to be solved at a large scale.

Usually, the idea emerges from a problem that the founder may have experienced themselves. They probably tried to find a solution but didn't encounter anything satisfactory. To validate if it's indeed a pressing problem, the simplest approach is to understand if there are other individuals equally troubled by it. This process is also known as *user validation*.

The objective of user validation is to understand if a hypothesized problem is actually being faced by a large number of people. And if that's the case, is the solution proposed by you practical and affordable enough for a sizeable chunk of the population?

At the smallest level, there are two ways in which you can establish some sort of user validation - by talking to prospective customers, and by offering a Minimum Viable Product (MVP) and observing its acceptance.

Let's delve a little deeper into the first method.

'Talking to prospective customers' is self-explanatory. You have a hypothesis of who experiences the problem and you talk to them to unearth insights. When talking to prospective customers, ensure that they're indeed the people you'll target. They must belong to the same demography to which you'll sell your product. Talk to as many people in this group as possible, but no fewer than 50-60 of them to establish a strong conviction internally. Make sure that they understand the problem and try to get unbiased, objective feedback on the proposed solution. If possible, get a sense of their willingness to pay for it.

Usually, if there really is a problem, it gets acknowledged unequivocally. However, a lot depends on how effectively such interviews are conducted. I've shared a few quick pointers on interviewing below:

- Use very simple, conversational language to inquire; no jargon!
- Don't feed them the solution, build up towards it
- Gauge how big a problem they think it is
- Get a sense if they'd pay for your proposed solution

- Beware of your own biases, don't shrug away an opinion because you personally don't agree with it
- Have a conversation, not an interview

If you're undertaking large-scale research, I'd recommend taking professional help in this regard if it's your first time.

Also, people seldom do what they say, especially when it involves any monetary transaction. So just talking to customers may give you some insights, but a more dependable validation can be obtained only after they use or experience the solution you build. If people are willing to accept it and pay for it, you have possibly identified a valid gap in the market.

The basic solution offered is what we also call a Minimum Viable Product or MVP, which we'll discuss later in this chapter.

But how do you discern average ideas from revolutionary ones? Kunal Shah, the founder of Cred and Freecharge, developed a simple but interesting theory around it.

The Delta-4 Principle for Market Disruption

Do you know how railway tickets were booked in the pre-IRCTC days? You may not have done this yourself, but ask your parents, and they'll tell you how they would need to physically visit a railway station and stand in long queues. Sundays would be especially painful.

How much more convenient do you think the IRCTC website made it for people? As a kid in high school, I remember my father marvelling over this phenomenal advancement. Considering the number of people who travel by train daily and the sheer inconvenience of the process, booking a railway ticket sitting at home was life-changing for millions!

If you were to rate the pre-IRCTC booking experience and the current method on a scale of 1 to 10, with 1 being extremely poor and 10 being outstanding, what scores would you give?

2 to pre-IRCTC, 9 to the current system - should I assume? If you

belong to my father's generation, it would probably be 1 and 10.

The difference between 9 and 2, i.e. 7, is what the 'delta' of the new solution is over the older one. Kunal says that for any idea to be potentially revolutionary, this delta should be 4 or higher. This is what he calls the Delta-4 framework.

We can think of more such examples which changed how we function on a daily basis.

Uber, for cab-hailing. The incumbent solution was venturing out, getting hold of a taxi driver, bargaining, and then hopping in if all parameters were met for both parties.

WhatsApp, for ease and affordability of communication. Phone calls and SMS were the incumbents when they arrived on the scene.

Google Maps, for finding directions easily. A far better and more reliable alternative to asking people for directions.

Measure your delta between the offered solution and the incumbent ones when these products arrived. Unless you're an outlier, they'll surely be over 4.

What Kunal also says is that once a new product has established itself as Delta-4, its additional value is so large that customers become completely unwilling to revert to the old solution, are more tolerant of the small inefficiencies in the product, and the product grows organically rapidly because of the positive word-of-mouth. Truecaller is a great example of a product growing fast just on the word-of-mouth, with almost zero marketing expenses initially.

If you are a founder or aspire to become one, evaluate your idea in terms of this Delta-4 theory. If you feel it doesn't satisfy it, what can you change so that it does, eventually?

I'd highly recommend you watch Kunal's talk at the Tech Sparks 2016 event by YourStory[2]. The video is available on YouTube.

What's your TG? - Understanding Customer Persona

When we think 'startup', we tend to imagine companies in their current avatar. Uber caters to anyone who wants a cab. Google's search engine is accessible to anyone with a device and an internet connection. However, startups seldom begin with a product or idea that works for everyone.

Facebook was launched as a personal networking platform specifically for the students of Harvard University. Its acceptance and craze in that one campus prompted the founders to expand to all the other Ivy League colleges. Gradually, all the universities and colleges in the USA and Mexico became its target market. And soon, anyone above the age of 13 with a valid email address could have a Facebook account.

Startups usually start off by building a product or service for a smaller, defined set of customers. They are also referred to as their target group or TG. The customer persona is basically the personification of this TG. Let's understand this in some more depth.

There are many products whose acceptance depend on the users that take to them. Often, these users can be divided into two categories. Men and women, boys and girls, job seekers and recruiters, educators and students, house owners and renters, drivers and riders, basically any aggregation platform that brings together the supply and the demand, or any social platform where a high number of users encourage more to flock to them.

For Uber to operate, they needed both the drivers and the riders to use their platform. In the beginning, there must have been a question on whom to onboard first - drivers or riders. Their initial tests suggested that riders were more willing to adopt the new solution and onboarding them in large numbers was easier than for drivers. Perhaps the drivers were still unsure of this new model. After all, their livelihoods depended on it, so it was a larger chasm to cross. Without enough drivers, a large number of riders would be left unserved and that would lead to a poor experience. Uber decided to focus their energy on onboarding drivers because that would anyway take care of the rider experience and bring in even more riders. In this case, drivers were the harder category to onboard[3].

The online dating platform Tinder observed that men swiped right to 45% of the women's profiles they encountered, while women did so for only 5% of the men[4]. I suspect these numbers would be more skewed in India since I have seen guys casually right-swiping every profile they came by. Clearly, women are the harder lot to impress here, and the overall number of matches depends on the ladies' choices. Continuously onboarding more men then wouldn't amount to much. So Tinder focused its efforts on getting more women on the platform by building in a better experience for them. More men would anyway follow if there were enough women. In fact, Bumble and Hinge used these insights to create women-led dating platforms, where they have more control over the entire process.

To build their user base efficiently, these companies designed their products to attract the harder category of users. And to make the development process even simpler, this user is clearly and precisely defined. This is how a customer persona is built.

For example, when Tinder commenced operations in India, they may have defined the customer persona as a certain Neha Singh, a 23-year-old female working in her first job, residing in Andheri East, Mumbai, single and independent, and with no major familial responsibilities or liabilities. Neha here represents a much larger target segment of young, independent, single women. All of them obviously don't possess the exact characteristics as Neha but are close enough to be clubbed in the same category. If Tinder contemplated adding a new feature, it must answer satisfactorily "How will this feature help Neha?" If it doesn't, the feature may be shelved in favour of more meaningful developments. A well-defined customer persona acts as an able guide for the product team.

> To build a customer persona for your product, identify the harder category of users if applicable. Design your product to incentivize them better.

As you grow, your product may necessitate defining multiple

customer personas. When I started writing this book, I visualized a 28-year-old male (mainly because over 90% of my Instagram followers are males, and most of them are in the 18-35 age category) who is contemplating starting up but needs answers to help him decide better. As I continued writing, it helped to define the customer persona for each of the three parts of this book. Part I was written with a 25-year-old in mind who wants to understand the basics of business and startups in general. Part II writes to the 30-year-old first-time founder contemplating raising funds and unsure of the pitfalls that surround the process. Part III was written for someone who has already started up but is unaware of the legalities and compliances that come with it.

That obviously doesn't mean the content wouldn't help anyone else interested in any aspect of starting up in general. It just helps me write with the right context.

> Interestingly, consumer motivations vary significantly in Indian and Asian markets from the Western markets. If consumer companies from the West use data from the US and apply it directly to the Indian context, they may witness unexpected results. Indians are highly status-driven and spend disproportionately on things that elevate their standing in society. Something that would baffle Westerners is that Indian families routinely spend about a quarter of their net worth on lavish weddings because that puts them on a societal pedestal. For the same reason, youngsters spend double their monthly salary to purchase an iPhone when a regular smartphone would fulfill their basic needs more than adequately. As a startup building in the Indian subcontinent or South East Asia, if you can help them look good in front of others, you could charge abnormal premiums and still don't see your user base shrink[5].

How Big is the Market? - TAM, SAM, SOM

Should you search for the river first and build a dam on it, or should you build the dam and then hope for the river to flow through? Interestingly, many founders fail because they build dams where the river is yet to arrive. And when it does, they realize a dam wasn't really needed[6].

The Ganges has 940 dams[7] and barrages built on it, and it still flows through to the Bay of Bengal, serving (and overcoming) the needs of all those obstructions. Similarly, Godavari navigates through approximately 350 large and small dams. Smaller tributaries too have these constructed on them, but they have limited ability to support or survive beyond a point.

Markets are like these rivers, and startups are like dams. Large rivers support a large number of dams adequately, while smaller ones support only a limited few. Similarly, large markets can support a large number of startups without letting any of them go thirsty. In fact, it's believed that a large market can even support average ideas and teams just on the account of the total market size. Many investors give the highest weightage to the size of the market the startup serves while evaluating it, and sometimes seemingly average executions get handsomely funded because the market size alone guarantees returns to some extent.

Once you have identified a problem at a small scale, you next need to understand the true scope of the solution - the potential of this idea. Estimating the total market of the problem and proposed solution lets you gauge that. There are essentially three terms pertaining to the market size - Total Addressable Market (TAM), Serviceable Addressable Market (SAM), and Serviceable Obtainable Market (SOM).

Total Addressable Market (TAM) is the total demand for your product in the market at the present. This ideally covers all the possible users across the world who face the problem that you are solving.

Serviceable Addressable Market (SAM) is the part of TAM that you can serve at present because it is within your serviceable limits (geographical/ demographical/ size constraints).

Serviceable Obtainable Market (SOM) is your Go-to-Market focus group. SOM refers to the exact group of customers that form your target group in the short term.

Have you ever experienced an upset stomach? I'm sure you have. I did, while working on this chapter, and found it convenient to use this episode to explain TAM, SAM, and SOM better.

When someone has a troublesome stomach, they have four remedial options - allopathic medicine, ayurvedic medicine, hot water, or doing nothing and allowing the body to heal naturally. For simplicity's sake and for my reluctance to consume them, I have kept homeopathic medicine out of this explanation.

Let's say you have developed a medicine that treats this ailment. In this case, regardless of the type of medicine, its TAM *is all the individuals experiencing an upset stomach at any given point.*

Let's assume yours is an Ayurvedic medicine. Additionally, we now know that only 30% of the TAM (again an assumption) will consider taking Ayurvedic solutions. These represent all the people who will consider taking the medicine today and can be potentially serviced by your company. The SAM then becomes 30% of the TAM.

Further, let's say you, the business owner, are based in NCR and have geographical constraints which only allow you to sell in the nearby region. The SOM, then, will be the number of people having an upset stomach in and around NCR who are open to treatment using Ayurvedic preparations.

Observe how small the SOM is relative to the TAM. It's also interesting to note that we considered 30% of the total population to be accepting of Ayurvedic treatments. If this acceptance increases over time, then the market grows commensurately with it. Founders and investors look for such trends and build or invest in markets that are poised to grow. An example today could be the acceptance of cryptocurrency among the masses. Only a tiny portion of the global population has accepted it wholeheartedly, but many investors are bullish on its growth prospects and are investing in startups in this space.

Many founders make the mistake of taking a highly simplistic approach to calculating their SAM and SOM. They estimate a TAM and simply assume they will acquire a certain percentage of it. "How hard is it to get just 1% of the total market after all?" This is a highly flawed approach.

For the exercise to be meaningful, all the numbers must have a clear rationale behind them. The assumptions must be thought through, and if applicable, suitable industry benchmarks must be considered. It works both ways - extrapolating from the current customer persona and estimating SOM first, followed by SAM and TAM, or taking the approach we took for estimating the market size for Ayurvedic stomach bug pills.

The objective of knowing the market size for a founder is to understand the true potential of the business, and if it makes sense for them to pursue it. Startups often fail after months and years of effort when founders realize that they had grossly overestimated the market's potential. A hallmark of such failures is large-scale hiring in early stages, all based on faulty market size assumptions, followed by mass lay-offs. The ones who suffer the most - the fired employees - are often the least at fault.

Launch Strategy - Go-To-Market (GTM)

The go-to-market (GTM) is often incorrectly perceived as the tactics which help you get the first set of users. The GTM itself essentially refers mainly to the M - Market, that you'd target first. The first set of customers that you'd look to acquire. Once you have done the idea validation, you'll have a hypothesis about which customers will form your very initial target segment. The low-hanging fruits. If you're diligent, you'll also build a customer persona.

The go-to-market strategy or the launch strategy is the 'how' of acquiring these users, which is the next logical step after identifying the go-to-market. The GTM strategy aims to target these customers in a manner that maximizes their chances of buying the product. It's mainly about identifying the most frugal way to reach them, help them discover your product, and hopefully get them to buy.

As an example, if you have created a packaged fresh juice brand, your go-to-market could be a certain locality having about a thousand residents, and the GTM strategy could be making the brand available in the local stores those residents frequent.

If it's a SaaS product like, say, Grammarly, then a plausible GTM could be professionals in a specific domain, and the GTM strategy could revolve around making the product discoverable on either social media or through Google Ads.

If you've started a legal firm specializing in consumer complaints, your GTM will be all the disgruntled consumers in your city, and the GTM strategy to garner more clients could be a promotion of your website through Google Ads. With smart SEO, you could target anyone in your city looking for answers on consumer forums.

In larger, more mature companies, there are teams dedicated to just identifying the right GTM and developing a detailed strategy to make a new launch successful. For early-stage startups, however, one need not have such elaborate plans. But a simple, scaled-down version clearly identifying the target segment, the discovery process, and the mode and motivation for purchase should still be established.

For starters, you can use this simple **3Cs checklist** to assess your right go-to-market and how to target them. For each of these, opt for the most cost-effective way to execute.

1. **Channel**: Identify the channel which will lead to maximum discovery among your initial target group. It can be either online (Google Ads, social media, or even closed WhatsApp groups) or offline (local Kirana stores, restaurants, malls, etc.).
2. **Content:** What content, when put out, will trigger or interest your target group into considering your product for purchase? When you put your product at the right channels, your customers should be fed the right information which maximizes their chance of trying it out.
3. **Consistency:** It's often said: Out of sight, out of mind. You

need to interact with your users with high frequency repeatedly. Make iterations and modifications to expand your data set and validate whether your initial set of inferences holds true with a bigger data set. This will help you generate meaningful feedback from early customers and refine your strategy as you grow.

Building the MVP - Minimum Viable Product

We touched upon the concept of Minimum Viable Product (MVP) earlier in the chapter to highlight its significance in idea validation. Its role, especially in very early-stage startups, doesn't stop there.

The correct MVP is essential to give any founder true, meaningful feedback on their pursuit. MVP helps in early validation of the demand, the business model, and the target segment among other things, and arms you with insights on building the right features in your product. It helps you course-correct early and saves the founding team unnecessary heartache. 'The Lean Startup' by Eric Ries is an excellent, comprehensive guide on building and using MVPs the right way.

Speed and frugality are the two critical characteristics of all good MVPs. If it's taking either a lot of time or money, then you're not building an MVP. As an example, if you're looking to build an app like Goodreads, the MVP is probably a WhatsApp group of book lovers where each member reviews a book of their choice regularly. For Ola, it was probably a single phone number operated by one of the founders where reservations were communicated to driver partners through phone calls. In fact, around 2015, phone calls were the only way to book Ola Cabs and the app was launched several months after its existence in this form.

If you notice, the MVP is not the product that can scale, and it's not supposed to. Its objective is to validate whether a simplified solution indeed has any takers at the smallest scale. If it does, it bodes well for the founders and they can build further based on the feedback from these early users. But if it doesn't give desired results, the founders need to objectively analyze if it's due to the wrong problem identification or due to devising an ineffective solution to the problem.

If the customers show no interest in the solution whatsoever, chances are that they don't face this problem. At this stage, the founder should test a different customer segment and see if there's a better response. If all such identified customer segments give cold responses, then the issue is with the problem itself. It's likely that the hypothesis was overstated, so the founders must return to the drawing board and assess if there really is anything to be solved.

On the other hand, if the problem has been validated but the product has failed to gain the desired traction, it's possible that the solution being offered is unsuitable to the customer for one of several reasons - cost, quality, convenience, friction, time, or something else known best to the customer. Understand the exact reasons for the low acceptance, and make changes to the offered solution on the exact pain points.

Investing some time in building and validating an MVP is always worthwhile. In the absence of one, the founders might end up creating a solution or a product which only aligns with their hypothesized specifications. If it does not provide tangible results to the target group, it eventually leads to painful, large-scale changes at an advanced stage, or even shutting down of the business.

Tally, the accounting software, in its early days used an MVP and derived insights that basically changed the landscape of its industry.

In an interview[8], the co-founder of Tally, Bharat Goenka once revealed that he had shared the MVP of the software with the accountant working at his father's factory. His father, Shyam Sunder Goenka, is also a co-founder of Tally.

When the accountant used the software, he added the date in the format DD/MM/YY. Bharat wanted him to use DD-MM-YY, a dash instead of a slash because that's how the software processed dates. But his father made a wise interjection: how will he ask every single user of the software to follow that format?

Bharat then collected all possible date formats that accountants use and integrated them into Tally. The software eventually became format-proof when it came to adding dates. More than just the dates, the mindset of testing a smaller version before building for the masses perhaps helped Tally become a market leader in this space. In spite of many other players arriving on the scene, it has continued to maintain its stronghold in the industry. It may not be the best-looking software, but it certainly strikes the correct chords with accountants. And sells.

2. Product Market Fit (PMF)

Once an MVP is ready, the founders can use it to take quick and consistent feedback and refine their products further. These incremental developments are aimed to make the product more attractive and useful for the target audience. When things go as per plan, a point comes when your customers become ardent users and start spreading positive word about it. But getting to this stage often takes a lot of effort, and several hits and misses. In fact, most startups that start out never reach this enigma called Product-Market Fit (PMF).

What is Product-Market Fit?

'Product-Market Fit' is one of the most commonly thrown around startup jargon globally. What does it even mean?

Founders across the world have different perceptions of it which are often incorrect. One founder, while explaining his product to me, claimed that they had achieved PMF and the time was ripe to raise funds. When I inquired about their number of users, it was less than 100 and hadn't grown significantly in the last couple of months. Moreover, none of them were paid customers. When I asked about his basis for considering it PMF, it was the positive feedback of users already onboarded. While good feedback is encouraging, I'm afraid it can't simply be considered PMF, especially when the number of users is so low.

Marc Andreesen, co-founder and General Partner of Andreesen Horowitz and one of the pioneers of PMF as a concept, says this about Product-Market Fit[1]:

> *"Product/market fit means being in a good market with a product that can satisfy that market."*

A good market, as we saw in the previous chapter, usually is one that's large and growing fast. A product that satisfies this market must be able to capture a large number of users fairly easily to achieve PMF. About the state of being in PMF, Marc says[2]:

> *"The customers are buying the product just as fast as you can make it -- or usage is growing just as fast as you can add more servers. Money from customers is piling up in your company checking account. You're hiring sales and customer support staff as fast as you can."*

As evident, Product-Market Fit is achieved when you have built a product that a lot of people want and are willing to pay for, if applicable. You are not struggling to gain users, your marketing spends are nominal, and your customers love the product so much that they spread a good word about it and get more for you. Going purely by business metrics, some of the indicators are high user growth rate, low customer acquisition cost (CAC), high virality coefficient, and low churn, all of which we'll discuss in detail in the next two chapters.

How do you measure PMF?

Before we get into measuring PMF, let me narrate an idea and take your opinion about its prospects. Sometime in March 2022, Prachi, an old friend, requested my feedback on it.

Prachi's younger brother often complained that he wasn't allowed to pursue his dreams. He was made to study foreign trade because the family had an import-export business and their father wanted him to carry forward the legacy. You too probably know people who took up a course or a vocation due to parents' preference. Prachi, being witness to it, too realized that there are thousands of kids who follow career paths not necessarily of their own choice.

But following one's own choice first requires clarity on their interest. Even if parents were supportive, which many are today, finding one's calling as a kid is not that straightforward. So how can that come about?

Prachi came up with an aggregator model where career counsellors would help children find their interests based on different assessments. They would then be enrolled in exploratory courses before deciding to commit to the field. These courses, however, could only be availed at a fee. The assessments, though, won't require any payment.

Do you think her product will achieve Product-Market Fit?

The problem that she is trying to solve is real. There is a large enough market. She has designed an MVP to test with early users, and there are signs that people are willing to try it out.

However, the question remains if they will be willing to pay for her product. If a child takes the assessments, gets some idea about her interests, but skips enrolling in a course, they wouldn't end up having a sufficient number of paid users. Moreover, the counsellors won't continue sparing time for kids for free. They would either need to be compensated directly through the consultations or by the company. Without enough paying customers, the startup won't survive for long, and obviously won't achieve PMF.

Does that mean it will never achieve PMF? No.

The purpose of MVP, as we discussed in the last chapter, is to build fast, get feedback fast, and iterate the product until it gets to a point that many people start paying for it. *Fast* is the crucial term here, and when you're small, you have the flexibility to communicate directly with the customers and understand quickly what they really want. Prachi must use the MVP to find quick answers, iterate, pivot to a different model, and help the product achieve PMF.

Product-Market Fit itself is not a stand-alone phenomenon or a single metric taking a certain value. But there are indicators that signify a product's proximity to it. While there are several frameworks proposed by experts around the world, I've presented two of my favourites here.

The 40% Test

This was popularized by growth hacking expert and author of *Hacking Growth*, Sean Ellis.

Ask your users: How would you feel if you could no longer use the product?

They have to choose one among:

- Very disappointed
- Somewhat disappointed
- Not disappointed
- I no longer use this product

If more than 40% of your users choose *Very disappointed*, you are on the right track. It, in a way, establishes that your product is a must-have for a considerably large section of your users.

As the founder, you should further profile who these customers really are, who claim would be extremely disappointed if the product did not exist. That is your ideal target audience, and the start-up should look to find more such people to offer the product and improve their chances of success.

Broadly, if 40% of your users will be very disappointed if your product were to vanish tomorrow, it's a strong indicator of being close to PMF. However, note that it may not necessarily apply to a consumer product that has very few users. It would still be an encouraging sign, but for it to be considered an indicator of PMF, there must be at least a few hundred users if not a few thousand.

Net Promoter Score

Net Promoter Score indicates customer satisfaction and measures how many of your users are also your promoters. That is, people who spread positive word-of-mouth about your product and help garner more users in the process.

Consider a customer survey question that asks: How likcly are you to recommend our product or service to someone you know? Score on a scale from 0 to 10 - 0 means not at all, and 10 means most definitely.

Customers with their scores are classified as follows:

0 to 6: Detractors

7 to 8: Neutrals

9 to 10: Promoters

NPS = % of Promoters - % of Detractors

Say, on a customer survey of 100 people, 30 were detractors, 20 were neutrals and 50 were promoters.

NPS = 50 - 30 = 20

A score of 30 or above is considered great. It shows that there are a significantly more people willing to promote your product than those who'd discourage others from using it. This is also an indicator that Product-Market Fit has either been achieved or is close.

The next two images have been taken from Andrew Chen's blog[3].

what P/M fit looks like

Consumer products:
Usage 3 out of every 7 days
Organic growth of 100s of signups/day
30% users are active the day after signup
Clear path to 100,000 users

what P/M fit looks like

SaaS products:
5% conversion rate from free-to-paid
3X CPA to LTV ratio
<2% monthly churn rate
Clear path to $100k MRR

Source: Andrew Chen's article titled "Zero to Product/Market Fit"

During fundraising, one of the factors investors consider is the closeness of the product to achieving PMF. One that has recently achieved PMF tends to be a hot property for investors. As we have understood so far, every product after achieving PMF is poised to scale rapidly and generate superlative returns. It also coincides with the rise in valuation of the startup. The investors who fund them at this stage stand to benefit from this growth. We'll understand valuation in detail in Chapter 8.

8 Types of Business Models - Which one are you?

To achieve PMF, it's imperative that founders track the right metrics and don't consider false positives as a sign of success. Similar to Andrew Chen's suggestions of PMF indicators for consumer and SaaS products, YCombinator presented 8 different business models and the key metrics that should be tracked for each of them. They are presented in the table on the next page. Identify your business model, and check if you're measuring the right ones[4].

Business Models	Description	Metrics
Enterprise	An enterprise company sells services or software to other businesses on a single-license basis. These contracts have fixed terms, designated contract values, and come up for renewal at the end of the term. Eg., Zoho, Freshdesk	a. Bookings b. Total customers c. Revenue
SaaS (software-as-a-service)	A SaaS (software-as-a-service) compny sells subscription-based licenses for a cloud-hosted software solution. Eg., Mailchimp, WebEngage, Whatfix	a. MRR (Monthly Recurring Revenue) b. ARR (Annual Recurring Revenue) c. Gross MRR Churn d. Paid CAC
Subscription	A subscription company sells a product or service, usually to a consumer, on a recurring basis. Eg., News apps, Netflix, Spotify	a. MRR (Monthly Recurring Revenue) b. MRR CMGR (Compound Monthly Growth Rate) c. Gross User Churn d. Paid CAC

Business Models	Description	Metrics
Transactional	A transactional company enables a financial transaction on behalf of a customer and collects a fee (usually a percent of the underlying transaction). Eg., Razorpay, UPI apps	a. Gross Transaction Value b. Net Revenue c. User Retention d. Paid CAC
Marketplace	A marketplace acts as an intermediary in the sale of a good or service between sellers and buyers, generally collecting a percent of the total transaction value. Eg., Amazon, Myntra, AirBnB	a. GMV (Gross Merchandise Value) b. Net Revenue c. Net Revenue CMGR (Compound Monthly Growth Rate) d. User retention e. Paid CAC
Ecommerce	An e-commerce company sells physical goods online. Generally, e-commerce companies manufacture and inventory those goods. Eg., Lenskart, Nykaa	a. Monthly Revenue b. Revenue CMGR (Compound Monthly Growth Rate) c. Gross Margin d. Paid CAC
Advertising	An advertising company offers a free service to consumers and derives revenue entirely, or predominantly, from advertisers. Common advertising companies include social networks and content sites. Eg., Instagram, Twitter	a. Daily Active Users (DAU) b. Monthly Active Users (MAU) c. Percent Logged In
Hardware	A hardware company sells physical devices to consumers or businesses. Eg., Fitbit, HP, Samsung	a. Monthly Revenue b. Revenue CMGR (Compound Monthly Growth Rate) c. Gross Margin d. Paid CAC

What is Product-Market-Founder-Fit?

Achieving PMF for a product may take a few months, or probably around a year. If the startup is building something useful in a market that's big, then following the right processes will eventually lead to PMF. But for a product to sustain beyond the PMF, or even to be driven towards it, it needs a founder or a set of founders who are determined to make it work.

The Product-Market-Founder-Fit (PMFF) is about how suitable the startup founder is to lead the growth and evolution of their product. It considers both the internal drive and the ability of the person to manage this particular product. While PMF indicates the potential of a startup to do well, PMFF signifies a higher probability of long-term success. It often comes down to the motivation of the founder to continue building right, much beyond PMF, fundraising, and all the vanity events they encounter in the journey. In my experience, the following three things are great signals of PMFF.

1. **Personal experience with a problem:** When a founder solves a problem that he or she had personally experienced, they understand the pain that comes with it and what customers really want. In many cases, the experience is also connected emotionally which lends them a drive much stronger than a simple desire to see the business grow. FirstCry, the online retailer for baby and kids products, was founded in 2010 by Supam Maheshwari. The startup intended to make the best baby products and baby care brands easily accessible to Indian parents. Back then, the options for buying such products online were limited. Supam would buy toys and other products for his son from the countries he visited for business trips. He realized the gap and the need for making similar products accessible in India. He plugged it by building an online platform that gave Indian parents access to the best baby care brands from across the globe[5]. Like Supam, there are many other founders who started with a strong customer perspective based on personal experience with the problem and have built thriving businesses.
2. **Industry Understanding:** When you work in an industry for a long time, you gain enough insight and experience of how businesses run. That's what Ashok Soota put to use when he

started MindTree in 1999. He had served as the President of Wipro Infotech for 15 years prior to this and was already a stalwart of the IT sector when he ventured out[6]. MindTree clocked $1.4 billion in revenue in FY '22, and Ashok Soota, at 79 as of August 2022, continues his entrepreneurial journey with his third startup Happiest Health[7]. His second is Happiest Minds Technologies Ltd., another successful venture in the IT domain. Having deep expertise in a field arms you with insights few others possess. When you venture out on your own with that amount of knowledge and experience, few situations would feel alien to you. Expertise often leads to success, and nothing motivates better than success.

3. **Intrinsic motivation:** Some founders are just inherently motivated to build a startup. They have probably grown up dreaming about it, are unafraid of risks, and always willing to sacrifice more for the sake of their venture. Such founders are highly resilient because they probably understand what it would take to succeed, and go the extra mile. When such resilience and tenacity combines with an astute mind, it usually results in a founder capable of solving any problem.

PMFF is not a popularized term yet. Founder-Market Fit (FMF) is more widely known which essentially refers to point 2 here. However, I feel PMFF is a broader, more encapsulating concept to predict long-term success than Founder-Market Fit alone. It considers not just the ability of the founder to operate in a particular market, but also their capacity to drive the product to PMF and beyond.

3. Getting Your First Users/ Customers

If your idea and hypothesis are valid, your MVP itself will get you your first few users. However, building upon this can be tricky as you search for the most cost-effective avenues to grow and be viable even at relatively small scales. If you operate in a crowded domain, the effort needed to gain the attention of your target audience will be higher and you'd constantly need to break through the barriers. Often, such efforts lead to indiscriminate spending which early-stage startups can ill-afford. In this chapter, we'll go through the concepts to know and the metrics to track while you try to gain a foothold in the market.

Type of marketing spends

Most founders, especially first-timers, evaluate the marketing spend of the start-up incorrectly. If your periodical financial statement has just one head for marketing or ad spend, you're only measuring the bare minimum.

Marketing spend can be potentially divided into 4 heads for better clarity and decision-making:

1. **Ad Spend on Customer Acquisition**: Money spent with the goal of getting new customer registrations/downloads. These customers may not be paying anything to you yet, but by signing up for your product, they become directly accessible and easy to target. This spend is used to calculate the Customer Acquisition Cost (CAC), which is explained in the next section.
2. **Ad Spend on Performance Marketing:** Money spent on ads with the goal of getting more sale orders or paid subscriptions. This spend is used to calculate the Return on Ad Spend (ROAS), which has been explained later in the chapter.
3. **Ad Spend on Branding:** Ads you run where there is no clear call to action, such as on billboards, magazines or different mobile apps. You do it purely for visibility with the right target audience and building awareness.
4. **Marketing Overheads:** Salaries paid to the manpower employed in marketing to run the function.

These demarcations are not set in stone and may vary from business to business. In some cases, boundaries will be ambiguous or no detailed data may be available to make this classification. Wherever possible though, it's advisable to further segregate your marketing spends.

Let's understand the different ad spends in more detail.

Customer Acquisition Costs (CAC)

Customer Acquisition Cost, or CAC, is the money spent to get a customer to register and/or download your app and start using it. A crude way of calculating the CAC is to take the total marketing spend of the company and divide it by the number of users onboarded in a given period.

CAC = Total marketing spend/No. of new users acquired

If a start-up spends INR 1 lakh on marketing and manages to get 1000 users to register on its app, the CAC of the start-up is Rs. 100 (1,00,000/1,000).

However, this doesn't consider some specific scenarios. Let's dive deeper.

Discounts under CAC?

Founders and marketers often wonder if discounts should be included under customer acquisition costs. Although there's no established rule, if the discount offered results in a loss in that particular transaction, the loss value is considered under CAC.

As an example, think of a fictitious international brand called Bringles which makes potato chips. The brand has just entered India and competes with the likes of Lays, Bingo, etc.

A packet of Bringles is priced at Rs. 100, and it costs Rs. 60 for the company to make one such packet.

But the company decides to offer a 50% discount to drive sales. This brings down the price to Rs. 50, thereby causing the company a loss of Rs. 10 on every packet of Bringles sold.

Since the company spends Rs. 10 from its pocket to acquire Indian customers, it should be considered a Customer Acquisition Cost.

Had the company given a discount of 30% instead, the price would be Rs. 70 but it would have still earned a positive contribution margin (or profit) of Rs. 10 per unit. In this scenario, since there was no loss incurred in the transaction, the discount would be considered a simple pricing decision and not count towards CAC.

The idea, again, is subject to independent interpretation. Some clothing store brands perennially keep a few sections on sale. Similarly, some restaurants always offer a discount on food delivery apps. Many products on Amazon or Flipkart offer discounts all the time.

Their objective is usually to make the offer look attractive and trigger a purchase. Where discounts are a norm rather than an exception, they usually don't count as CAC.

Cashbacks under CAC?

Cashbacks are a popular way to attract new users. Companies understand that the average Indian consumer loves freebies. Payment apps like PayTM and Google Pay, e-commerce stores like Amazon, food delivery apps like Zomato and Swiggy, and even D2C platforms offer cashback in different forms.

From a purely business perspective, a cashback is similar to a discount. But they too are subject to interpretation and depend on their source.

Google Pay, in its early days, gave a cashback for every referral made. While the individual cashback for each of those referrals would almost always result in a loss for Google on that transaction, over the long term, if the newly acquired users became active, they would easily compensate for that initial loss. Should Google count that cashback as a CAC? Ideally, yes. Because that investment was made to acquire more users.

Later, Google Pay reduced the cashback amounts for referrals significantly after a large number had onboarded. They then limited their cashback to only a few individual transactions. Consider that the company takes 2% as commission from the merchants using its platform. If a customer makes 10 transactions cumulatively worth Rs. 2000, the company earns a total of Rs. 40.

Let's say after the 10th transaction, the customer is given a cashback of Rs. 10. So the net revenue that this customer has generated for Google Pay in these ten transactions is Rs. 30. Should the Rs. 10 cashback then account as a CAC? In my view, no. Because the company hasn't spent anything from its pocket for that. And also because it's an already active user and no 'acquisition' has happened.

However, these are again subject to interpretation and the company may account for it differently. As long as it's backed by sound logic, it's not a problem.

Blended CAC

Everything covered so far considered the Customer Acquisition Cost as a single entity. You can move a step down the ladder and calculate the CAC for each of the different marketing channels of the product, say Facebook, Instagram, Google Ads, influencer marketing, etc.

Suppose that a product company has a total ad budget of Rs. 5 lakh per month. It spends 2 lakhs on Facebook, 2 lakhs on Instagram, and the remaining 1 lakh on Google Ads.

On Facebook, let's say 10 lakh users saw the ad. 10% of those users (1 lakh users) clicked on the ad. A further 20% or 20,000 users checked out the product and registered on it. With an ad spend of Rs. 2 lakh, the product acquired 20,000 new users.

So CAC on Facebook = 2,00,000/20,000 = Rs. 10

Similarly, you can calculate the CAC for Instagram and Google Ads.

The combination of these individual Customer Acquisition Costs from across channels is called the **Blended CAC**.

Blended CAC = Total spend on user acquisition across channels / Total users acquired from all channels

The Blended CAC gives the overall efficacy of your customer acquisition efforts, while the metrics for individual channels elucidate which platforms work well and which don't.

Paid-to-Organic Ratio

We understand now that the Customer Acquisition Cost (CAC) is based on the amount spent on different marketing channels to acquire customers. However, there will also be users who will onboard organically, without additional spending by the company. And that's who you want more of.

Ideally, a business should have a paid-to-organic user ratio of no less than 1:1. This means every paid acquired user gets one more to onboard through word-of-mouth referral and helps cut your CAC in half. If the paid-to-organic ratio is even better, say 1:2, then it means each paid acquisition is getting two more to use the product. The more they get, the lower the CAC for you.

While starting out, these metrics on customer acquisition should be enough to keep you in good stead. Knowing these will give you a good top-level view of your marketing operations. A well-versed marketing professional can help you operationalize them properly.

Customer Carrying Cost (CCC)

This is one type of marketing spend very few talk about. While CAC accounts for the ad spend on acquiring a customer, there may be further costs incurred by a company to retain that customer over the duration they are associated with the brand.

This becomes especially critical when there are multiple players offering exactly the same thing. Take the case of all the grocery delivery platforms today - Big Basket, BlinkIt, Zepto, Swiggy Instamart, Amazon Fresh, and Dunzo Daily. Most of these companies initially offer freebies in the form of cashback and discounts to lure new customers. Even though a customer may get acquired for once, if they find a better deal elsewhere, they'd not hesitate to switch.

To ensure that a customer continues to be active on their platform, these startups have to then continue incentivizing them in some form, and that usually means spending additional money on marketing. The Customer Carrying Cost (CCC) is the advertising spend made by the company to retain an existing customer.

Performance Marketing & CAC

The objective of ad spend on customer acquisition is to acquire a customer, but not necessarily a paid one. Performance Marketing, though, is about selling your product or acquiring paid users. The metric which measures this "performance" is called the Return on Ad Spend or ROAS.

ROAS represents the return obtained per every rupee spent on ads. Usually, ROAS is calculated by dividing the revenue generated from marketing by the total ad spend.

Let's consider the example of our fictitious Bringles again. Assume that the company spends Rs. 1 lakh to sell 3000 packets of Rs. 100 each.

The revenue generated is Rs. 3 lakhs, and the ROAS you'd calculate here is 3 (3 lakhs divided 1 lakh). Note that we have considered the revenue and not profits.

However, by considering revenue or sales in the numerator, you consider the cost of the product as a part of the 'return' or profit, which isn't correct. The ratio of the Contribution Margin (or the profit component) to the Ad Spends, rather, is a better way to calculate ROAS since the Contribution Margin only considers the returns and discounts the costs incurred by the company.

ROAS = Total Contribution Margin/Total Ad Spend

In our Bringles example, the Contribution Margin on each packet was Rs. 40. So the Total Contribution Margin on the sale of 3000 packets comes out as Rs. 1,20,000, and with an ad spend of Rs. 1 lakh the ROAS becomes 1.2.

D2C brands often put performance marketing to use to drive sales. There are websites where you do not need to sign up to make a purchase. You can directly add the items to your cart, make the payment, and get the product delivered. There's no customer acquisition for getting an app download, but there is still a sale.

There are even small-scale businesses that run ads on Instagram and take orders on DMs. Delivery details are shared over a chat and payment is made electronically.

Running ads for your product on Amazon can potentially generate great returns on performance marketing. The chances of sales are higher because users are anyway browsing Amazon to shop. When they search for a certain category and see your product promoted on top, there's a good chance that it triggers a purchase. The sale made and the associated ad spend is taken into account for calculating ROAS then.

It has been noted that ROAS is high initially - early adopters buy without much spend - but later starts to plateau and may eventually reduce. One should ensure that the ROAS in no case goes under 1:1, as that implies a loss on your spending. If it gets close to 1.5, it may be time to start making new ads with new visuals, new narratives, and trying creative ways to increase conversions. Barring exceptions, when an ad runs for too long, they tend to lose the novelty factor and stop delivering desired results.

Branding and its impact on CAC

We have been talking about Bringles, so let's continue with that example.

Assume that Bringles has grown in India and is now launching new flavors to complement the flagship product. The company puts up a large hoarding on a busy Delhi road announcing the new offerings. There's no accurate way to know how many people exactly purchase those flavours after seeing the ad. The objective here is not to make a quick sale but to generate awareness about the product and increase its *recall value*.

So even if customers do not buy immediately, the hoarding has ensured that Bringles occupies some space in their mind and when they do buy potato chips next, chances of that being Bringles would be higher.

If you use the CricBuzz app to follow cricket news, you're likely to come across several pop-up ads which you'd never click. Last I checked, I saw one of Bet365, Century Real Estate, and a little-known brand presumably selling women's apparels. No one really opens CricBuzz and proceeds to purchase a promoted product. The purpose behind these ads, again, is generating awareness. Such companies may have the insight that a large number of these cricket lovers comprise their target audience. These ads seek to get into their minds and increase the chances of a future purchase.

Measuring brand marketing

> *"Half my advertising spend is wasted; the trouble is, I don't know which half." - John Wanamaker*

The quote above holds true in many cases, especially if most of the advertising spend is on branding activities.

Some even feel brand advertising is useless as the real impact cannot be measured. But by doing brand marketing well, the conversion of performance marketing improves. Performance marketing is where you drive sales, and branding helps create the recall value that feeds into the purchase decision.

Brand marketing expense should ideally be evaluated in terms of this impact. If conversions in the 'site visit -> add to cart -> purchase' journey have improved for your product after incurring branding expenses, it's a sign that it's working. Quantifying this improvement would help you measure its efficacy accurately.

Targeting Ads Optimally

We have so far discussed how to measure the relevant advertising metrics right. Let's now understand how to target your advertisements to maximize their performance.

There are broadly three aspects to targeting your ads:

i) Target Audience

Who you're targeting your ad to should be very clear. Your past customer data would reveal clearly their demographic break-up, and who among them is likely to buy more.

Some common parameters to identify the right demography are age, gender, residence, income level, educational qualification, occupation, etc.

Further, you can develop the persona of your target customer by considering other more subjective aspects of their personality. These may include their hobbies and interests, favourite cuisines, favourite travel destinations, books they read, music they like, movies they watch, etc.

You may not be 100% accurate with the subjective traits, but they will still come in handy when making finer targeting decisions. So when deciding your target audience, be clear about the demography and the persona.

ii) Channel

On what channels do you run your ads? If your target customer is a gentleman in his 50s, running ads on Instagram will give you terrible returns.

Channel selection follows naturally from target audience identification. Once you know clearly who your target is, you can broadly figure out where they spend maximum time offline and online.

For offline, some places or activities they may spend a considerable portion of their time can be TV, shopping, office, commute, park, books, newspapers, etc.

Once you narrow down to one or two such places, again dig deeper into that activity to find insights. For example, if your customer spends most of their time watching TV, which channels do they spend the most time on? What hours of the day do they watch TV? This will help you identify precisely the time and place to run your ads for maximum returns.

For online, similarly, you can do a first broad selection by considering social media platforms, other websites, mobile apps, OTTs, and YouTube.

If you know that your customer spends maximum time on Instagram, then knowing their interests and who they follow will help you identify the best channel within Instagram. For example, if your customer watches a lot of comic skits, it may be a good idea to use a popular Instagram comedian for influencer marketing.

For channel selection, the key is to consider all possible places where your customer spends time, and then narrow down further to the most optimum channel.

iii) Filters

While setting up ad targeting on Facebook or Instagram, you can set the right 'filters' so that the platform targets those ads correctly. These filters can be set for demographic targeting, like location and gender, and also for specific interests by setting the right keyword filters. For example, if your customer is an avid reader, 'books' can be a keyword.

While this seems straightforward, some creativity here can potentially generate phenomenal returns. A D2C Indian t-shirt brand, March Tee, showed us how[1].

March Tee sells t-shirts in just 3 plain solid colours with no logo at all. Yet, it has become a 10 Crore per annum business, doubling its sales year on year, while being bootstrapped. How?

It's because they've positioned their brand such that they don't even use filters such as "tshirt" or "fashion" as keywords while doing Facebook customer targeting. Instead, words like "outdoor travel" or "foreign films" does it for them.

Their lowest-priced T-shirt sells for Rs 1200 and they have a repeat purchase rate of over 50% with less than 5% returns, which is unheard of in the online fashion retail space. Their conversion rate is 10%+ on their website, which is much above the industry average of 1-2%. Their repeat rate is an astounding 70% and 30% of their customers own more than eight March Tees.

Make it Viral - Viral Coefficient

It must be clear by now that at a very fundamental level, you want your product to be used by the maximum number of people by making minimum spends on marketing activities. One way this manifests is when your existing customers help get new customers aggressively.

Viral coefficient helps quantify the extent to which this may be happening.

Businesses often run referral campaigns to effect a high virality of the product and achieve a high viral coefficient.

Have you used the CultFit app? If a friend signs up to its app using your referral code, you get a service of 15 days free of cost. Since it's run digitally, you get data on the number of users who view your campaign, the users who refer, and even the ones who refer without the campaign's push.

You can then calculate how many users referred your product, and how many of those referrals signed up. A simplistic formula for the viral coefficient is then given as:

*Viral coefficient = Number of users * % of users who have referred * % conversion*

The calculation of viral coefficient varies by business and product type, and it mostly pertains to B2C companies.

There's one company that uses referrals very smartly.

Tally, as we discussed earlier in Chapter 1, is an accounting software product. The company figured that Chartered Accountants held tremendous influence over their sales. If the CA recommends Tally, the client usually buys it. So the company shares referral codes with CAs and keeps track of how many new customers they bring in. Despite being a B2B product, they created a B2B2B distribution network and their presence today is unmatched in the Indian market.

While I'm no expert on anything pertaining to marketing or virality, I can recommend an excellent, insightful book that has helped me immensely in my content creation journey: *Contagious - How to build word of mouth in the digital age*, authored by Jonah Berger. He has admirably explained the different psychological elements that lead to virality and are applicable to any type of product or content. A must-read if you want to make anything go viral.

Burn Rate and Burn Multiple

Burn Rate is the measure of net cash a company lost in a period, usually a month. If a company is said to have a Burn Rate of Rs. 5 lakh, it means it's losing this amount every month on average.

Burn Rate is calculated as net expenses incurred by the company in a month (or any defined period) after accounting for the cash flow.

Burn = Expenses - Cash inflow

When the above is normalized for a month or any other defined period, it is referred to as the Burn Rate.

Burn Multiple is a ratio of the revenue earned and the amount of money burned to earn that revenue.

If a start-up burns Rs. 5 lakhs per month and earns a revenue of Rs. 1 lakh, then its burn multiple is 5.

The Burn Multiple is an indicator of how much money a start-up is burning to generate one unit of sales.

The ratio indicates capital efficiency (or inefficiency, for many startups), and the number must decrease as the startup matures. A founder should evaluate their Burn Multiple relative to that of their competitors. For the ones looking for investors, this would be one of the parameters VCs would evaluate your business on.

Burn Multiple (SaaS) = Net Burn / Annual Recurring Revenue

Burn Multiple (D2C) = Fixed Costs / (Sales-Variable Cost)

A burn multiple under 2X in the early stages may be good, but a multiple above 3X after a product is developed may need introspection on the product-market fit, and whether a cost-optimisation exercise needs to be considered.

Own Website vs Marketplace

D2C brands encounter several instances that compel them to prioritize selling either through their own website or through the larger e-commerce marketplaces. Take a step back and think about why D2C startups have to sell on marketplaces in the first place.

Every D2C business has to acquire customers during its initial months. They may employ ads on social media platforms for this purpose. However, the organic CAC for D2C startups for their own website can be considerably high, especially in the beginning since they are virtually unknown and need to spend on marketing to be discovered. Hence, they prefer to sell their products on marketplaces like Amazon, Flipkart, etc. These platforms enable higher discoverability and a lower CAC, especially if the product is differentiated. In the first few months of the life of a D2C startup, marketplaces become a great channel to sell such products without incurring a high CAC.

The big downside of being reliant on marketplaces is that the control is largely in their hands. The customers who make the purchase on their website are their customers, not yours. Mostly, they retain that customer data sharing very little with you, just enough to let you make educated guesses at best. They have complete authority over the commission rates they wish to charge, and if they become a monopoly, you'd have no other option but to continue paying higher commissions. They can choose to promote your competitor's products if that aligns better with their business goals. They can partner with the most prominent logistics partner in the delivery space and drive up delivery costs. In extreme cases, they may even ban you from the marketplace.

In the long-term, thus, it is preferable for every D2C startup to drive sales through one's own website. The higher the dependency on marketplaces, the lower your control. As the founder of a D2C startup, there's no perfect model or framework to follow. You may start your business with the help of marketplaces if that offers you a better unit-level profit. Over the long-term, however, strive to gain more control of your business by driving more sales through your own website. It can be a gradual process and might cost more, so closely track the CAC being incurred on both marketplaces and your own channel. Once there's more parity between the two, you can start pushing for more volumes through your own channel. It may still be a good idea to have some presence on Amazon, Flipkart, Myntra, or any other relevant marketplaces as that allows more people to discover you, but it would be ideal if you're not dependent on them for your survival. Investors too prefer businesses that have more control.

4. Building an MIS

We understood the critical metrics to be tracked while onboarding your first set of users and even beyond in the previous chapter. Like those, there are many other metrics that signify the health of your startup in different aspects. To use them effectively though, they must be prepared in a manner that allows easy access and decision-making. A Management Information System or MIS helps you do that. In this chapter, let's understand what it is, the metrics that startups usually include in it, and the investors' perspective on them. Also, note that the next chapter on Financial Ratios and Accounting explains in detail the different metrics and ratios purely related to Finance and Accounting. Although they are not included as part of this chapter, they should too ideally feature in your MIS.

What is an MIS? Why is it important?

Folks having worked with larger corporates would have encountered some version of MIS during their tenure. Many companies have this system of monthly and quarterly 'MIS reports', where all the critical parameters of the business or a particular function are laid out visually for the management to study. The ones with elaborate automated processes allow such reports to be downloaded in one click. CXOs, at least the diligent ones, seldom take decisions without comprehensively studying these reports.

Even for startups, MIS fulfills similar objectives. It is a report or a dashboard containing all the important data points and metrics that the founders need to track for a complete understanding of their startup's health. It allows them to track progress, identify patterns, and simplify decision-making.

Having an MIS doesn't mean that all the metrics need to be prioritized. Doing that would defeat the purpose of having one. Different companies prioritize different metrics based on their short and long-term goals. Early-stage funded startups will probably have aggressive growth targets and prioritize metrics relevant to them. They can then design the MIS around such parameters. However, even simply being aware of all the other business fundamentals will prevent them from taking measures that may harm their long-term prospects.

In the subsequent sections, we'll understand the different business metrics that usually constitute the MIS for startups. We'll start with financial metrics and move to the operational ones after that.

Explaining Financial Metrics - GMV, LTV, GM, CM, ...

GMV, Sales, Revenue

GMV stands for Gross Merchandise Value. It was popularized after the advent of e-commerce and is now commonly used in both online and offline retailing. GMV refers to the total sales done on an e-commerce platform or any website or retail store for that matter.

In e-commerce, the marketplace cannot claim the sales done as their revenues. It's the sellers that host their products and this company provides the platform to sell. It's similar to a real estate company or a landlord offering rental space for physical stores. GMV is the total value of sales done on this platform. Revenues for them comprise of the commissions they take from this sale in different forms - e.g. closing fee and referral fee that Amazon charges, and any other additional services offered.

For D2C brands, whether they host their products on their own website or on an e-commerce platform, the sales and GMV will be the same for each. This is because all the merchandise sold belongs to them. Such companies use GMV and Sales interchangeably. But if they have a website and start hosting other brands' products, it becomes a marketplace model and GMV and Sales won't be the same then.

Some companies also consider Sales the same as "Revenues". Although there are no rigid rules on this, I reckon Revenues should be considered after deducting the commission payments and any transactional charges. That's the amount that actually hits the account and is often significantly lower than Sales. Many investors consider Revenue to be this figure, and unless clarified early, can lead to confusion and even disagreements on valuation. My recommendation, hence, would be to keep Sales and Revenue separate if applicable.

To summarize simply,

- GMV refers to the total value of goods sold (the total amount customers paid) through a platform
- Sales refers to the total value of goods sold (again, the total amount customers paid) belonging to that company
- Revenue is the amount that a company receives in its bank account after a sale is concluded, after incurring the transaction costs and any commissions paid immediately on sale

Gross Margin (GM)

Gross margin (GM) is calculated by deducting the Cost of Goods Sold (COGS) from the Revenue. COGS is the amount it took you, as the company, to get that product made. It only includes the direct input cost incurred to get it made.

As an example, if you're a brand selling cricket bats, you would normally place an order to the manufacturer and they'd get the pieces made and delivered to you. You would then package it with your brand stickers, put on the rubber grips, and place it inside a cover to be sold in.

Let's say you placed an order of 1000 bats with the manufacturer. You paid Rs. 10 lakhs for them to be made and delivered to you. You then incurred another Rs. 2 lakhs for all the packaging needs. The COGS for you, in this case, is Rs. 12 lakhs, because all these costs have been incurred to create the final set of products. The COGS per unit becomes Rs. 1200 (12 lakh/ 1000). Note that Sales and Revenue are the same in this case.

Now, if you sell these bats through your retail outlet at Rs. 4000, your Gross Margin is Rs. 2800, i.e. Sales - COGS. If you sold them at the same price through an e-commerce website which deducted 10% as transactional costs, your revenue will be 4000-(10% of 4000) = Rs. 3600. Your Gross Margin in this case would be Rs. 2400 (3600-1200).

Note that in both the scenarios, there would be other expenses incurred in the form of storage, logistics, and even marketing costs, but they don't get included in the GM calculation because only the costs directly associated with making the product is considered.

LTV and CM

I have an elderly uncle in his 70s now, living a blissful retired life. He held several respectable positions with the government when he was active and earned enough money to never be financially dependent on his children. Like many other service-class folks from his generation, he never prioritized materialistic pleasures. Except for one - his Omega watch.

He has 9 expensive watches of this brand in his collection, with the first one dating back to the late 1960s. He drives a humble Honda City, but takes uncharacteristic pride in these watches, and wears one of them to all kinds of occasions in life. He once told me that the watch 'feels like a part of him'. He was introduced to the brand by a friend who used to wear one in college, and it somehow became aspirational to him.

Every brand longs for such customers. Over his lifetime, my uncle has purchased Omega watches worth over Rs. 15 lakhs. And he may still buy more. Remarkably, Omega didn't spend a single rupee to acquire him.

In the previous chapter, we understood that Customer Acquisition Cost (CAC) is the average cost a startup incurs to gain one customer. But how do you know if this cost is justified?

Suppose you acquire a customer and they register on your app or website. The CAC, let's say, amounts to Rs. 100.

If the customer makes a product purchase at Rs. 500 and your Contribution Margin (CM) is 20%, i.e., Rs. 100, then you have managed to recover your CAC in this single sale. Contribution Margin, in simple terms, is the profit you make on a sale. It only considers the costs directly attributable to making that sale, thus excluding the overheads, salaries, or any notional costs, and including only variable costs.

However, if the CM on this sale was just 4%, you'd earn only Rs. 20 on the sale. To recover the CAC of Rs. 100 alone, you'd need the customer to make 5 such transactions.

Startups often incur high Customer Acquisition Costs in hope that most such acquisitions will become active users, and over the lifetime of their association with the product, the number of transactions they do would far outweigh the initial CAC. The total profits a customer generates for a startup through such transactions over a lifetime is referred to as the Lifetime Value of the customer, or LTV.

*LTV = Average CM per order * total number of orders over the lifetime*

In my uncle's case, if we assume that the average Contribution Margin of his 9 purchases is Rs. 30,000, Omega would calculate his LTV as 30,000x9 = Rs. 2,70,000.

A more relatable example would be that of the food delivery app Swiggy. In the past 12 months, I have made 18 orders through the app. Let's assume I'd remain a Swiggy user for a total of 10 years. If the average Contribution Margin is Rs. 20 across all orders, and 18 is my average annual order count, then Swiggy calculates my LTV as Rs. 20x18x10 = Rs. 3600.

Now whether this LTV makes sense or not depends on the marketing expenses incurred by Swiggy to acquire me as the user. The metric which measures this is the LTV to CAC ratio, which has been covered later in this chapter.

Also note that Contribution Margin here has been taken as the final profit made on a sale. Many times, the expenses for a company to make a sale occur at different stages. COGS is the cost of making the product which when deducted gives the Gross Margin as we saw in the previous section. The next expense could be in the form logistics costs like storage and delivery. Another could be any royalty to be paid to a collaborator. And then there could be promotional expenses undertaken specifically to promote this product. To signify each of them, businesses often calculate different margins for each of them as Contribution Margin 1 (CM1), Contribution Margin 2 (CM2), and Contribution Margin 3 (CM3). We'll learn more about these in the next chapter on Financial Ratios and Accounting Statements. However, if only a single term 'Contribution Margin' is mentioned, you can assume it to include all such costs.

Explaining Operating & Cohort Metrics - DAU, MAU, Churn, ...

DAU and MAU

All startups which have digital offerings as products are directly or indirectly dependent on the number of users that use them. These include all social media platforms, digital media websites and apps, OTT platforms, fitness apps like HealthifyMe, and many more. A large volume of users usually translates to higher overall usage, which then leads to more cumulative time being spent on the product or higher purchases being made through it. More time spent can eventually translate to higher ad revenues for the company.

However, not all users are equal. Although I'm a user of the Cred app, I open it just once a month for a couple of minutes to pay my credit card bills. Cred would prefer if I visited their platform more often so they get a chance to cross-sell or upsell something. Low frequency makes that hard and it potentially reduces my LTV for them.

Daily Active Users (DAU) is essentially the count of unique users who visit and use your app daily. Higher the DAU, more the time they spend on your app, and greater the opportunity to make them habituated with your product. Once this behaviour becomes a habit, the LTV of the customer tends to rise significantly.

Similarly, Monthly Active Users (MAU) is the count of unique users who used the product at least once in a month. Normally, growth teams of such companies are tasked to increase the frequency of usage for the users who only visit a handful of times every month. A metric that helps them track the ratio of highly active users to the not so active ones is DAU/MAU. A high ratio indicates the ability of the app to become habit-forming, and is an attractive proposition for investors.

Like DAU and MAU, startups may also choose to track the Weekly Active Users (WAU) for more clarity. They can then track DAU/WAU and WAU/MAU metrics separately and take specific growth measures considering each.

Recurring Revenues

The portion of revenue generated by a company that is expected to continue in the future is called Recurring Revenue. Let's consider a simple example.

Country Delight, a milk delivery platform that has also expanded into other dairy products and grocery items, offers its customers a subscription model as well as one-time purchases of any item. I know that my household requires milk daily, so I subscribed to their daily milk delivery service where I get a half-litre cow's milk delivered every morning at my doorstep. Once in a while, I also order ghee and coconut water for which I pay separately.

The daily milk delivery service here counts as a Recurring Revenue for Country Delight, whereas the coconut water and ghee are one-time purchases and don't get classified similarly.

CAC is often high for SaaS companies. For a B2B SaaS company, for example, acquiring a customer may mean multiple trips to the prospective customer's location who may be based out of a different city. Many of those attempts may not yield any result. The recurring subscription model, however, ensures that a single purchase made once continues to generate revenue over a considerable period, ranging from a month to even a few years. For B2B companies, the transaction value is especially high because the software would be used by potentially hundreds of employees.

It's important to note that often, software companies take up one-time consulting or freelance projects to beef up their cash flow while their main product is still under development. These earnings help them fuel the cost of building the product. But while reporting their Recurring Revenue, they can't consider this income as it's not recurring in nature.

The Annual Recurring Revenue is the total revenue generated from a customer or a contract annually. If the duration of the subscription is monthly, then it's the Monthly Recurring Revenue that is usually calculated.

In my Country Delight subscription, if one packet of milk costs me Rs. 30, and I have a monthly subscription, then the Monthly Recurring Revenue would be around Rs. 900. If the subscription was an annual one, the Annual Recurring Revenue, assuming the same price, would be Rs. 10,800.

Run Rate

The Run Rate of a company is basically a projection of the annual revenue based on the most recent performance, assuming nothing changes - no churn, no expansion, no variability.

This figure, however, may vary considerably in real terms for startups when compared to the annual revenue actually obtained. In startups, growth tends to happen faster, and they are also more vulnerable to volatilities which makes it hard to project accurately. However, the Annual Run Rate (ARR) is a widely accepted and used metric to analyze the current performance of a startup. In fact, many investors consider the ARR to arrive at the valuation of a startup.

Annual Run Rate (ARR) is usually calculated as the last month's revenue times 12.

*ARR = Last month's revenue * 12*

'ARR' is used interchangeably for Annual Run Rate as well as Annual Recurring Revenue. D2C startups and companies that rely on one-time purchases mainly consider the former, while subscription models consider the latter. Fundamentally, the only difference is that the Recurring Revenue is a more accurate projection, since the customer may have actually signed up for an entire year. The same goes for MRR as well.

For a more accurate calculation, it would make sense for companies to average the revenue of the last 3 months instead of 1 and multiply it by 12 to get the run rate. If the product has seasonal sales, then the calculation must also normalize the calculation for seasonal distribution and multiples, and not calculate using a straightforward 12 times of the last monthly revenue. If a mango delivery startup, for example, shows an ARR of June sales times 12, you know the figure would be wildly inaccurate.

Bookings

SaaS companies, especially in the B2B space, may take a considerable amount of time to actually become operational for a client. There may be specific setup challenges which take a few weeks or sometimes months. In such cases, even though the sale has been closed, revenue wouldn't start coming in until the client actually starts using the product. In such cases, 'Bookings' becomes an important metric. They represent a letter of intent from a prospective client and act as a strong indicator of future revenue.

How you account for these Bookings in your statements must also be clear. The client may have signed up for the product for a certain period, say 2 years. For a 2-year contract, even if you get the entire amount at once, you will need to pro-rate this revenue across the 24 months. If you are starting operations right at the beginning of the current Financial Year (FY), half of the amount received will be accounted for in the current FY, and half in the next. If you start right in the middle of the current FY, then a quarter of the amount received gets accounted for in the current FY, half in the next FY, and the remaining quarter in the FY after that.

Churn

Churn represents the number of users who fall off a product and stop generating business for you. When this is averaged out as a percentage of the total active users for a specific period, say a month or a year, it is referred to as the Monthly Churn Rate or the Annual Churn Rate respectively.

For example, consider that you have 1000 Weekly Active Users (WAU) on the app your startup has built. Your data suggests, on average every week 25 users are dropping off. In this case, your weekly churn rate will be (25/1000)*100% = 2.5%.

Every startup looks to minimize this metric for optimum performance.

Net Promoter Score (NPS)

We have covered NPS previously in Chapter 2 and saw how this score can be a strong indicator of Product-Market Fit. Its relevance, however, doesn't just end with PMF. For products that have already achieved PMF, it's still a reliable way to understand how satisfied your customers are.

Let's revisit how NPS is calculated by startups.

Customers are asked to respond on a scale of 0 to 10 to the question: How likely are you to recommend our product or service to someone you know?

0 indicates they're not at all inclined to recommend, while 10 means they definitely will.

Based on the scores they give, customers are classified as follows:

0 to 6: Detractors

7 to 8: Neutrals

9 to 10: Promoters

NPS = % of Promoters - % of Detractors

Say, on a customer survey of 100 people, 30 were detractors, 20 were neutrals and 50 were promoters.

NPS = 50 - 30 = 20

A score of 30 or above is considered great. It shows that a considerably larger number of your customers are willing to promote your product than those who'll discourage it. So the net effect is positive, hence the 'net promoter score'.

However, the process doesn't end here if you wish to get into the depths of what works for your product and what doesn't. Ideally, customers should be asked why they rated your product so, and be given enough space to express themselves freely. This can happen either through an accompanying open-ended question in the survey or even through direct interviews with randomly chosen customers.

Compounded Growth Rates

Compounded Annual Growth Rate (CAGR), in simple terms, is the mean annual growth rate of any metric - revenues, profits, number of customers, units sold, etc. - over a specified period, usually a few years.

Usually, startups don't grow in a linear fashion. The month-on-month growth rates for any metric over any 6-month period will vary every month. This phenomenon may continue in the first few years of its existence and gradually achieves stability with maturity.

The CAGR puts one value on the growth rate and presents a uniform, summarized picture of the growth story.

Consider a startup that registered a revenue of Rs. 1 Cr* in the first full year of its operations, 3 Cr in the second, 8 Cr in the third, and 10 Cr in the fourth.

If you consider YoY growth for every subsequent year, the number would be 200% for year 1 to year 2, 167% for years 2 to 3, and 25% for years 3 to 4. However, while calculating the CAGR from year 1 to the end of year 4, you only consider the revenue in these 2 years - 1 Cr and 10 Cr, and the number of years it took them to grow, i.e. 3 years.

The formula for the Compounded Annual Growth Rate is given below:

$$CAGR = ((Y_n - Y_1)/Y_1)^{1/n} * 100$$

where

n represents the number of years over which the change happened, Yn represents the value at the last year of consideration, and Y1 represents the value in the first year of consideration. The values here can represent any metric that needs to be calculated.

In our example, the CAGR over the 3-year period, using the for-

*Cr = crore = 10 million

mula above is (((10-1)/1)^(1/3))*100% = 208%

The formula for CAGR can be replicated for Compounded Monthly Growth Rate (CMGR) by simply replacing Years with Months.

CAGR is usually more relevant to slightly mature companies which have been in business for at least a couple of years. For an early-stage start-up with existence of fewer than two years, CMGR would be a better way to track growth.

Rule of 40

SaaS companies do not incur much in terms of variable costs once the product is developed and ready. After that, it's the marketing expenses that comprise most of their variable spending.

According to the Rule of 40, a SaaS company's growth rate when added to its EBITDA margin in % should be at least 40%. It has become quite popular in the SaaS industry as it, in a way, measures the balance between growth and profitability.

As an example, if a SaaS company has a growth rate of 60% but the EBITDA margin (or profitability, for simplicity's sake) is -50%, indicating it's incurring a loss in its operations, the sum of both these metrics is 10%. This is not desirable and indicates an imbalance between growth and profitability. The burn here doesn't justify the growth.

For this growth to be acceptable, the company would need to either improve upon its growth rate (increase to 90% at the same -50% EBITDA) or reduce its losses (improve to -20%, at the same 60% growth rate).

Unit Economics

Every business must make money, either immediately or at some point in the future. That can only happen when it is left with a surplus after making a sale, or in other words, has positive *unit economics*. Positive unit economics also means having a positive Contribution Margin.

CM, as we saw earlier in the chapter, is the profit remaining after accounting for all the variable costs associated with a sale. This profit, when scaled to a large number of products, is expected to eventually cover all the fixed costs that are not considered for operational calculations.

There's a notion that VCs fund "loss-making" startups. These losses, in most cases, are not at the operational level but on the overall organizational level. Large amounts are spent on hiring employees and on marketing activities to enable faster growth in the present and hopefully reap the rewards in the form of superlative profits in the future. When VCs scout for startups to fund, they always look for a high positive unit economics business as that indicates their ability to cover the losses that may be incurred in the near future. Negative unit economics simply denotes that the company loses money on every sale. When scaled, it would magnify the losses further. Startups must have positive unit economics, or at least a path to it, to have any investor's interest.

I usually advise startups to work under the following constraints while building:

- Material and packaging costs (COGS) should not exceed 35% of the selling price
- Logistics cost should be under 15% of the selling price.
- CAC should be under 25% of the selling price
- The above would result in a contribution margin of at least 25%

The better the unit economics, the easier it becomes for you to run the business and also to attract investors.

LTV/CAC Ratios & Everything else that an Investor wants

Understanding LTV and how it's used with different marketing costs gives you an idea of the things critical to retain a customer for a long period. The metrics mentioned in this section are necessary to capture the growth efficiency of a company.

Let's go back to my Swiggy example where I showed that I ordered 18 times in the last 12 months. Assume that I'd remain a Swiggy user for 10 years. If the average Contribution Margin is Rs. 20 across all orders, and 18 continues to be my average annual order count, then Swiggy calculates my LTV as Rs. 20x18x10 = Rs. 3600.

If we go a step deeper in this, I probably made the first purchase on the app as a result of a heavy discount and cashback which was being offered. I noticed that one of my favourite restaurants in Gurgaon had its items listed about 50% cheaper on Swiggy with free delivery. On top of that, I was also being offered a Rs. 100 cashback for the first transaction. It seemed like a no-brainer to try it out.

On a meal priced otherwise at Rs. 400, I had it delivered to me at Rs. 200, in addition to a cashback of Rs. 100. So the net cost I had to incur was only Rs. 100.

Swiggy, on its part, absorbed the difference in price, the delivery person's fees, and the cashback obviously. From the restaurant, it could have earned a commission, which is usually a % of the final order value. Let's assume it was 10%, which translates to Rs. 40.

Let's calculate my CAC for Swiggy now.

Commission earned = 40

Price difference absorbed = -200

Cashback = -100

CAC = Rs. 260

Now, compare this with my LTV for Swiggy, which is Rs. 3600. An LTV to CAC ratio of 3 or above is usually considered acceptable. In my case, the LTV to CAC ratio is almost 14, which is phenomenal. But is it a true reflection of Swiggy's performance? Can just the LTV/CAC ratio justify the startup's performance?

Accounting for CCC

As startups grow and mature, more competitors enter the industry, and additional efforts are needed to prevent one's customers to deflect to competition. CAC, then, is needed to be supplemented by Customer Carrying Cost (CCC) for retention.

In the example above, Swiggy knows that Zomato is always breathing down their neck. Complacency would result in me becoming a Zomato customer in no time. To prevent this, Swiggy keeps me interested with more offerings and freebies. Let's say that every year Swiggy spends an additional Rs. 100 as CCC to retain me as their customer.

The true indicator of my worth to Swiggy can now be calculated as follows:

LTV/(CAC+CCC)

Does the total amount spent on me by Swiggy justify their efforts? Let's find out.

We have calculated my CAC as Rs. 260. Considering they spend an additional Rs. 100 annually as my CCC, the total amount spent by Swiggy becomes (100*10)+260, or Rs. 1260.

As per the formula above, the ratio is (3600/1260), or 2.86.

Every rupee spent on me by Swiggy is actually earning them Rs. 2.86. Profitable still, yes. But certainly not as lucrative as LTV/CAC alone suggested.

LTV in action

It must be clear by now that every business must look to maximize the LTV and minimize the CAC as well as CCC for their customers.

LTV, as we can see, is a function of three things: frequency of use or number of sales orders, average transaction value (ATV), and the duration of association.

The duration of association largely depends on how strong a brand a product can build, the customer experience they offer over a long period, and the success of the company itself - how long it thrives. While these are obviously important things for the management to work on, we would for now focus on how a founder can approach the other two variables of LTV.

Frequency of Use and Average Transaction Value (ATV) combine to give the average revenue generated by a user over a given period. Revenues directly impact the profits and cash flow, and every business wishes to maximize this. Every tactic employed by any business to increase revenues from existing customers aims to increase at least one of these two factors.

E-commerce companies like Amazon use customers' data to understand their preferences and suggest them additional items to purchase accordingly.

Frequently bought together

These items are dispatched from and sold by different sellers. Show details

- **This item:** Atomic Habits: The life-changing million copy bestseller by James Clear Paperback ₹624.00
- The Psychology of Money by Morgan Housel Paperback ₹270.00
- Ikigai: The Japanese secret to a long and happy life by Héctor García Hardcover ₹415.00

Source: Product page on Amazon's website

If a customer follows up on any of these suggestions, it contributes to increasing their Average Transaction Value (ATV).

Similar tactics are employed by Zomato and Swiggy when they suggest additional items to try while you're ordering on their app.

The other lever that startups can use to increase their ATV is the frequency of purchase.

When Urban Company started, its primary service was AC maintenance. People usually get their AC units serviced once or twice a year at most. If they continued offering only this service, the frequency of sales would be limited to just one or two annually.

To increase this frequency, they started considering other categories they could enter within the ambit of home services, and one among these was personal grooming.

For example, a girl may have her hair cut every 3-4 months or so. For men, the frequency could be around 30-45 days. Clearly, entering this category could help increase the frequency of usage of their app by active customers. Having more categories also gave them the option to cross-sell other services on the platform and further drive up the frequency of sales.

Another tactic used by startups like Swiggy, Zomato, and Urban Company to drive up frequency of usage is offering special memberships at an initial price, with special discount benefits. Swiggy, for example, offers a 'One' membership (as of July 2022) where your delivery fees get waived off and you get some additional discounts. By paying Rs. 299 up front, you get these benefits for 3 months.

If you make a conservative estimate, the average delivery fee on an order is around Rs. 40. If you order even once weekly, you can potentially save upwards of Rs. 500 in just delivery fees. Additional discounts count separately. It obviously appears to be a good deal for you, the customer, but how does Swiggy benefit?

Swiggy benefits when you increase your frequency of orders. If you purchase one such plan from Swiggy, chances are you won't do the same with its competitor Zomato. So you'll have a clear incentive to order via Swiggy. Also, since you know the delivery fees are waived off, the overall propensity to order might be slightly higher.

So what Swiggy may seem to lose in terms of delivery fees and other benefits, it aims to cover up with a higher frequency of usage. A higher frequency multiplied by the average contribution margin in turn increases LTV of the customer.

Of course, not all customers end up behaving the way these companies want them to. That's where closely measuring each relevant data point helps refine these models further.

How to Build an Internal MIS vs. Investor MIS

An internal MIS is meant to serve the startup's management and decision-makers. It should ideally contain all the possible metrics that signify the different functions' performance, and should be designed such that the elements contributing to each function can be drilled down to reveal the smaller components. In the very early stages, it's the founding team itself that starts tracking the important metrics in an Excel file or Google Sheets. As the startup matures and more complexities get added, the MIS creation and management gets a dedicated Analyst or is undertaken by the Business Finance team. With time, the startup may also need to rely on customized tools and software for its management.

For founders, the answer on what metrics to track in an MIS is quite simple - all of them. But what varies is the prioritization of metrics depending on the phase of the startup, as discussed in the beginning of the chapter. Visually, the MIS can be designed to naturally focus more on the most important metrics, with the others too available for study but not seeking attention. A sample internal MIS I created for a startup has been shared at the end of the next chapter.

After a startup raises funds, it is normally required to submit a monthly MIS to its investors. Many investors have their own format for all their portfolio startups which they adhere to. In such a case, the MIS format is simply the template they share.

In cases where it's not specified, the information to be shared depends on the business model. The north star metric for a fintech startup would probably be the Gross Transaction Value. A marketplace would probably prioritize GMV, whereas a social media platform would optimize for DAU. Depending on the nature of your business, identify the metrics that best indicate the overall health and share with them. If they specifically ask for more, you may do so but never reveal more than what's needed. Sometimes, such information gets leaked unwittingly in conversations with other portfolio startups in the same domain and that can potentially harm you.

Secondly, in the early stages, the business hasn't yet matured to a level where some of the metrics can be looked at on a month-on-month basis. If you share low CAC values for one month, the investor would probably expect it to be lower in the next. But that may not happen probably because you were lucky the previous month and got an unexpected shout-out from a celebrity which drove up sales. Identify and share only those metrics which truly reflect the business performance, and don't over-reveal.

5. Understanding Financial Ratios & Accounting Statements

An important component of a company's MIS is its financial health. At its very core, it's tracking all the incomes, expenses, assets, and liabilities in a structured manner. In the initial days, the complexities are minimal so any founder with basic knowledge of finance can keep track of all of it. As the startup grows, things start getting complicated and require specialists.

Finance and Accounting are something many founders shy away from though. There's a perception that it's either too hard to learn or too menial to do on your own. I don't endorse either of these views.

Every founder, I believe, should be comfortable reading and understanding their company's accounting statements. These statements give the true overall picture of the company's health from operational and financial perspectives. They are also standard sources of truth considered by any entity auditing or assessing your business in any way. Investors too need them when they conduct their financial due diligence if they have agreed to fund. Understanding accounting for founders, unfortunately, is not really a choice.

Learning Accounting and Financial Ratios, contrary to what people believe, is just plain common sense and structure. In this chapter, let's understand everything a founder should know about these.

There are primarily 3 accounting statements:

1. The Profit and Loss (P&L) Statement
2. The Balance Sheet
3. The Cash Flow Statement

All three offer different perspectives of the business.

P&L Statement tells you how profitable your business is and broadly identifies the heads that contribute to costs.

The Balance Sheet shows you where, how much, and in what form the assets and liabilities of your business exist. It also gives a clear picture of how your funds have been used to create assets.

The Cash Flow Statement helps you segregate your cash flow from different activities and also the expenses incurred on each of them. This statement becomes especially important to gauge the operational health of your business.

Let's go deeper into each of them.

The Profit and Loss (P&L) Statement

As the name suggests, the P&L Statement talks about the profit that your business is earning or the loss it has incurred during a specific period. For a better understanding, let's construct a P&L Statement step by step.

I have shared an example of the P&L format[1], but know that the exact line items may change as per the business's requirements.

Creating a P&L statement

Statement of Profit and Loss for the year ended March 31, 2023			
Particulars	Note No.	Year ended March 31, 2023	Year ended March 31, 2022
REVENUE			
Sale of products		38,041	32,949
Less: Excise duty		4,005	3,512
Net sale of products		34,036	29,437
Sale of services		309	137
Other operating revenue		21	15
Net revenue from operations	17	34,366	29,589
Other income	18	455	465
Total Revenue		**34,821**	**30,054**

EXPENSES			
Cost of materials consumed	19	21,012	17,603
Purchases of stock-in-trade	20	2,114	2,632
Changes in inventories of finished goods, work-in process and stock-in-trade	20	(292.00)	(321.00)
Employee benefits expense	21	1,583	1,262
Finance costs	22	7	3
Depreciation and amortisation expense [includes impairment loss of Rs. Nil (PY Rs. 75 million)]	23	645	661
Other Expenses	24	4,346	3,904
Total Expenses		29,415	25,744

Profit before exceptional items and tax		5,406	4,310
Less: Exceptional items (net)	33	39	92
Profit before tax		5,367	4,218
Less: Tax Expense			
Current Tax		1,580	1,378
Deferred tax (credit)/expense		106	(24.00)
Earlier year's (excess)/short provision		6	(2.00)
Profit for the year		3,675	2,866.00
Basic and diluted earnings per equity share of Rs. 1 each	37	21	17

Revenue (and GMV)

Revenue is the first line item which features in a P&L statement. It's presented on the top and is also referred to as the *top line*.

If there are multiple businesses or revenue streams, then ideally the breakup of the total revenue or sales should also be provided in the statement.

Basically, revenue is the total money that you get through sales. Sometimes, the Gross Merchandise Value (GMV) of a marketplace business is incorrectly considered as the sales or revenue of the company. Let's understand this using Flipkart's example.

Flipkart, as we know, is a marketplace which connects sellers and buyers on its platform. Products worth many crores are sold every day on its platform. But all these products don't belong to Flipkart, and hence the sales don't count in their revenues. That's Flipkart's Gross Merchandise Value.

The company takes a fee for providing the marketplace to its sellers and enabling them to reach more customers. This fee is what counts as its revenue. If we assume that Flipkart takes a flat 10% of the total sale value as its commission from the seller, then the revenue of Flipkart is basically 10% of the GMV.

Similarly, if I pay a merchant on PayTM, the company may take, let's say, 1% of the transaction value from the merchant for enabling this transaction. Of the Rs. 100 that I transfer, the seller gets 99, and PayTM keeps 1. This Re.1 contributes to PayTM's revenue and not the Rs. 100 I paid to the merchant.

If it's your own product that you're selling, then this value goes under Sales. For example, if I'm a seller on Flipkart selling my book, then I'd account for all the sales of the book as my revenue and include it in the top line of my P&L statement.

For a marketplace like Flipkart or Amazon, or a payments enabler like Razorpay, the Revenue is what they actually earned from providing the marketplace service.

Variable Costs

The next line item is the Variable Cost. This is also listed as *Cost of Goods Sold (COGS)* for businesses selling physical products. Usually, COGS considers only the direct material costs but ideally, it should constitute all the variable costs associated with a product. For example, if you're selling a product online, then each such sale will also include the logistics costs which don't get accounted for under COGS, and hence may not provide a complete picture. If there are different items that contribute to the variable costs, then the breakup specifying their contribution should be shown.

Variable Costs are all the expenses that change in proportion to the volume of the products a company sells.

Let's further clarify the different variable costs a simple business can incur through an example.

Assume a small business named Gale Drinks which makes packaged ginger ale drinks and sells them at a price of Rs. 100 per bottle.

Now, what's the cost to actually produce the drink in its bottled form? Since the drink and the bottle both go to the end consumer, both count as direct costs. Consider that the sum of the raw material cost (for producing the beverage) and the primary packaging cost (bottle) comes up to be Rs. 35 per bottle. That's the variable cost or the direct material cost or the cost of goods sold for the product.

Let's say Gale Drinks purchased Rs. 35,000 worth of raw materials for the beverage and bottles which helped them stock 1000 (35,000/35) bottles of the drink. Although they expected to sell the entire stock in the financial year, they managed to sell only 600 and were left with 400.

The finished products (400 bottles) that are lying in their inventory is the **closing stock**.

It will be reflected in the balance sheet as a short-term asset, assuming that the business can sell them in the next few months. The value of the closing stock will amount to Rs. 14,000 (Rs. 35 * 400 bottles).

In the next year, this closing stock will act as the **opening stock**. Even before making any purchase or producing any beverages, there will be 400 bottles ready to be sold in the market.

Let's go back to the main question that we were trying to answer. What's the cost to the business to actually produce the beverage?

Cost of Goods Sold = Opening stock + Purchases - Closing stock

In the current year, the opening stock is Rs. 0 since there was no stock to start with. Purchases worth Rs. 35,000 were made up front, and the closing stock is worth Rs. 14,000. Therefore, the Cost of Goods Sold (COGS) by my business amounts to Rs. 21,000.

Intuitively, it can also be understood as the cost of the products actually sold to customers.

Next, we calculate the *Gross Margin* of Gale Drinks.

Recall that the selling price of the ginger ale drink is Rs. 100. Each unit has a cost of Rs. 35. Which leaves me with a gross margin of Rs. 65. This is the **Gross Margin (GM)**.

GM = Sales - Material Cost

Now, Gale Drinks is a D2C company, and the bottles need to be shipped to the customer's address. Let's say this costs an additional Rs. 10 for each bottle delivered. This brings down the profit margin to Rs. 55 (65-10). This margin is also called Contribution Margin 1 or CM1.

CM1 = Sales - Material Cost - Logistics Cost

As a D2C brand, Gale Drinks would need to advertise its product for generating sales orders. This performance marketing again costs them, say, Rs. 15 per bottle on average. So the profit margin, after considering all the variable costs, is finally Rs. 40. This is called Contribution Margin 2 or CM2.

CM2 = Sales - Material Cost - Logistics Cost for Delivery - Ad Spend for Performance Marketing

The final contribution margin, in all cases, must be positive for the business to make economic sense. If you make a loss on every unit's sale, then at higher volumes the losses would be massive.

Note that your business can have other variable costs which this example doesn't cover. Each of them should be accounted for while calculating Contribution Margins at different levels.

Fixed Costs

Next on the P&L statement, we account for the Fixed Costs. These are all the costs that the business will incur regardless of the volumes produced and sold. These can comprise salaries of employees, rent of the workplace, any software subscriptions for employees, fixed server costs, utilities like electricity, water, etc. There may even be fixed marketing expenses that a company incurs, like sponsoring ongoing events or paying a contractual fee to a brand ambassador.

On the P&L Statement, all these costs should be separately listed out and rolled up into the Fixed Costs head.

After deducting the fixed costs from CM2, the amount remaining is called *Operating Profits* or *EBITDA* (Earnings before Interest, Tax, Depreciation and Amortization).

Why is Interest not considered for calculating Operating Profits?

Interest is dependent on how the capital of the business is structured and not on the business performance from an economical point of view.

If Company A is bootstrapped and has taken a loan from a bank, it needs to pay some interest to the bank every month.

If Company B, operating in the same industry and catering to similar customers, is a funded start-up with no debt, then it doesn't pay anything as Interest.

The only difference between the two companies is how they have chosen to fund their business. Operationally, they are dependent on the same factors to deliver good business results.

It would be unfair to compare the operational performance of these two by including their interest expense, considering the difference is just in the capital structure. That's why EBITDA or Operating Profits does not take interest expenses into consideration.

Why is Tax not considered for calculating Operating Profits?

Taxation varies from business to business and considers factors that may have little to do with operations. Bootstrapped firms, like Company A in the example above, need to generate profits to reinvest into the business for the future and also to compensate promoters in some way. The profits left for the equity holders are taxed by the government.

On the other hand, Company B, being externally funded, may reinvest the entire profit generated from operations into marketing and growth to scale faster. Due to the presence of surplus funds from investors, there may be no immediate pressure to generate profits. Since there are no profits left at the end, there are no taxes to be paid.

Operationally, again, there's no difference in how the two companies function. It's just how they are capitalized which creates this difference.

Business Entity	Taxation Rates
Partnership Firms	30%
Companies	25%
Individual	Own slab rate

Tax structure also changes based on the business entity. Here's a table of the tax rates payable by different business entities.

Taxation, as shown, is not uniform for different business entities. It makes sense, then, to disregard the taxes paid when comparing the operational health of the two businesses.

Why are Depreciation and Amortization not considered for calculating Operating Profits?

Depreciation aims to take into account any asset that has a certain life span. For example, a given machine in a factory may only be used for 10 years, after which it gets replaced. Since the asset is in use for 10 years, it would be unfair to account for the entire expense of purchasing or building that in the year that it gets deployed. Instead, this expense is distributed through the life span of the asset, 10 years in this case, for a fairer allocation of this expense.

Depreciation is also a notional concept. If the asset is newly purchased, there's no depreciation to account for. So a company which is newly established and has new equipment may have no depreciation, while another company which has been in the same business for a few years will have some depreciation to show. Operationally, there's no difference in how the business itself gets done.

Depreciation is also not necessarily uniform, i.e. the expense may not (and in many cases, should not) be distributed evenly across all the years of its lifespan since its usability may reduce towards the end.

Amortization is like depreciation but on intangible assets. Let's say you have a deal with a brand where they have allowed you to use their name for a period of 10 years. This access to the brand then becomes an asset for your business. The cost of this asset will amortize over the 10-year period.

Both these concepts aren't governed by strict rules and are dependent on numerous non-quantifiable factors. Moreover, they don't have any direct significance on day-to-day operations. Hence, they are rightfully kept aside from the calculation of Operating Profits or EBITDA.

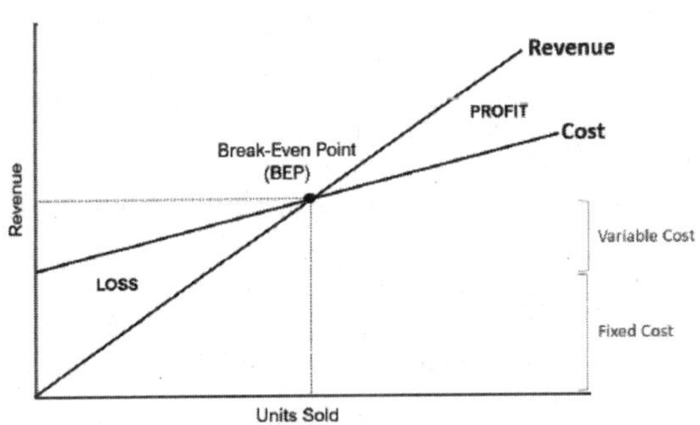

Break-even point

A business breaks even when the total fixed cost of setting up gets completely recovered by profits from sales. The point at which that happens is called the break-even point. It's normally denoted in terms of units sold. Let's consider Gale Drinks again to understand this phenomenon.

To start the business, the company must have incurred some initial costs - like purchasing equipment, renting an office space, perhaps renting a kitchen, and possibly other compliance costs. For operations, they would need to pay salaries to staff, purchase or rent office equipment (like laptops), software subscriptions (like a Google Workspace account for everyone), and possibly other server costs. All these contribute to the fixed costs of Gale Drinks.

Gale Drinks earns money in the form of Contribution Margin 2 (CM2), which is sales minus all the variable costs - material costs, logistic costs, and marketing expenses.

The break-even point, for Gale Drinks, is the number of units sold to earn an amount equal to the fixed costs incurred by them.

Break-even point = Fixed Costs/Contribution Margin per unit

Let's say, all the fixed costs incurred by Gale Drinks amount to Rs. 40 Lakh.

We found earlier that their CM2 after accounting for all variable costs is Rs. 40.

The break-even point for Gale Drinks then is (40,00,000/40) or 1 Lakh units in sales.

As an entrepreneur, you must ensure that the unit contribution margin is large enough so that the business reaches its break-even point faster and become a profitable enterprise.

This wraps up our P&L Statement section. As you can see, it's simple enough to understand as well as prepare, regardless of how big your business is. You just need to know clearly how you earn and where you spend.

Balance Sheet

The Balance Sheet of your company basically shows how your assets and liabilities are balanced, and what the shareholder's equity is, on a given date. In a more crude way, it shows what a company owns and how much it owes.

It's important to note that this statement is created to show the financial status of any company for a given *date* and not a specified *period.* In isolation, it does not indicate anything about the operational metrics of a business like the P&L Statement but gives a good account of its financial health.

Let's understand the Balance Sheet by understanding its two main components - Liabilities and Assets. The example shared here demonstrates it well[2], but as with P&L, the exact line items will vary across organizations.

Balance Sheet as on 31st March, 2023			
			As at 31.03.2022
		Rs. crores	Rs. crores
EQUITY AND LIABILITIES			
(1) SHAREHOLDERS' FUNDS			
(a) Share Capital	971		959
(b) Reserves and Surplus	51,650		45,807
(c) Money received against share warrants	-		178
		52,621	46,944
(2) HYBRID PERPETUAL SECURITIES		2,275	1,500
(3) NON CURRENT LIABILITIES			
(a) Long-term borrowings	21,353		24,499
(b) Deferred tax liabilities (net)	970		936
(c) Other long-term liabilities	216		373
(d) Long-term provisions	1,851		2,201
		24,391	28,011
(4) CURRENT LIABILITIES			
(a) Short-term borrowings	65		149
(b) Trade payables	5,973		4,465
(c) Other current liabilities	8,798		6,262
(d) Short-term provisions	2,066		2,219
		16,904	13,095
		96,191	89,552

ASSETS			
(5) NON-CURRENT ASSETS			
(a) Fixed Assets			
(i) Tangible Assets	11,142		11,532
(ii) Capital work-in progress	16,058		5,612
(iii) Intangible assets	224		272
	27,425		17,417
(b) Non-current Investments	49,078		43,565.15
(c) Foreign currency monetary item translation difference account	405		-
(d) Long-term loans and advances	6416		10,453
(e) Other non-current assets	3		3
		83,327	71,439
(6) CURRENT ASSETS			
(a) Current investments	1,204		3,000
(b) Inventories	4,859		3,954
(c) Trade receivables	904		424
(d) Cash and bank balances	3,947		4,139
(e) Short-term loans and advances	1828		6,459
(f) Other current assets	122		138
		12,865	18,113
		96,191	89,552
Notes to Balance Sheet and Statement of Profit and Loss			

Liabilities

Simply put, a *liability* is what a business owes to others.

Liabilities fall under two segments: Capital or Shareholder's Funds and Borrowed Funds.

A Shareholder's Fund is the money that the shareholders have invested in the company to promote its growth. For example, in a bootstrapped business, the founders may put in funds from their personal savings. This would be classified under Shareholder's Funds. The Borrowed Fund is what you may have borrowed from people or entities not associated with the company, for example, a loan taken from a bank.

Let's understand both of these Liabilities in detail.

Shareholder's Fund

The Shareholder's Fund can be of three types:

- Equity Shareholder's Fund/ Promoter's Shareholding

- Preferred Stock/ Investor's Shareholding
- Reserves and Surplus

The *Equity Shareholder's Fund* is what the founders invest as equity to build the company. In bootstrapped startups, founders pool money to set the business up and get the operations running. This money goes under the Equity Shareholder's Fund.

Preferred Stock refers to the investment of Angels or VC investors. Preference shares, which make up the preferred stock, have a preference over equity shares. This means that if the company is sold to a buyer, the money received has to be distributed among the preference shareholders first. After they get their money, whatever amount is left is then distributed to the equity shareholders (for e.g., founders). We'll cover this topic in detail in Chapter 12, *Fundraising Instruments & Mechanics.*

Reserves and Surplus refers to all the accumulated profits of the company on the given date.

In the first year of operations, if your company ends the financial year at a profit of Rs. 1 Cr, this will be noted under the head of Reserves and Surplus on the Balance Sheet as of the last date of this financial year. If the company generates another 2 Cr in profits in the next financial year, the Balance Sheet would have Rs. 3 Cr under the Reserves and Surplus.

A loss, similarly, reduces your Reserves and Surplus. And if the entire Reserves and Surplus gets wiped out due to any major event, the loss then starts eating into the preference shares and equity shares capital of your company.

This is why the founders and investors of loss-making enterprises need to continuously pump in funds to compensate for the losses and still keep growing.

Borrowed Funds/Debt

Borrowed Funds comprise all the loans taken by the company.

This needs to be further segregated into *long-term borrowing* and *short-term borrowing.*

Long-term borrowing refers to the loans taken for purposes that would serve the company for a period of at least 12 months. If a logistics company like Delhivery or Xpressbees borrows a certain amount to build a fleet of motorbikes, we know that these bikes would serve the company for at least a few years before being upgraded. The amount borrowed then falls under long-term borrowing on the Balance Sheet.

Short-term borrowing comprises loans taken to address immediate or short-term needs. Working capital loans, for example, fall under this. A garments manufacturer would pay for raw materials and other manufacturing processes up front and will be able to sell the finished product only after incurring these costs. While the sales would recover these costs, the manufacturer would still need to finance the upfront costs first. This could be facilitated by a short-term working capital loan from a bank which can be repaid once the sales happen. This loan goes into the Balance Sheet as a short-term borrowing under Borrowed Funds.

We have covered everything that constitutes the Liabilities on a Balance Sheet. Let's move to the next major component, Assets, and understand how it is structured.

Assets

In simple terms, an asset is what a company *owns*. Ownership should not be confused with things that you have taken on rent or on lease. Sometimes, entities take real-estate space on very long-term leases, even 100 years in some cases. That may give the perception of ownership, but in financial terms, it's not.

Assets, again, can be classified as *long-term* or *short-term*.

Long-term assets are those which are expected to benefit a company for a number of years. Delhivery's fleet of motorbikes, or any equipment purchased to serve you for at least a few years, are classified as long-term assets.

Short-term assets also referred to as *current assets*, are those assets which are held for a year or less and are expected to be converted to cash within this period.

An amount of money yet to be received after the sale of a product or a service, also known as *accounts receivable*, is an example of a short-term asset. Inventory balances, like the 400 units of Gale Drinks bottles that we considered in our closing stock, are also a form of short-term assets as the company expects them to sell and generate cash flow soon.

Cash in the bank is also a short-term asset.

If you have borrowed money for the short term and need to repay it within 12 months, you must never use it to finance a long-term asset. For example, a fleet of motorbikes for delivery is likely to stay as an asset for at least a few years and the incremental returns will be spread across this time period. The terms of short-term loans are kept considering a shorter payout period, which in this case would probably be a year. As with any debt that doesn't get repaid on time, there are penalties which keep adding to the cost. So if a short-term debt is taken to fund a long-term asset like this delivery fleet, the company would either have to find a different way to repay the loan or incur additional costs that come with it. However, if it's used appropriately, like using it for working capital expenses to facilitate large-volume orders and reduce unit costs, it's likely that the increased operational revenues would be sufficient to pay this debt out.

All the money borrowed must be bifurcated into the two heads of long-term and short-term borrowings and managed accordingly. Use the short-term funds to finance short-term assets and the long-term funds for long-term assets. Working capital loans, for example, would fall under short-term borrowings, and the founders must ensure that the amount is not utilized anywhere else. Similarly, a larger borrowing amount for the fleet of motorbikes should be categorized as long-term borrowing and must be used accordingly.

At all times, the liabilities and the assets should balance each other.

Assets = Liabilities

This is a strict accounting rule. If you have borrowed money or your investors have put money in your company, the assets created must always be equal to the liabilities (funds infused), whatever that number is.

This brings us to the end of the section on the Balance Sheet. If you observe closely, preparing a Balance Sheet of your company for any given date clearly shows how the funds are being utilized and paints a true picture of the overall financial health. It's simple enough to prepare and understand, as long as you know the things that constitute Assets and Liabilities.

We move next to the last major accounting statement - the Cash Flow Statement.

Cash Flow Statement	
For the Year Ended March 31, 2023	
Cash Flow from Operations	
Cash receipts from customers	86,772
Cash paid for inventory	(7,400)
Cash paid for wages	(53,000)
Net Cash Flow from Operations	26,372
Cash Flow from Investing	
Cash receipts from sale of property and equipment	13,500
Cash paid for purchase of equipment	(17,500)
Net Cash Flow from Investing	(4,000)
Cash Flow from Financing	
Funds received from Investors	5,000
Cash paid for loan repayment	(5,000)
Net Cash Flow from Financing	0
Net Increase in Cash	22,372

Cash Flow Statement

The Cash Flow Statement helps you understand exactly how much cash your company received and spent in a given period.

People often get confused between profits and cash flow. Profit is the notional money left with the business after considering all the expenses incurred. Cash flow, on the other hand, indicates the net flow of cash into and out of the business.

It's not uncommon for businesses to have a net cash in-flow but still incurring losses, or have net cash out-flow but are still profitable.

Let's take an example of how this can manifest. Suppose you own a factory and have purchased machinery worth Rs. 1 Cr. Now, you have already paid for this and incurred a cash outflow. But this is an asset that you intend to use for the next 25 years. So technically, in the P&L Statement, you'll show an expense of, say, Rs. 4 lakhs as depreciation at the end of the year. Assuming your business this year generates Rs. 90 lakhs in sales, and after considering all the expenses, the P&L Statement indicates you made a profit of Rs. 10 lakhs. But since you had paid Rs. 1 Cr upfront as cash, there was actually a *net cash outflow* in the business.

Even though your company is operationally profitable, there is a net cash outflow.

You must have by now guessed that net cash outflow happens when the cash inflow is less than cash outflow, and *net cash inflow* happens when the inflow exceeds outflow.

A Cash Flow Statement has 3 parts:

1. Operating Cash Flow
2. Cash Flow from Financing Activities
3. Cash Flow from Investing Activities

We'll understand each of these in detail.

Operating Cash Flow

This is also referred to as *Cash Flow from Operating Activities*. This measures the cash generated by the business from its regular business operations. It indicates whether a business can generate sufficient cash flow from its operations to grow, or whether it needs external funding.

In the Gale Drinks example, the cash generated from day-to-day sales of the beverage constitutes the cash inflow, while the expenses incurred to make the sale happen are the cash outflow. These expenses, in this case, are the raw material costs, logistics costs, and marketing expenses incurred to sell the drinks. If you notice, all these expenses are directly related to the core operations of the business. We have left out the fixed costs like rent, equipment, salaries, etc. since they are not operational expenses.

Cash Flow from Financing Activities (CFF)

Cash Flow from Financing Activities (CFF) tracks the net change in cash flow used for funding activities, i.e. equity or debt.

When investors pump in money in the form of equity, it is accounted as a cash inflow under CFF. Similarly, cash coming into the company in the form of a loan from a bank or any other entity is also cash inflow under CFF.

When the company repays a debt to its lenders or pays out dividends to its equity holders, it is accounted as a cash outflow under CFF.

The difference between the outflow and the inflow determines the net cash flow under CFF. As you must have understood, if the outflow is greater than the inflow, it is net cash outflow, and if the inflow is greater then it's net cash inflow under CFF.

Cash Flow from Investing Activities (CFI)

Cash Flow from Investing Activities tracks the cash spent or generated on investing activities. Investing activities usually refer to any sale or purchase of long-term assets, or anything pertaining to investment securities like mutual funds, fixed deposits, bonds, etc.

Some of the cash outflow items may include any purchases of long-term fixed assets such as machinery, a new office building, a factory, investments into security markets, or even the acquisition of other businesses. All these expenses are expected to generate returns for the business over the long term but necessitate cash outflow immediately.

Cash inflow items may include earnings from the sale of any fixed assets, like office equipment or machinery, sale of investment securities, collections of loans, collection of rent on office space, etc.

With this, we come to the end of the Cash Flow Statement, and also of all the major accounting statements. Preparing a Cash Flow Statement, like the two statements before it, is again a matter of classifying the right items under the right headers. I hope that going through this chapter so far has equipped you with the knowledge to understand major accounting statements.

Financial ratios

Financial ratios don't come under Accounting, but entrepreneurs without a background in finance usually struggle to understand the ratios and jargon thrown around by professionals. I have added this section as a reference guide for anyone wanting to get a quick primer on such terms.

This section is also inspired by the content on the finance web site investopedia.com. I'd recommend it to any beginner looking to understand the basics of finance.

Liquidity

Liquidity is *"the ease with which an asset can be converted into ready cash without affecting its market price"*, as articulately defined by Investopedia. Cash is the most liquid of assets, while other tangible items are relatively less so.

Selling stocks of public companies is fast and straightforward, so you'd consider stocks as a relatively liquid asset class. But selling real estate in the form of a plot of land is not so much. It may take months or even years to find the right buyer. Real estate, thus, is relatively less liquid.

Liquidity ratios

Current Ratio

A current ratio measures whether a company has enough resources to meet its short-term necessities.

Current Ratio = Current Assets/Current Liabilities

The current ratio helps understand the liquidity of a company and how easily that company will be able to pay off its current liabilities. A current ratio greater than 1 means that a company owns enough assets that it can sell off to pay all its liabilities.

Quick Ratio

It is defined as the ratio between quickly available or liquid assets and current liabilities.

Quick Ratio = (Current Assets - Inventory - Prepaid expenses)/Current Liabilities

The quick ratio is similar to the current ratio. It provides a more conservative assessment of the liquidity position of firms as it excludes inventory. A quick ratio greater than 1 means that a company owns enough assets that it can use or sell off instantly to pay all its liabilities.

Cash Ratio

Cash Ratio is the ratio of a company's total cash and cash equivalents to its current liabilities. Cash equivalents refer to the sources of money that can be converted into cash immediately, e.g. savings or fixed deposits in a bank account.

Cash Ratio = Cash and Cash equivalents/Current Liabilities

The cash ratio is more conservative than other liquidity ratios as it only considers a company's most liquid resources.

Other ratios

Debt-to-Equity (D/E) ratio

The Debt-to-Equity (D/E) ratio is the ratio between a company's total liabilities to its shareholder equity.

D/E ratio = Total Liabilities/Total Shareholders' Equity

The Debt-to-Equity ratio is most often used to understand the extent to which a company has taken debt relative to its total equity value. A high D/E indicates that the company has financed its growth mainly through debt.

Return on equity (ROE)

The return on equity (ROE) is a measure of the profitability of a business relative to the shareholder's equity. It indicates how efficiently the company generates profits.

ROE = Net Income/Shareholder's Equity

ROE of 15–20% and above is generally considered good.

Return on capital employed (ROCE)

It is a financial ratio that measures a company's profitability with respect to its capital.

ROCE = Earnings Before Interest and Tax (EBIT)/Capital Employed

ROCE is a useful metric to measure the returns a company can generate on the capital put in or used. If two companies start with the same amount of capital, the company with a higher ROCE generates more return than the one with a lower value. High ROCE companies are usually preferred by external investors for their return-generating capability.

Return on assets (ROA)

The return on assets (ROA) shows how profitable a company is relative to the assets owned by them.

ROA = Net Income/Average Total Assets

This ratio indicates how efficiently a company uses its assets to generate profits. An ROA of 5% or above is broadly considered good, but a comparison with companies within the same industry would be more apt.

Accounting is hard to cover in a single chapter. B-schools dedicate an entire trimester of classes, B.Com graduates study it for at least a semester, while Chartered Accountants breathe it day in and day out. This chapter, as the cliche goes, is like a drop in the ocean. But for entrepreneurs, it does cover the basics which can help them in at least understanding, and possibly preparing their company's accounting statements in the early stages.

In the subsequent pages a sample MIS format used by one of my clients in the D2C space, is shared. If you observe, the different sheets shown here present different types of business information, and all sheets combined comprehensively cover everything a founder needs to know about their business.

Sheet 1: Profitability Analysis	
Total Order Values (TOV)	
Less: Returns to Origin(RTO)	
RTO/TOV (%)	
Gross Sales (as per GST)	
Less: GST Output	
Net Revenue for Business (NR)	
% increase in revenue month-on-month (MOM)	
Operating Stock	
Add: Purchases (Material + Packaging)	
Less: Cl. Stock	
COGS	
COGS/Net Revenue (%)	
Gross Margin (GM), i.e., Net Revenue - COGS	
GM%, i.e., GM/NR	
Less: Logistics Cost	
Contribution Margin 1 (CM1),i.e., GM-Logistics Cost	
CM1%, i.e., CM1/NR	
Less: Ad Spend (Facebook, Instagram, Google)	
Contribution Margin 2 (CM2), i.e., CM1-Ad Spend	
CM2%, i.e., CM2/NR	
Less: Fixed Costs (FC) (other than Partners' salaries, Staff welfare, business promotion, office rent/utilities, all other business expenses)	
Net Operating Profit, i.e., CM2-FC	
OP%, i.e., Net Operating Profit/NR	
Less: Fixed Assets Purchased	
Less: Partners' Salaries	
Less: Advance Income Tax paid	
Surplus/Deficit	

Sheet 2: Sales Analysis	
Net Revenues (NR)	
Top SKU 1	
Top SKU 2	
Top SKU 3	
Top SKU 4	
Top SKU 5	
All other SKUs	
SKU wise analysis	
No. of Orders (Gross)	
No. of Returns	
Net No. of Orders (Gross - Returns)	
Selling Price (SP) per unit (incl. GST)	
Total Sales for SKU (SP x Net Orders)	
Customer wise analysis	
B2B sales	
B2C sales	
B2B sale & Channel Analysis	
Customer wise split (B2B only)	
Customer A	
Customer B	
Customer C	
Channel wise split	
Instagram to own website	
Own website direct	
Amazon	
Flipkart	
Nykaa, etc.	

Sheet 3: Inventory Ageing					
SKUs	**Value (Rs.)**	**0-30 days**	**30-60 days**	**60-90 days**	**>90 days**
SKU 1					
SKU 2					
SKU 3					
SKU 4					
SKU 5					
SKU 6					
SKU 7					
Cl. Stock Total					

6. Setting Yourself Up - Co-Founders & Advisors

So far we have covered the basics of what one needs to know if they have started up or plan to in the future. Although being abreast of those concepts keeps you in good stead, in all honesty, I don't believe knowing or not knowing them would be decisive in your success. Concepts can be learned on the go, and mistakes once made can usually be rectified. But relationships gone awry are harder to mend and lead to disastrous consequences.

Among all things, co-founder conflict is believed to be the number one reason for startups failing. Intelligence and ability aside, if you can't work well with your co-founders, your startup will not see much success. Here, we shall understand the major co-founder dynamics crucial to a startup's health. A great founding team with the right ingredients to build a great company is perhaps the single most important marker of success.

Let's go deep into what comprises a great founding team, but before that, let's see if you even need a co-founder.

Going Solo or with a Co-founder

According to research by Ali Tamaseb[1], Partner at DCVC and author of "Super Founders", of the 195 startups which became unicorns (valuation of USD 1 billion) between 2005 and 2018 in the US, about 20% of them had just one founder, 35% had 2, and 30% had 3. The rest, obviously, had 4 or more founders.

In another 2016 article on Techcrunch by Haje Jan Kamps[2], however, data of 7,348 companies which had raised at least USD 10 million in funding showed that almost 46% of those startups had a single founder, almost 32% had 2, and 15% had 3.

If we consider both these data sets to be true, and if we assume that all startups that became unicorns had raised at least USD 10 million (a fair assumption, I believe), two things become clear.

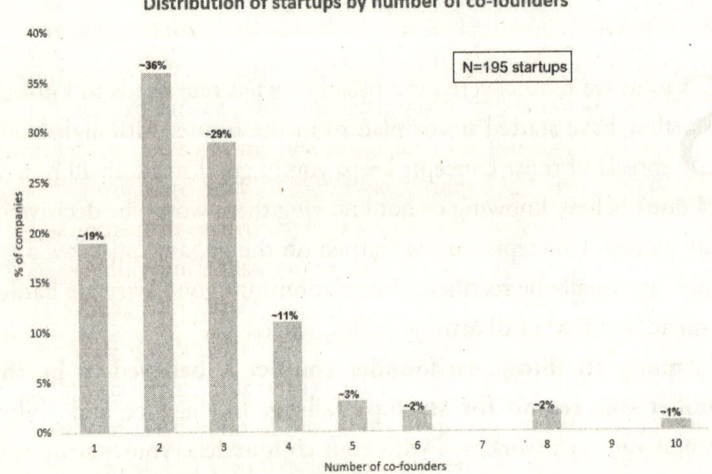

Source: Ali Tamaseb's post on Medium

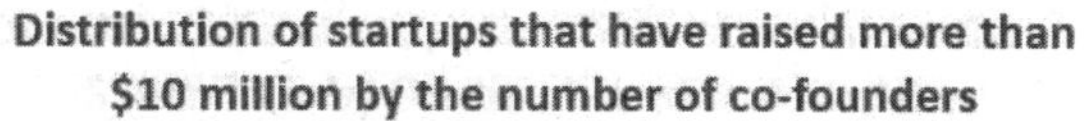

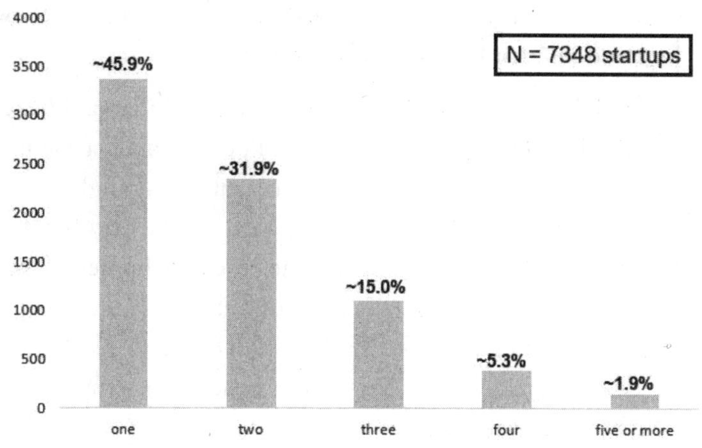

Source: Techcrunch, article titled "Breaking a myth: Data shows you don't actually need a co-founder"

Firstly, it appears as if a higher number of solo-founded companies are able to raise at least USD 10 million in funding, but from among them, chances of further becoming a unicorn are highest for startups with 2 co-founders followed by 3.

Secondly, the number of founders does not conclusively determine how big or successful the startup would be, at least when the number is 3 or fewer.

Going solo as the founder or going ahead with one or two co-founders then, comes down to the individual starting out. There are numerous examples of successful startups with 1, 2, or 3 founders. 4 or more may not be ideal, as we see from both data points, and we'll discuss why later in this chapter. Firstly, let's understand why having co-founder(s) can be helpful, and when it makes sense to go solo.

Perks of having a co-founder

Building a company is inherently a difficult process. It takes a toll mentally, physically, financially, and emotionally; and handling it all by yourself only makes it harder. When you have someone reliable and capable alongside, it gives you the necessary support on all fronts. The following points cover why I believe having a co-founder or two may be the right approach to building a startup.

1. **Division of labour:** This is the most straightforward benefit one obtains. No single person is equipped to build a company all on their own. If they can find a capable co-founder to lead one of the core aspects of a company - product development or business - while they handle the other, the burden of managing different things reduces drastically and makes the process a lot more efficient. Each co-founder leads the function they are great at, and the startup benefits in terms of both speed and expertise.
2. **Fewer bottlenecks:** When there are 2 or 3 leaders equally driven to run the company, it allows all of them a timely breather when they need one. They know that they'd be ably substituted temporarily and work wouldn't stop. Going solo doesn't give one that luxury.
3. **Complementary skill-sets:** When 2 or 3 capable people with complementary skill-sets but common goals come together, it creates a base for healthy conflicts and creative outcomes. While a solo founder is usually left to their own wits when making a decision, having a co-founder protects the company from the consequences of sometimes impulsive choices made by one.
4. **Easier bootstrapping:** Startups usually start bootstrapped. It's the founders' limited personal funds that take care of expenses early on. If there are 2 or 3 co-founders, this load gets distributed and allows more breathing space for the startup to mature. It also allows one of the co-founders to continue working in a regular job and fund the business from their salary, while the others put their entire energy into building it.
5. **Emotional support:** This is probably a more underrated aspect

of building a company with co-founders. It's hard enough to build a startup with a great founding team, and if you do this alone it becomes even more challenging. During difficult times, and a startup faces many of them, having co-founders who can egg you on may just be the difference between giving up and soldiering ahead. The collective enthusiasm of the entire team ensures that one never feels alone, and it is a huge asset to have.

All the factors above, though, work only if there's excellent chemistry between the co-founders. While having co-founders can benefit a startup immensely, it's not mandatory. Let's understand in what scenarios going solo may be a better option.

When solo makes sense

When should you consider doing things alone? I have listed some points below that, if you observe, are connected with the ones in the previous section on the perks of having a co-founder. If one can find alternative ways to address the pain points that co-founders solve, it may make sense to do it alone.

1. **Complementary skills not necessary:** While most startups would require a 'builder' and a 'seller' in the founding team, it's possible that one of these two things does not take as much effort. For example, if a product has been built quickly by the founder, and they have found paying customers quickly with the MVP, it may not be necessary to bring a co-founder on board. The revenues would probably allow them to hire individuals who can manage the two tasks dedicatedly. The founder need not go out of the way to look for a co-founder in such a case.
2. **Greater access to funds:** If a founder has more funds at their disposal, either in a personal capacity or through external means, then they could possibly hire smart people and build a founding team without making anyone the co-founder. This

founding team can then collectively cover most of the benefits that the co-founders would have provided.

3. **Deep expertise in industry:** When the founder has relevant, deep expertise in the industry themselves, and are well-versed with all aspects of the business, then they may not need a co-founder early on. They probably know exactly how to get the job done and are confident to get the ball rolling on their own.
4. **Control freaks:** Some individuals just like having more control and want to have a say in all aspects of running the business. If you belong to this category, then it may be a good idea to build a company by yourself, because co-founders would surely not appreciate that and the association may not last long.
5. **Inability to find someone:** It's possible that despite your best efforts, you are not able to find that one person to share your startup journey with. The worst decision you could make then is to bring in someone you're not convinced with. Chances of a conflict become much higher, and as a result, the company may even have to shut down. In such a scenario, it's actually better to keep building solo with the help of advisors and freelancers until someone worthwhile comes along.

While these pointers may not cover everything that can go right or wrong, you probably get the idea of when to build as a team and when to go solo. The following sections in the chapter address the co-founder dynamics that are critical for a startup's success.

The Ideal Co-founder Mix

Any business, at its core, basically does these two things: build and sell. If it's a product-based business, like a tech startup building a SaaS product, it needs an engineer who can 'build' the product and a business person who could 'sell' it. If it's a D2C business selling a packaged food item, the building involves creating and manufacturing the product, while selling involves making it available and visible in the right places. Either building or selling cannot work in isolation to run a company.

When a startup has co-founders, the most basic segregation of tasks is that of a 'builder' and a 'seller'. In fact, if you observe, most businesses with 2 co-founders that achieved some level of success have a builder and a seller at the helm. In tech startups today, they assume the positions of a CEO and a CTO.

But how you define the builder and seller roles also becomes important. In tech startups, it seems straightforward that the engineer is the one who'll build, while the business guy will sell. It's the responsibility of the CTO to handle everything pertaining to product development, while the CEO takes care of all things business. Here, the identification of the builder and the seller is clear.

But not all startups are technology-driven. For a D2C fashion brand, the builder would not be a CTO but someone who's managing the creation and manufacturing processes, while the seller would ideally be an adept marketing professional since that's what would drive sales.

Clearly, in a two-co-founder setup, the mix should always be that of a seller and a builder. It also must be noted that being the designated builder doesn't forbid one from being involved in the selling process and vice-versa. It just identifies their primary responsibility and the decision-making authority when it comes to either of the aspects. In a startup, after all, you just do whatever it takes to run the company successfully, regardless of how skilled (or unskilled) you may be at it.

When does a third co-founder come into the picture?

The way I see it, when one of the building or selling processes has two clear building blocks within itself, it may require two individuals to manage that process completely and efficiently.

For example, a FinTech product that helps one save and manage taxes efficiently may need both a Chartered Accountant and an engineer to actually build it. The CA will help functionally design the right product while the engineer will actually build the product.

An AI-based SaaS product will probably require both an AI expert and a software developer to build it right.

Similarly, manufacturing-based startups may require one person to supervise the operational aspects of manufacturing while another manages the R&D for the product.

In an FMCG startup, the selling process comprises both visibility (marketing) and availability of the product (retail sales). The company may then consider having two individuals manage these separately.

Before considering a third co-founder for your startup, always check whether that person is coming in with a complementary skill-set that is indeed adding value and will increase the speed and efficiency.

Should you ever consider a fourth co-founder? I personally don't think a necessity should arise. Three is the maximum number of complementary skills any startup would need in the beginning. If you're considering a fourth co-founder, chances are that the skills of at least two of the four are either overlapping, or one of them will be relevant only after the startup attains some maturity. In either of these cases, bringing in a co-founder for that purpose will be unnecessary.

Historical data also suggests that two is probably the best number under most circumstances, and three could be considered for reasons we discussed. Anything more than that will probably cause redundancy, which no startup can afford.

How to Check Co-founder Fitment?

While one may find a co-founder that fits the bill perfectly on paper, at the end of the day, it's about 2 or 3 human beings working together to build something extraordinary. It may still be easier to find potential co-founders that are a functional fit, but it's more important for them to have a more holistic fitment for the startup to succeed. They should be able to work seamlessly in a professional setup while also having good rapport on a personal level.

Investors often look for some relevant history between the co-founders when assessing a startup for investment. Their favourite manifestation of this is a past working relationship. If the co-founders had been colleagues at an organization previously for a considerable duration, it's a clear indicator that they decided to start up together knowing exactly what each brings to the table. Chances of professional conflict, in the investors' eyes, are minimum in such a setup.

Another good indicator of fitment is how well and for how long the co-founders have known each other personally. College friends starting up together is a common occurrence and investors also view it positively, as it at least indicates a good personal relationship.

Some co-founder team-ups trigger instant alarm bells. Examples can be:

- Met on a co-founder dating site
- No prior working or personal relationship
- Vast difference in age or experience level
- Different goals and aspirations with the startup

While the first three points are easy to spot, it's important for the co-founders to be aligned on the fourth. Even individuals with a solid history together may end up having differences if this is not addressed in time.

One way to do this is to clarify each person's motivation to start up and what they wish to achieve from it. Rizwan Virk, in his book 'Startup Myths and Models', shares 7 motivations for starting up[3].

1. Money Driven
2. Creativity Driven
3. Technology or Market Driven
4. Fame or Respect Driven
5. Independence Driven
6. Competition or Empire Driven
7. Social Mission Driven

It's important that the co-founders are clear about each other's motivation to start up. If there are clear differences, the end may not be far.

As an example, if you are driven by a social mission to impact the world, whereas your co-founder is driven by money, a few years down the line, you may want to reject an acquisition offer outright while your co-founder would be in its favour because of the money! It will result in a stalemate.

It's possible and understandable that the co-founders have multiple motivations from the list given. They should still have an open discussion upfront about them, play out different possible scenarios - good and bad - and understand what each one would prefer. If there are differences, then it would be good to map alternate courses for those scenarios well in advance when things are still nice and amicable.

Optimum Equity Split between Co-founders

A bone of contention for the co-founders is often the equity split between them. While many co-founder teams have an equal or an almost equal distribution of equity, it's not so evenly shared among others. What is the right way to approach this? Let's first understand some of the reasons why some startup founders settle for an uneven distribution of equity.

Founders may justify lopsided equity splits with a reason that will fall into one of the following buckets:

- Joining the startup at different times
- Difference in investments in the company
- Difference in experience or expertise
- Difference in salaries drawn

While all these reasons may seem justified, it's important for the founders to consider that the equity split should be fair enough to keep each co-founder engaged and motivated for the long term. It's often hard to intuitively account for this in the beginning. If one of the co-founders has invested more time and effort, then the others involved may agree to an unequal split. But as the startup matures, the initial few months of extra effort appear increasingly insignificant in the face of what they're building towards. A 5% difference in equity shareholding in a 100 Cr company results in a difference of 5 Cr between the co-founders if a payout happens. If the basis of this 5% was a 3-month difference in tenures, do you think the split was justified?

If the skills of the co-founders involved are complementary and core to the main business idea, I usually advise founders to keep the split as equal as possible. They may choose to give a slightly higher share to the CEO to indicate a higher decision-making authority if they deem fit. Normally, a 50-50 or 51-49 share for 2 co-founders, and a 34-33-33 share between 3 is what I advise under most circumstances.

However, if any of the reasons mentioned is indeed significant, it may warrant a wider equity split. For example, if a co-founder joined more than a year after operations commenced, or after a round of funding was raised, then clearly they undertook less risk than the one who took the plunge early. Or if the investment made by one of the co-founders was significantly larger in the business, then they may justifiably expect a larger share of the equity.

Another scenario is if the product under development is based on a patented Intellectual Property owned by one of the co-founders, then additional equity is justified. In all these cases, the motivation of all the co-founders for the long-term should be taken into account, and the decision should be taken keeping the best interests of the startup in mind.

Finding and Compensating Advisors

Despite one's best efforts, one may be unable to find the right co-founder for their startup. In such scenarios, founders are forced to rely on freelancers and advisors for help. While freelancers can be useful to obtain clear deliverables related to product development, finance and accounting, or legal work, advisors are usually more strategic to the business and may help in more ways than one.

Advisors are professionals who have at least 3-5 years of experience ahead of you in the industry of your startup. Their main task is to help you steer your startup in the right direction with their experience and guidance. A good advisor will be able to provide valuable insights into the industry and help you avoid the pitfalls that come with relative inexperience. If they strongly believe in your startup, they may also help with industry connections and at times with their credibility.

Based on the stage at which your company is, or the primary business goal, you can consider having different advisors as per the table below.

Stage / Goal	Advisor
Ideation	An industry expert to give relevant insights
MVP	A product or tech advisor to help build the product efficiently. OR A seasoned tech entrepreneur who successfully scaled a product.
Fundraising	Fundraising expert / Seasoned CA who has worked with startups, Startup legal expert
Growth	Growth marketing expert
Brand building	Brand marketing expert

It must be noted that advisors may not always be officially appointed. If you have a founding team to run the business with, then you could reach out to individuals you regard highly in your field and seek advice whenever necessary. An exception to this, though, would be for fundraising. Unless you have an experienced entrepreneur who has raised funds in the past, it would be prudent to hire a financial and legal advisor to help you with the process.

What does an advisor take?

Advisors can sometimes help you without any monetary rewards or they take a small fee in return. At times, advisors may take equity in the startup, which is called advisor equity. If you offer shares to advisors, do keep in mind that even at the early stages, the advisor pool in total should ideally not exceed 2% of the total shareholding of the company.

Ideally, the equity they receive should be based on achieving certain milestones. If an advisor adds strategic value to the company and is making tangible, measurable improvements, you can possibly offer them 0.5% of the company. If an advisor is for the brand name and to validate thoughts and ideas once a month, I recommend not giving them more than 0.25% of the company. These thumb rule benchmarks are based on the assumption that you have not over 4 advisors and a total pool of 2%.

Ultimately, before giving away equity, always consider the value they'll add over the long-term. Founders are sometimes tempted to offer significant equity to early advisors only to later realize that their contribution in the larger scheme of things was commensurately much smaller. I advise founders to be highly protective of their equity. Use cash wherever possible and feasible.

I have shared a link to the Founder Advisor Standard Template (FAST) prescribed by the Founder Institute (fi.co), a founder education and networking platform, in the Annexure 6.1 to refer to points to negotiate and terms to agree on before onboarding advisors.

Understanding and optimizing the dynamics between co-founders is extremely critical to a startup's success. While a lot of the points mentioned in this chapter may appear obvious or even trivial at first, always remember that provisions need to be made for the bad days in good times. If you run a startup which doesn't abide by the suggestions mentioned here, I'd urge you to consider the points of difference and assess any possible conflict areas at the earliest. It helps to be clear and prepared when things are good and amicable.

I have not covered the co-founder's agreement in this chapter. It's a legal document that every startup with two or more co-founders must have. It has been covered in Chapter 16, *Fundraising Paperwork & Compliance*.

7. Understanding Employee Stock Options (ESOPs)

All founders have some primary skills of their own. But no one person has all of them to run a business successfully. In the long-term, there are only two ways a founder can have the complete gamut of necessary skills to build their startup - have co-founders with complementary skill-set and/or hire people who possess them.

Hiring people is especially challenging in the beginning. Startups are usually bootstrapped first and are limited in funds to offer a proper market salary to their key hires. Getting inexperienced or underwhelming candidates to save on salary costs is not a good idea either. There must be some way to both attract great people and not be handicapped by salary payout constraints.

Also, regardless of the stage of the startup, employees who have stayed for long and contributed heavily to its growth expect to be compensated fairly for their role in building it.

Employee Stock Ownership Plan, also called ESOP or ESOPs, exists for such purposes. They have been used by startups and established companies as a critical tool for employee compensation and retention. In this chapter, we shall learn in detail about ESOPs, and how they can be utilized to benefit startups and their employees.

Understanding the Need and Basics of ESOP

ESOPs ensure a sufficient partake of employees in the startup's profits.

By choosing to work at a startup over a more established firm, an employee, similar to the founder, also takes a risk. While the founder's risk is higher, they also stand to get rewarded the most if the startup grows and does well over the years owing to their high ownership stake. Employees who help build the startup with them should also similarly be rewarded for the risk they undertook during its early stages and their contribution to building it over a considerably long period.

ESOPs give the employees an option to claim an ownership stake in the company. It allows them to be compensated on the basis of their contribution to its growth. With ESOPs, as the company grows in value, the employees' individual net worth also grows. Also, unlike variable pay, ESOPs don't have the upside capped. So it gives the employees the opportunity to generate a large amount of wealth if things do work out for the startup.

Due to ESOPs' immense wealth-generating potential, employees who get them often harbour the sentiment to work hard, build the startup into a success, and then reap the rewards. Such employees stick to this company and work with the founders to make it successful. This significantly helps in retaining the key people and reduces the hiring cost.

Founders, on the other hand, can plan and set aside an ESOP pool to be distributed among their key hires. It often reduces the burden of paying out huge salaries entirely in cash. Also, issuing ESOPs doesn't immediately give equity to the employee. It only means that they have the right to claim a stake in the future if they meet certain criteria. Lastly, issuing ESOPs is a fairly simple process and doesn't involve high costs.

It's not hard to see why ESOPs have become a critical element of employee compensation today, especially in startups. Let's understand its technicalities in detail.

ESOP Basics

ESOP, as mentioned earlier, stands for Employee Stock Ownership Plan or Employee Stock Option Plan. Having ESOPs permits the employees that hold them, or gives them an *option*, to convert those into shares of the company or *exercise* them. Technically, what employees have are not stocks but *stock options.*

Every company which issues ESOPs needs an *ESOP policy* which clearly defines the terms, conditions, and circumstances under which those can be exercised. In this section, we cover all such elements that constitute the ESOP policy and what each of them means.

Eligible Employees

A startup founder may not want to give ESOPs equally to each of their employees. In fact, it's not necessary they give ESOPs at all after a point. There could be several bases for giving ESOPs - time of joining, performance, seniority, etc. - depending on the founders' preferences. ESOPs, in the end, are only given to *eligible employees.*

By definition, eligible employees are those who the Board of Directors collectively agrees to be eligible for the ESOP scheme.

Here is a simple example that you can refer to define the eligible employees of your company.

1. Employees who have been with the company for 2 years or more
2. All employees at managerial levels and above
3. Employees who are marked above 8 out of 10 in the annual appraisal report
4. Any employee nominated by their manager for exceptional contribution

Grant letter

Grant is the event when the ESOPs are offered to the employee by the company.

Grant letter is the legal document or the agreement of the issuance of ESOPs to employees. It contains the terms and conditions of the ESOP policy.

Vesting Period

The *vesting period* refers to the length of time an employee must spend with the company to earn the right to exercise the ESOPs in full.

The basis of having this vesting period is to ensure that employees holding ESOPs stay long enough to be able to exercise them in full or in part, depending on the length of time they stay. It thus acts as a tool to incentivize employees to stay longer with the company, while fairly tying the rewards with their period of association.

The vesting schedule refers to what portion of the ESOPs get vested over specified periods.

As an example, if a person has 100 ESOPs vesting over 4 years following an annual vesting schedule, the employee may earn ESOPs as follows:

On completing

Year 1: 25

Year 2: 25

Year 3: 25

Year 4: 25

If the employee leaves the company before the first year, they get no ESOPs. If they leave the company sometime between year 3 and year 4, they get 75 ESOPs. You get the idea.

Such vesting can also be monthly or half-yearly or quarterly.

In half-yearly vesting, for example, the same 100 stock options will vest completely over 4 years, but there will be fresh vesting every 6 months. So instead of waiting for one full year, the first set of vesting will happen at 6 months with 12 (or 13) stock options vesting first.

Then again, at the end of 1 year, when the total vested stock options become 25. At the 1.5-year mark, another 12 (or 13) stock options will vest, taking the total to 37. If the employee leaves at this point, they'd be eligible to exercise 37 stock options in half-yearly vesting, whereas with annual vesting they could have only exercised 25 stock options. Similarly, quarterly or monthly vesting also happens. The higher the frequency of vesting, the more favourable it generally becomes for the employees since they lose less in opportunity cost.

Vesting can also happen in a staggered manner instead of a linear way as exemplified here. Some companies allow their employees to vest a much smaller portion of their ESOPs in the initial two years and then significantly increase this value in the final two years. Amazon, for example, has a vesting schedule which looks like this:

1st year: 5%

2nd year: 15%

20% for every six months thereafter

Similarly, some companies follow a 10-20-30-40 vesting schedule to incentivize employees to stay longer.

A staggered vesting schedule dissuades employees to leave within the first few years. However, many startups are now moving towards more employee-friendly vesting rules. Meesho, for example, allows their eligible employees to convert up to 25% of their salary to special ESOPs (called MeESOPs) which vest 100% in 1 year[1].

Cliff

Cliff refers to the minimum period an employer needs to be employed with the company to earn any ESOPs at all. 1 year is a standard most companies keep.

Modifying the example from the previous section to monthly vesting with a cliff of 1 year, the person will earn 25 stock options at the end of year 1. But if they leave the company before completing a year, even in the 11th month, they will not get anything. If they leave in the 13th month, however, they will receive ~27 stock options, 25 earned after completing the cliff period, and 2 for the 13th month.

Exercise

Exercise refers to the event when an employee converts the ESOPs to shares.

Let's say an employee possesses 100 stock options with a vesting period of 4 years and a cliff of 1 year. After the first year is complete, 25 of these stock options get vested. Now the employee has an option to convert these options to shares, or in other words, to exercise their options. Note that exercising your options doesn't mean selling your shares, it just means that your options get converted to proper shares of the company.

What happens when an employee doesn't exercise their options?

Vested ESOPs, if not exercised, may extinguish if the ESOP policy defines a timeline for mandatory exercising of ESOPs. However, if there is no such timeline, then such vested ESOPs may remain vested, to be exercised immediately before a liquidation event, such as an IPO, or an acquisition of the company, when all shareholders get money in return for their shares.

Exercise Price

The exercise price is the price an employee needs to pay to buy their vested shares.

This is the discounted share price, usually a nominal value, decided by the company at the time of issuance of the ESOPs and mentioned in the ESOP grant letter. This price depends on the *fair market value* of the shares at the time they are being granted but is usually less.

The shares that the employees receive on exercising their ESOPs can be equity shares, preference shares, or equity shares with Differential Rights, based on what the company decides.

Employees usually purchase these vested shares only when they have found a buyer who's willing to pay a much higher price for those than the exercise price. In some cases, even the company, whose vested shares they have, offers a loan to enable such employees to purchase the shares. Since they're aware that the shares will be sold at a premium to the exercise price, they're confident of getting the amount repaid.

Fair Market Value

Fair Market Value is the price the market is willing to pay for the shares on their exercise date. For listed companies, the fair market value is simply the share price at any given time in the stock market. For startups, most of which are unlisted, the price is usually calculated by a Registered Valuer, Merchant Banker, or Chartered Accountant. They consider the company's profits, revenue, growth metrics, and other performance parameters to arrive at the value.

Once the fair market value is known, the employees can purchase the vested shares at the exercise price and sell them to a willing buyer at the fair market value, or a price close to that. The wealth generation opportunity for the employee obviously depends on the difference between the exercise price and the selling price.

Finding a buyer for vested shares may not be easy for an employee on their own. But if a startup does its IPO, all employees with vested stock options can easily trade these stocks after exercising them. That's why it's a highly anticipated event for long-serving employees and shareholders of any startup.

What should be the Size of the ESOP Pool?

Once the founders have decided to use ESOP as a tool for compensation, they next need to be clear on what share of their startup they wish to keep aside for their employees' ownership. This becomes the *ESOP pool* of the company.

In bootstrapped startups, the founders have complete authority on how small or big they wish to keep this pool. It becomes a strategic business call for them and depends on how they believe ESOPs may help in the overall progress of the company.

In funded startups though, external investors also have their say.

Most investors, in the first funding round, ask the founders to create an unissued ESOP pool of 10-15% from the pre-money valuation. Many founders who are not well informed about ESOPs and how they work may simply give in to this demand, which may not be the best decision always. One need not set aside 10% or any arbitrary number just because it is considered an "industry norm".

One way to rationalize the ESOP pool size is to make it a function of the cash component of employees' expenses. In the early days, especially, it makes sense to give an employee ESOPs equal to their salary in the cash component.

The following steps clarify how to calculate the ESOP pool by making it a function of employees' salaries.

Step 1: Estimate the resource cost

How many people do you need between the current fundraise and the next, i.e., during the proposed runway?

Assume this is your first round of funding and you are building a runway for 12 months. Since these are early days, you might just need a 5-person team with an average salary of Rs. 12L per annum to get through the next 12 months.

That's a total manpower cost of Rs. 60 Lakhs.

Step 2: Calculate the post-money value of your startup

What will be the post-money value of your startup after the current fundraise?

Let's assume that it is Rs. 12 crores. If you raised Rs. 2 crores at a pre-money value of Rs. 10 crores, you give the investors 16.67% holding in your company.

Step 3: Divide the step 1 value by step 2

Divide the Core Team Manpower Cost calculated in Step 1 by the Post Money Value calculated in Step 2.

In this example, it comes to (0.6 crores/12 crores), i.e. 5%. This 5% should ideally be the size of your unissued ESOP pool in this round.

Note that in this case, we have considered the cash component of employees' salary to be equal to the stocks component. However, it may not always be the case. If the employees are getting paid well below their market standards, it makes sense to give out more in stocks. In that case, in step 1, you multiply the runway by the premium you deem fit - could be anywhere between 1.2x to 2.5x, depending on what you think is fair.

Similarly, if your employees are already getting market salaries or above, it may not be necessary to set aside a large ESOP pool. In that case, you could reduce the Step 1 value by a percentage you think is fair.

This is one way to rationalize and negotiate the size of the pool. There can be other methods too, where industry standards and employee wealth creation incentives may be given a higher multiple.

With time, the value of your shares increases and you'd be able to issue a higher value of ESOPs without giving away as much in terms of the number of shares as you did the first time. During subsequent fundraises, I believe, you should have the unissued part of the pool at half of the issued part of the ESOP pool, assuming you're doing rounds every 18-24 months.

For example, if you've issued 8% from the first pool, then you need to maintain about 4% unissued in the next round. This 4% will be used to issue more ESOPs to new hires.

This is not an absolutely foolproof method, but just one way to logically think through the ESOP pool size rather than blindly adhering to existing standards.

How many ESOPs should you give your Employees?

Once you have created an ESOP pool, the next decision is how much to give to employees.

While there are no rules set in stone, the following factors can be considered to decide the ESOP component of employees' compensation:

a) Salary

The difference between the salary drawn by the employee with the market salary they would otherwise command should be taken into account. One way to arrive at the number is to consider a multiple of this difference. For example, if you're interested in a person who would otherwise command a CTC of 12LPA in the market but your budget is only 9LPA, then the difference of 3LPA can be considered as the base. To make the offer attractive, you could offer a 2x-4x of this difference in ESOPs. If this number is 2x the difference, then you can offer 6L worth of ESOPs in addition to the 9LPA cash component of the pay.

What the multiple should be is again a call to be taken on the other two factors mentioned here.

In case the employee is already being paid a market salary or above, then offering ESOPs is a strategic call to make the offer even more attractive so that it acts as a tool of motivation. The other two factors can again be taken into account to make this offer.

b) Seniority/ Criticality

If an employee is being hired at a senior position to handle a critical role, then the goal of the founder is to make them stay and keep them motivated for the long-term to build this startup into something great. To achieve this, they're usually offered a high ESOP component. For someone heading a critical function, like a head of product in a tech startup, you could even keep aside a certain percentage of your company for them. If they have joined at a very early stage and are drawing a salary much lower than market standards, then they'd expect a higher stake in your company. It's not uncommon for startups to keep aside anywhere between 0.5% to even 5% or higher, keeping other factors in mind. If it goes beyond 10%, then they may be worthy of being called a co-founder.

If someone is being hired at a more mature stage, then the ESOPs could be considered based on their value. You need not give a significant portion of your company away in such cases.

c) Time of joining

Usually, the earlier the stage, the larger the stake you offer. In the beginning, shares of the company won't have much tangible value, so critical employees and co-founders need to be given larger chunks of the company to keep them interested. As the startup matures and the company's shares have a price, it becomes simpler to offer ESOPs based on their currency value. At later stages, high ESOP values can be given at very small percentages of the company, potentially making the offer attractive for joiners and not costing the company much either.

All three factors above can be considered to compute the final ESOP component for any employee. In fact, ESOPs can also be used creatively to offer more attractive increments or to even restructure one's CTC. We saw earlier in the chapter how Meesho allows their eligible employees to convert up to 25% of their salary to special ESOPs (called MeESOPs) which vest 100% in 1 year. Employees who are bullish about the company's growth and wish to stay for long can opt for such offers.

Management Stock Options (MSOPs) & ESOP Top Up

Management Stock Options or MSOPs are the ESOPs granted to the top management of any startup or even a large company. These employees may not be a part of the founding team, but many companies keep aside a separate pool for the ones heading critical functions. They often constitute a healthy portion of their overall compensation and give them a reason to stick longer with the company. Simply put, MSOPs refer to the ESOP pool set aside for the top management.

In many companies, additional ESOPs are also rewarded as part of annual increments or good performance over a period of time. When employees already holding ESOPs are given more of them due to any reason, it's also referred to as an ESOP top-up. In simple terms, it's a reward mechanism aimed to retain good performers.

What happens when an Employee Leaves?

Exit clauses specify the exact terms under which the exiting employee can avail of the benefits of their vested ESOPs. They also depend on the nature of the exit - resignation, retirement, termination with cause, or death.

When an employee retires or resigns from a company, they are usually given a specific timeframe after exit within which they can exercise their vested ESOPs. Companies keep this as 30 days or 90 days. If they don't exercise in this duration, the ESOPs stand cancelled and the employee doesn't get any monetary benefit. The unvested options are automatically cancelled on the date of termination and go back to the ESOP pool of the company.

There are relatively uncommon cases where an employee gets handed a "termination with cause" on the basis of any wrongdoings. ESOP Governing Board or the Board of Directors can cancel all their vested options in such cases. The vested shares of the employee are withdrawn and sold to promoters or other shareholders. This sale can also occur at the exercise price subject to the provisions of the Companies Act.

In the case of an untimely death, companies transfer all the vested options of the employee to their nominees. It is then the nominee's responsibility to exercise the options. Sometimes, as a mark of solidarity, companies may transfer even the unvested options to the nominee.

A possible exit clause table can look like this:

	Vested options	Unvested options	Exercised options
Retirement	Can be exercised within a specific time period after exit.	Cancelled on the date of termination.	Held as shares or sold by the employee.
Resignation	Can be exercised within a specific time period after exit.	Cancelled on the date of termination.	Held as shares or sold by the employee.
Termination with cause	Cancelled.	Cancelled.	Transferred to Promoters and other shareholders at face value or bought back by the company at face value.
Death	Transferred to the nominee.	Transferred to the nominee.	Held as shares or sold by the nominee.

Any other exceptional terms must be clearly mentioned in the exit clause document.

Paperwork & Records for ESOPs - Manual & Computerized

While ESOPs are a great tool to compensate and retain employees, managing the complexities of record-keeping can be cumbersome. Whenever new ESOPs are issued or any dilution event (fundraising or acquisition) happens, the ownership stake of every individual holding ESOPs changes. The more the number of such folks, the higher the complexity. In such scenarios, maintaining an accurate cap table can be a challenge.

When the startup is nascent, there may just be a handful of employees apart from the co-founders. At this stage, it is possible to maintain all the stock ownership records in Excel. But as the company grows, it becomes imperative to manage the cap table digitally. While Excel can do the job, the process would be manual, tedious, and prone to errors. Today, there are digital tools specifically catering to cap table management that automate all the necessary calculations and can act as the single source of truth. Qapita and Carta are two reliable SaaS tools for equity or cap table management.

Taxation of ESOPs

Like any other source of income, ESOPs also get taxed when they result in some form of tangible income for an individual. This can happen on two occasions - when one exercises the ESOPs and when shares are sold.

When an employee decides to exercise their ESOPs, i.e., they decide to convert them into shares by paying the exercise price,difference between the fair market value of the shares and the exercise price gets taxed.

As a simple example, if an employee decides to exercise 100 shares at an exercise price of Rs. 10 but with a fair market value of Rs. 100, then the difference between the two, i.e. (100x100)-(100x10) is taxed. In this case, Rs. 9000 is the taxable portion of the ESOPs. This amount, as you can see, represents the profit the employee has made by exercising the stock options. The tax rate depends on your total taxable income in the year. It must be noted here that this taxation happens regardless of whether you sell these shares or not. So you would not actually earn anything yet, but you still pay the tax.

The next instance of taxation happens during its sale. In the example above, if the shares are sold at a price greater than Rs. 100 per share, which was the fair market value at the time of exercising, then a Capital Gains tax is levied on the difference.

So if the shares were finally sold at Rs. 110 per share, then (110x100)-(100x100) is the amount that is taxable. In this case, Rs. 1000. This amount again represents the profit further made on selling the shares. If the shares were sold at Rs. 100 instead, there would be no tax as the gains were already taxed when the options were exercised first, and no further profit was made by the seller.

If you notice, an employee benefits only after they sell their shares. If not, they pay a hefty tax upfront without even encashing them. If you're an employee considering exercising your ESOPs, it would make sense only if you have a ready buyer, or are confident to find one in the near future.

Buy Back of ESOPs

Although ESOPs act as an incentive for employees to work for a startup, they may harbour certain inhibitions.

What is the real worth of the shares?

Will the start-up ever reach an IPO?

Who will buy the shares of the start-up from me?

ESOP Buyback is an event where the company itself offers to buy back the vested stock options of its employees. It gives such employees an opportunity to encash their shares without having to wait for an IPO.

ESOP buyback events generate confidence among other employees with unvested stock options as well as incoming employees. They know that ESOPs may not be just notional wealth after all. On the other hand, it helps the founders maintain their shareholding power in the company.

A buyback event is usually offered when a startup plans to raise a new round of funding. It helps them make additional space for the incoming investors on the cap table, apart from helping founders gain some more control over the company.

Alternatives to ESOPs - RSU, SAR, Phantom Stock

It's possible that a founder doesn't want to offer ESOPs to employees but still wants to reward them for their efforts outside of their fixed pay. Consultants and contract employees can't avail of any ESOP benefits, so are there alternatives to compensate them sufficiently, apart from cash? Some of these alternatives are listed in this section with a brief explanation of each.

Sweat Equity

Sweat equity is an instrument to award anyone, whether an employee or not, for their contribution to building the startup. As the term suggests, sweat equity is about rewarding work done with the equity of the company.

The main difference between ESOPs and sweat equity is that the former is deferred compensation, whereas sweat equity is transacted without any delay. You work and you get the shares worth your efforts that very day.

Restricted Stock Units

Restricted Stock Units (RSU) are like ESOPs but with additional 'restrictions'. For example, RSUs, like ESOPs, may have the same vesting schedule as regular ESOPs but are also subject to achieving certain performance milestones at work, in other words, are like ESOPs with milestone-based vesting.

Phantom Stock and Stock Appreciation Right

Phantom Stock is a way of giving many of the benefits of stock ownership to employees without giving them actual shares. They are a performance-based compensation tool that aims to reward the employees based on the company's growth during their association.

Phantom stocks, when offered, have a price attached to them which is usually the existing share price. With time, this price rises along with the increase in the value of the business, thus also increasing the value of these phantom stocks.

So let's say an employee or an advisor is given 100 phantom stocks priced at Rs. 100, the current value is Rs. 10,000. In 2 years, let's say the company's value and consequently the share price increases to 200. The phantom stocks too now have a value of 200 each, valuing the phantom stocks at Rs. 20,000.

Another way phantom stocks could be awarded is by promising the employee a payout equivalent to the value of a certain number of shares instead of the increase in the price.

Their final payout is linked to the value of the shares, but they don't get any real shares. They are "phantom" or "ghost", only representing the actual share value.

Stock Appreciation Rights(SAR) also follow a similar concept, except that the payout is always linked with the increase in the monetary value of the shares over a specific period of time, as shown in the first phantom stock example.

Drafting an ESOP Policy

The important considerations for drafting an ESOP policy are listed here. If you're getting it done for your company, it's highly recommended that you get proper legal assistance. You can refer to the points below as a checklist for important clauses you can't miss.

- The objective of the Policy
- Definitions: Terms like an Eligible Employee, Grant, Vesting, ESOP, Exercise, Nominee, Shares, Termination, etc. are defined in this section.
- Quantum of the ESOP Pool: What % of the total ownership of the company has been set aside to issue ESOPs?
- Grant procedure and process for acceptance of options
- Vesting Period and Vesting Conditions
- Exercise Period, Process, Valuation and Exercise Price
- Conditions for Transferability
- Exit Clauses: Retirement, Resignation, Death, Disability or Termination due to Cause
- Benefits and Obligations of Shareholders: Reference to the Shareholder's Agreement and Articles of Association
- Appointment of Nominee
- Explanation of Tax Liability
- General terms and conditions like confidentiality, jurisdiction, etc.
- Drafts of documents like grant letter, acceptance letter, exercise letter, letter requesting sale, nomination letter, etc.

Steps for Issuing ESOPs

The steps to set up an ESOP Scheme for a private unlisted startup are shared below.

1. Draft an ESOP Policy with terms on eligible employees, vesting and cliff, exercise terms and price, terms on resignation or termination, fair market value determination, etc.

2. Approve the policy in a Board Meeting and then in an Extraordinary General Meeting (EGM) through Special Resolution.
3. Ensure the Articles of Association allow for ESOPs, and amendment of the Memorandum of Association to have an unissued ESOP pool as part of Authorized Capital.
4. File Form MGT-14 with the Ministry of Corporate Affairs (MCA) for these resolutions. You may need to file the form SH-7 to increase your unissued authorized capital.
5. Issue Grant Letters to eligible employees.
6. Maintain a register of ESOPs in Form No. SH-6.
7. Track the ESOPs vesting schedule, exercise and conversion in Excel or software for it such as Qapita or Carta.

Part II
Starting the Fundraising Journey

8. Sources of Finance

What comes to your mind when you think 'funding'? Possibly media reports celebrating a large funding round closed by a startup, with the founders' smiling, and sometimes jubilant, pictures displayed in an expression of triumph. The ones who have 'backed' them, are invariably one or a few of the usual suspects - there are not too many marquee Venture Capital firms going around. In fact, the fundraising bug has bit some aspiring founders so bad that their ambitions are now tied to raising funds from a known VC, getting published in YourStory, and wearing it as a badge of honour for the rest of their lives. If you have started with vanity as the goal, I'm not sure how much I can help. But if you truly want to build a great company and view funding as a means towards it, this chapter and the subsequent ones in Part II will help streamline your efforts.

Although VCs are the most popular source of external funds today, they are not the only ones. Depending on the stage and needs of your business, you may find other sources more suitable. We'll find out about them in this chapter.

But before we get into the different sources of finance, let's first understand how to calculate what you need.

When and how much to raise?

In my conversations with founders, I have heard statements like "No matter what, I want to raise at least a million dollars", and "I think we should be good with just a 6-month runway." Often, founders tend to either grossly overestimate or underestimate their funding needs. Many look at it as a matter of pride to raise as much as possible and be in the news.

How much of funds to raise should always, always be derived from nuanced calculations based on your best understanding of the expenses your startup would incur over a defined period, depending on the milestones you want to hit.

It should never be a reverse calculation from an arbitrary, aspirational number you may have in your head, and it doesn't need to be strictly confined to the 18 months runway norm.

An effective method to ascertain your financing requirements would be to map your milestones against a timeline, and figure all your resource costs you'd need to hit them. It could look something like this:

Milestone	Timeline	Additional costs (Rs.)	Major expense heads
Basic working protoype/ MVP	2 months	40,000	Research, no-code tools
First 100 paid users	4 months	60,000	Product development, marketing
Product rollout to a small target segment	6 months	3,00,000	Product development, marketing
5K paid users at CAC of Rs.20 or lower	8 months	6,00,000	Product development, marketing, IT infra
Roll out updated version of product	12 months	25,00,000	Product development, marketing, PR, overheads
25K paid users at CAC of Rs. 15 or lower	15 months	15,00,000	Product development, marketing, PR, overheads
ARR of $1Mn	18 months	40,00,000	Product development, marketing, PR, overheads

This is a simplified guide on how to think through your requirements. Ideally, each of the expenses in the third column should be broken down and properly calculated. For example, to roll out your product in a small market, how do the product development expenses exactly stack up? If one of the co-founders is the CTO, then 1 or 2 interns may help in building this adequately. Otherwise, the development may need to be outsourced to a freelancer. Unless all these cost components are individually split into their finer constituents, it will be hard to make an accurate estimate. Note that the 'additional costs' in the table don't include the ones for the previous milestones. So in this example, the total amount needed to hit the ultimate milestone of ARR $1Mn is Rs. 90 Lakh - summation of all costs in the third column.

In Chapter 11, Building a Financial Model, you'll understand in depth how to make these calculations. But in the earliest stages, a simple exercise like this would suffice.

It's always prudent to add roughly six months of buffer cash to this amount because that's the average time it takes for a founder to complete a round of funding. Not accounting for it may lead you to overshoot the runway if the money hits the account later than expected.

To calculate your fundraising ask, work backwards from the

milestone you want to hit, and ascertain all the costs you'd incur to hit that; add a 6-month buffer to this value.

Sometimes your ultimate milestone may be highly ambitious and your estimates may suggest you'd need a 36-month runway to achieve that. In such a case, you can present your ask accordingly, but investors normally don't fund runways that long. So they may help you break it down into shorter term milestones and promise to fund the next 12 months, initially, and then back you for the following 24, if you achieve X.

Series of Fundraising based on Stage of the Startup

Startups raise funds in stages or rounds.

The table below lists the different rounds of funding, the investors involved in each of those stages, and the possible objectives of raising that particular round.

Round	Investor	Objective
Pre-Seed	Friends and Family	1. Build a prototype of the product. 2. Refine the product. 3. Achieve Product-Market Fit
Seed	Angel Investors and Micro VCs	1. Acquire the first paying users of the business. 2. Rapidly scale the number of users. 3. Build features and fixes that would help the business serve a high user base.
Series A	At least one marquee VC firm	The focus of the business shifts from scaling users to scaling revenue.
Series B	Marquee VC firms	1. The business will rapidly spend on marketing, branding and top tier talent to hopefully become a well-known name in the market. 2. Might also make small acquisitions.
Series C and beyond	Marquee VCs, Private Equity firms, Strategic Investors	1. The business cash flows and financial models are studied with tight scrutiny. 2. Valuations start rationalising to multiples of profitability expectation, rather than to multiples of revenue or users.

A VC firm is a Venture Capital company whose business is to identify promising startups with potential for growth, invest in them in return for a stake in the company, and then sell their stake in whole or in parts to obtain a healthy return on their initial investment. The money that they invest is generally pooled in from several high net-worth individuals (HNIs) and institutions with a promise of giving them exceptional returns within a promised timeframe.

Micro VC firms are those that have relatively smaller cheque sizes, usually between 100K to 1 million USD, and typically invest in early-stage startups. 100X.VC and Titan Capital are good examples in India.

Marquee VC firms have the capability to write larger cheques. They typical lead rounds at the Series A and later stages, although there's nothing stopping them to do the same in the earlier ones either. Sequoia Capital, Elevation Capital, Blume Ventures, Accel, Matrix Partners, and Kalaari Capital are some of the top names in this space.

Angel Investors are individuals who invest in startups in their personal capacity either directly or through Angel Syndicates, which are basically representative groups of certain Angel Investors.

Apart from the stages shown, startups may also raise money between two large rounds, like a pre-Series A, or a pre-Series B. Known as bridge rounds, they help startups extend their runway to the next.

If you study the above table, you'd understand broadly the objectives at each funding stage and who gets involved in the process. Today, the instances of startups deviating from the older norms are higher, so don't be surprised if you immediately recognize some not adhering to the thumb rules I mentioned here or anywhere else in this chapter.

Understanding differences between Debt and Equity

Financing is the process by which you fund your business activities. It can happen in two forms: Debt or Equity. Let's quickly understand how each of them works.

Debt Financing

Debt Financing simply means that one borrows funds from another entity - an individual, a bank, or any other institution - with a promise to return that money over a specified period with a certain interest. Regardless of the business' performance, the borrower is obligated to repay the money due within a given timeframe. All types of loans fall under debt financing.

Debts are mainly of two types: secured and unsecured.

In secured debts, the borrower offers security or collateral to the lender. One example of secured debt is a gold loan, where you offer gold as collateral to the lender to borrow a certain amount of money. If you are unable to repay, the lender is granted the ownership of this gold.

In unsecured debt, the lender trusts you to repay the money and does not take any collateral. Since the risk is higher, the rate of interest charged is usually, but not always, higher too. Since there are no assets involved, if the business fails, the lender may not be able to recover even the principal amount of the loan.

Debt financing in startups happens in the form of venture debt, about which we'll learn later in this chapter.

Equity Financing

Equity financing happens when an investor invests money in a company in return for a stake in it. Angel Investors, Venture Capital firms, and Private Equity firms invest in startups in this mode.

An equity investor does not expect a fixed return on their money. As the startup grows, so does the value of their investment. At an exit event (investment by a larger investor, IPO, or, acquisition), the investor can sell their stake in the business and potentially pocket a multifold return on the principal investment.

Unlike debt financing, there is no assurance or obligation of a fixed return in equity financing by the founders. If the startup fails, the investor may even lose the entire investment. Equity investors make use of their conviction and analysis of startups to find the right opportunities which hold the most potential for success. At the same time, they also take protective measures like liquidation preference to safeguard their interests. This is talked about more in Chapter 12, *Fundraising Instruments & Mechanics.*

A mix of debt and equity financing to a hybrid form of financing, mainly carried out through convertible securities. The investor puts money in a startup as a loan (debt financing), and as the company grows, the invested amount is converted into shares (equity financing).Funding instruments like the one stated above have been discussed in detail in Chapter 12.

In the following sections, we'll understand the different sources of finance.

Founder's Funds

Startups are generally incepted as a side hustle to a full-time job or studies. The founders use their existing skills and time to build something they believe in. In such initial stages, the real and only investment going into the startup is the founders' own time, which has a cost of its own. On top of that, any other expenses are borne entirely by the founders.

With time, the demands of the startup (or the side hustle) start increasing, both in terms of time and money. The founders usually put their own money from past savings or any existing salary to fund the business. This is what we call bootstrapping. This source of funds is generally referred to as 'Founder's Funds'.

Most people, though, are financially limited in their individual capacity. After a point, it becomes hard to manage everything on your own, and you don't have enough funds to hire employees and pay salaries. If the business revolves around a tangible product to be sold, working capital challenges arise. If it's a tech product, you'd be constrained to hire the right people to build it out.

This is the point when it becomes critical for the founders to consider external sources of funds to survive. While funding happens at different stages of maturity with different objectives at each point, the overarching purpose can almost always be classified under one of the two: survival or growth.

In the subsequent section, let's understand the different sources of external funds and the characteristics of these investors.

Raising from Friends & Family

As discussed before, there comes a point when the individual financial limitations of the founder prevent them to make any meaningful progress. Count yourself lucky if you have friends and family who believe in you and may be in a position to support you financially. If you have a concrete plan to move forward and strong conviction in your idea, approaching them is probably a good idea.

It's likely that they agree to fund just on the basis of their relationship with you. Needless to say, it's important that you do things the right way and give them the maximum chance of success.

Mode of investment

As mentioned before, they may or may not believe in your idea, and probably don't even understand your work. Their willingness to invest is a result of their faith in you as the person.

The financing by friends and family can either be debt-funded, which is the more common method, or even an equity transaction where they're formally allotted shares of your startup.

Usually, founders take the former route as it's easier to execute. Also, since they have borrowed money from friends and family, it's likely that there's no pressure of any additional interest to be paid. This debt is usually of a convertible nature that later converts to equity instead of being repaid. A purely equity round can also be done if the founder doesn't want any liability whatsoever.

Equity Issued to Friends and Family

Figuring out the valuation of an early-stage startup is tricky. The founder's investment into the business may have been only through their time and efforts. They may not have invested a substantial amount of money of their own.

In such a case, if friends and family invest Rs. 10 lakh whereas the founder invests only Rs. 5 lakh, does it does not mean that friends and family take up 67% of the company. If this happens, the founder will not be left with any meaningful equity, and their motivation to build for the long-term will suffer, probably vanish.

Founders should retain significant equity on their part to leave sufficient room for future rounds of investment. An even better alternative, though, is to defer the valuation to a later stage.

This can be done through an iSAFE round or any of the Convertible instruments covered in detail in Chapter 12, *Fundraising Instruments & Mechanics*. These methods also allow you to execute the round faster while also ensuring a fair transaction.

Also, since this is a friends & family round, it becomes the moral responsibility of the founder to give these earliest investors an option to exit at the Series A stage. Their motivation to invest was just you, and prioritizing them is only justified.

Contingency planning

No matter how generous your friends and family are, chances are that the funds obtained would likely not last beyond getting you the initial push. If you haven't raised a sufficiently large amount, you'd still need money and resources to grow your business to a meaningful scale. If you struggle with marketing due to shortage of resources, your target users may never discover your product.

It's possible that everything goes as planned, and you use your funds judiciously to build what you initially set out to, but you also realise that raising the next round of investment from an Angel or a VC may take a lot more time.

As a founder, it is your job to evaluate whether the funds you have raised from your friends and family in the first round are enough to sustain until you raise the first external round or until the business becomes self-sustaining. You should have a reasonable idea under what circumstances you may need another round of investment from friends and family, what the amount would be, and how that will be used.

Your family and friends too should have prior knowledge of these possibilities, so they can be prepared to put in more money when the need arises. If they do not have that capability to fund you sufficiently again, you'll need to prepare accordingly and plan your progress around it.

Protect your relationships

Money is a sensitive topic and often becomes the root of sour relationships. Raising funds from people you're related to also entails the same risk.

No matter how much conviction you have in your startup, statistically, especially at such early stages, you're more likely to fail than succeed. And when a startup fails, usually the entire money put in goes down the drain. 100% of the wealth is eroded.

It's imperative that your family and friends know these risks in no uncertain terms. Whether it's debt or equity through which they have funded, there is no certainty if they will get their money back.

Secondly, be transparent and clear about how you plan to use the funds. If you take Rs. 10 lakhs from them, how exactly will you invest it into the business? What outcomes do you expect to achieve from this? Your family or friends, here, your investors, should be aligned with your plan of usage of the funds. They should match your vision from both the perspectives of business rationale and family support.

Raising from Angel Investors

As we discussed in the previous section, the funds from your friends and family may only take you so far. To grow and acquire your first set of serious customers, you need more resources at your disposal. This is when you look to raise the Seed round and secure a substantial amount to hit your next milestones.

The objective of the Seed capital is usually to help you market your product and acquire the first large set of users. A Seed round can comprise Micro VCs as well as Angel Investors. Let's understand who these Angel Investors really are.

Traditionally, Angel Investors have primarily been High Net-worth Individuals (HNIs) having large personal wealth (at least a few million dollars) and investments across different asset classes. As with any regular retail investor, the objective of HNIs is also to optimize their investments based on their risk appetite and multiply their wealth in the process over a period of time.

When these HNIs invest in startups in an individual capacity, they are referred to as Angel Investors, especially if the investment has been done in the early days of the startup. For most such 'Angels', startups are just another way to diversify their investments while supporting something that they believe in. Since startups are a risky asset class, they usually constitute only a small portion of all their total investments.

To maximize their overall chances of success with their startup investments, these Angels usually invest in a host of startups they find promising, and believe have a chance to succeed. Statistically, most of these startups fail and the money invested goes to dust, but the ones that succeed often end up compensating for the losses made and still deliver a decent (>2x for successful investors) return on the total capital invested.

Where and how much do Angels invest?

The motivation for a prospective Angel Investor to invest in a startup can vary. If you have watched episodes of Shark Tank India, you'd have noticed that different sharks (or Angels) present different reasons for investing or rejecting, which essentially includes one or a mix of the following:

- Belief in the founder's profile and track record
- Belief in the founder's vision
- Recent performance of the startup
- Expertise and interest in a particular domain
- Positive outlook for a particular industry
- Attractive business model and scope to scale

- Support for a larger cause

From my experience of working with early-stage startups, Angel Investors tend to put a higher weightage on the team solving the problem. Other factors are also relevant but weigh slightly less at this stage. However, it's inappropriate to give a blanket statement that applies to all Angel Investors. A lot depends on their individual beliefs, biases, preferences, and principles.

The base amount for an Angel investment starts usually at around INR 5 lakhs and could go up to INR 20, 30, or even 50 lakhs and upwards. The exact value depends on the total worth of the investor and their conviction in the startup. However, today there are modes through which individuals can invest even much lower amounts into startups.

Many Angels are highly industry-specific due to their experience in that field. If one is a stalwart of the healthcare industry and is looking to invest INR 50 lakhs in startups, they may opt to invest 5 lakh each in 10 different **health-tech** startups. This is the factor of industry or market fit of an investor at play. Because of their expertise in the area, their ability and confidence to judge the potential of a startup building in it is higher.

Other than industry fit, while looking for prospective Angels, the portfolio of companies invested in by them also gives an indication of their preferences. Founders can use this information to determine if a particular Angel may be interested in their startup or not.

If an investor hasn't invested in any business in the past 12 months, it is probable that they may have burnt their fingers somewhere, incurred loss, and hence, put a break. Such deals may be difficult to crack. Prefer targeting Angels who have put money into startups in the past two months.

How much to raise in Angel/Seed Round?

The amount to be raised follows the same methodology that we discussed earlier in the chapter. Identify the milestones you want to hit, then work backwards to calculate all the expected expenses, and finally add some buffer for safety. Usually, any round of investment should at least cover the runway for the next 18-24 months.

If you seek a relatively larger amount, say Rs. 10 crores or more, one Angel will not be enough for the purpose. You will have to look for multiple Angel Investors to put in relatively small cheques and make up the amount, or possibly get a Micro VC firm to lead the round with these Angels pitching in too.

A typical Angel round falls in the range of INR 50 lakhs to 2 Crores. If the amount significantly exceeds 2 Cr, it may be difficult to raise entirely through Angels and a VC may be needed.

Finding Angels

Angels can either be approached individually or through Angel networks. Angels often invest in groups, so if you convince one influential Angel, chances are that they would get more from their circle to invest in your startup.

Angel networks have several Angels as members who meet periodically where the shortlisted startups are presented on Pitch Days or Demo Days and discussed internally for possible investment.

A list of Angel syndicates is given in the Annexure 13.1 of this book.

Typically, Angels can be individuals in very senior positions in well-known organizations, entrepreneurs who have either had successful exits or are running highly profitable businesses, founders who have raised Series B, C funding rounds and beyond, or celebrities in the fields of entertainment and sports.

To find individual Angel Investors, you can scour through LinkedIn, TechCrunch, Tracxn, Crunchbase and AngelList. On LinkedIn and AngelList, companies often name their investors in their profiles, so if you are building in a domain that has several other startups which raised from Angel Investors, you may find their names in some of these startups' profiles. It works the other way too - a number of

Angel Investors mention their portfolio startups in their LinkedIn profiles.

Incubators & Accelerators

Incubators

Incubator programs are generally set up by trust funds in educational institutions. Some of the most popular incubators are run by the IITs, IIMs, and other top colleges in the country, and usually accommodate student founders. Even companies like Google (Google Launchpad), Microsoft (Microsoft Accelerator), and Cisco (Cisco Launchpad) have their own incubation centres where they support startups that align with their long-term strategy.

Incubators select founders with promising startup ideas. They supply them with office space to work out of, which also houses other similar startups giving them networking opportunities. They also invite industry experts periodically for interacting with the students and guiding them in their entrepreneurial journey.

An important benefit provided by these incubators is the access to Angels and other early-stage investors. Investors are always on the hunt for good startups and often approach top incubators to invest in the promising ones.

In return, incubators take equity in the startups that varies from 2% to 12%. The percentage of equity is usually defined per cohort in the different institutions. Incubators that have a larger corpus, either donated by alumni or through surplus funds, may also invest in the startups alongside the investors in the first round. Normally, the investment is made in the form of convertible debt since assessing the valuation of early-stage startups is not easy. (More on these in Chapters 9 and 12 respectively)

Industry associations and larger companies also set up incubators within their premises.

Accelerators

Accelerators are spaces where founders and early-stage startups get access to Angels and VC networks, professional guidance, and investments. They are usually run in the form of multi-week programs. Y Combinator, 500 Startups, Sequoia's Surge, Accel Atoms, and Techstars are some of the most popular accelerators in India and across the world.

Founders accepted to an accelerator program go through training classes and sessions to refine their processes. They are guided in all aspects of the business - business model, customer journey, product development, marketing, hiring, leadership, and everything else you could think of - and given access to an enviable network of resourceful fellow founders and alumni.

Accelerators also invest a certain amount of money in the startups and take equity in return. YCombinator invests $125,000 in return for 7% of the company, and put in another $375,000 in an unvalued capacity through a SAFE (covered in Chapter 12).Startup's standard accelerator deal is a $150,000 investment in return for a 6% stake. Techstars takes 6% of the company's stock for $20,000. All these figures are as of August 2022.

In some ways, getting into one of these coveted accelerators is akin to getting into a reputed institute, like an IIT. It's a strong indicator of the promise of the startup, and the training and network provided by these accelerators enhance the chances of success further. It thereby gets easier to raise money from VC firms and investors in the future. Back in 2011, Yuri Milner and an angel fund SV Angel offered every startup in the Y Combinator cohort $150,000. Although such rewards are rare, it indicates the belief in the selection process of Y Combinator.

Venture Capital Firms

If you invest in or know about mutual finds, you probably know there are hundreds of schemes offered by many large and small firms - DSP, PPFAS, HDFC, Axis, SBI, Mirae Asset, ICICI, SBI, and scores of others. To invest, you pick the best ones based on any parameters you have and put your money in them. Each such mutual fund scheme has a fund manager who, on your behalf, allocates your money into different assets based on your risk appetite.

VC firms work similarly. They consist of professionals who raise a large sum of institutional funds from HNIs, insurance firms, university endowment funds, pension funds, etc., and invest the money on their behalf into startups. VC firms promise returns to their investors in a timeline of 7-10 years. Hence, they themselves need to generate enough returns to give back to their investors.

For this purpose, VC firms constantly lookout for startups that show potential for success. They employ what is popularly called the "Spray and Pray" strategy. They spray their funds over the identified startups and pray that at least some of them give phenomenal returns.

Well, not literally. Each investment made by a VC is a calculated risk based on proper analysis and due diligence. When they invest in a startup, they do so with the belief that it would be a success. But since the chances are low statistically, they hope that at least some of the startups they have invested in generate abnormally high returns.

VC firms have traditionally invested in startups that are relatively mature and established - a proven product, a good user base, and promising growth metrics - but lately, more and more VC firms have started investing in startups that are pre-revenue or do not even have a product ready. The sooner they invest, the larger the multiple they can generate from the principal invested. But such bets also entail a higher risk so they often take a larger chunk of equity in return.

While startups compete with each other to raise money from VCs, VCs compete with each other to find the best startups to fund. A VC firm usually would not want a competitor to invest in a pre-revenue startup they may be targeting and get early access to it. We'll understand more about why VCs have started including early-stage ventures in their portfolios later in this section.

How VCs identify promising startups

The factors that VC firms look for are almost the same as those of Angel Investors. But Angels, being individuals, can choose to stay out of the investment game at times. Investing is not their main occupation. VCs, though, are in the business of making money from money, so they are always active.

Most times, when VC investments are made, it's because of either or both of the following reasons.

- The VC is already looking for an opportunity to invest in a particular industry for its portfolio - e.g. gaming, fintech, crypto, etc. - and you happen to be the lucky one who showed up with a decent pitch first. This is why one needs to know a prospective VC's portfolio in detail and see if you plug in a missing gap.
- The founder has a warm intro to the VC through a credible connection, or possible commonalities like the same alma mater, social interests, etc. So find commonalities on LinkedIn and other public profiles so that you can pull the right levers and have a better connection.

But that's not all. If one thinks about the metrics or exact factors that a VC looks for in an early-stage startup, the following three points come to the fore.

1. Past Achievements of the Founders / Founding Team

This is more relevant in the earlier stages. VCs back a competent team even before they look at the product or the market. If there was just one deciding factor, it would be the founding team. Therefore, it helps if you have either solid academic credentials (IIT, IIM, Ivy League), or successful past exits.

If not, it helps if you've achieved something at a national or at least state level, or if you've built something great as a part of an organisation in your employment.

It's similar to showing a spike on your MBA application or your resume. Past achievements that differentiate you and show that you can hustle and execute better than the others instill confidence in VCs about your ability to run the startup. This is especially important if you're trying to raise money at the early stage and have little to show in terms of traction or product.

2. Serving an Unmet Need in a Growing Market

Most startups die because they're building a product that not enough people want. It's not the best product that wins, it's the product that can sell the most, which does, or, the founder, who can sell it the best, who does. This is why the size of the market and its growth rate is more important than the product, at least in the beginning. The product can be worked upon, but the market is not in one's control.

3. 10x Product

Your product (or at least the conceived product) must be 10x better than the existing solution - 10x faster, 10x cheaper, 10x more efficient. Thus, it always helps to have an MVP and traction numbers that indicate these success factors before you approach a VC for funding.

As the startup matures, the preferences of VC firms also change. Initially, they focused on the profiles of the founder and the founding team, but the emphasis shifts to the business performance of the product in the later stages. When you raise funds in a Series A or further round, it can be assumed that your startup has been up and running for a considerable period. Hence, the investors will look at the past performance of the startup and the potential it holds through future projections of revenues and profits.

Why marquee VCs are investing at the Seed stage

Some of the marquee VCs like Sequoia, Accel, Elevation Capital, Tiger Global, and many more now have separate arms that focus exclusively on early-stage investments at the seed and pre-seed stages. Let's understand why.

As explained earlier in the chapter, when an investor gets a stake in a startup early for a relatively smaller sum, and if the startup does well, then there's a good chance that the investor generates a multiple in excess of 25x, possibly much more. This way, with a much smaller investment, they are still able to generate returns that they may get by investing in proven, established startups. Needless to say, the risk is commensurately high as well.

However, the motivation for a marquee VC to invest at such early stages may not necessarily be getting a larger stake early. If they identify any promising pre-revenue startups, they may choose to write cheques as low as Rs. 5 lakhs, which is an amount more typical of Angel investment. By investing even a small amount, the VC gets access to data and metrics of the startup which is then evaluated to consider any future investments at later stages where they could possibly lead the rounds. The amount invested then is just a small price to pay to improve their chances of success at later stages.

But what also happens at the next stage is that the same VC that put in a tiny amount earlier may not follow on. It's not uncommon for VCs to invest early in startups solving similar problems in the same domain, and then only choose to back the best performers in the next round.

As an example, let's say a VC firm is looking to invest Rs. 50 lakh in the FinTech space. It comes across 10 startups that are solving similar problems. However, since the startups are nascent and don't have any meaningful data, the VC can't ascertain which one will succeed in the future. It can take a larger bet on one or two of these, but the risk of failure is high. So the firm decides to hedge its risks and invests equally in all 10 by allocating Rs. 5 lakh to each of them. It thus gains access to the monthly performance data of all the 10 startups. It can now track their progress and earmark the best 2 for the next round of investment.

Although this works perfectly well for the VC, it leaves the rejected startups in the lurch. Those startups agreed to take money from them, albeit as a small amount, probably because a known VC as a backer lends them higher credibility which they could use to attract more investors. However, if the same VC doesn't top up their investments in the next round, it sends a clear signal that they don't consider them promising anymore. By accepting the meagre sum of Rs. 5 Lakh, the startup eventually did themselves more harm than good, since they have to now build their credibility afresh.

I always advise the founders working with me to pass on any such small offer a marquee VC makes in the early stages, regardless of the credibility that it may bring initially. The invisible costs associated far outweigh the more visible benefits in such cases.

Strategic Investors

Sometimes larger companies look to expand their footprint into adjacent domains inorganically. They acquire a minority or majority stake in startups who are building in such spaces. The objective of these larger companies is an expanded presence and higher diversification, and these startups already have the necessary expertise of such domains. They become suitable, low-risk vehicles for the larger companies to explore these spaces. Such companies that acquire a stake in a startup by investing money into it become Strategic Investors.

Unlike VCs, Strategic Investors don't have any target to exit the startup and generate returns. They are more likely to be interested in acquiring these startups if they satisfactorily fulfill their objectives. Startup founders opting for such investments must be aware of these possibilities and be willing to lose control in due course.

Conglomerates such as Reliance Industries Limited, Tata Group, and Aditya Birla Group make numerous such investments every year. Reliance does it through its subsidiary Reliance Strategic Business Ventures Ltd. and has acquired majority stakes in several startups. Aditya Birla's subsidiaries have been similarly active. For example, in 2021, their fashion and retail company ABFRL acquired 51% stake[1] in Sabyasachi Couture, a firm specializing in designer bridal dresses founded by the renowned fashion designer Sabyasachi.

9. Valuations - What Is Your Startup Really Worth?

Open, a neo-banking fintech startup, became the 100th Indian *unicorn* in May 2022, when it announced its Series D fundraise of USD 50 million, at a *valuation* of just over USD 1 billion[1]. A unicorn, as you'd probably know, is a startup valued at USD 1 billion or more.

News about fundraising and valuation, in the last few years, has been so rampant that many founders now start with the motive of raising funds and becoming a unicorn, rather than building something truly worthwhile. Recognition can be a massive driver, and the sensationalism of valuation has lured many young founders to chase it with impunity.

People like me, who help startups raise funds, do benefit from abnormal valuations and colossal funding rounds. But my involvement usually ends with the conclusion of a round. Venture Capital firms, however, are fundamentally dependent on the growth of the startups they fund. They make a sizeable return on their investment only when the valuation of the startup grows multifold between funding rounds. Outrageous valuations are highly favourable to these VCs and other shareholders in most cases.

Some call it a frenzy, others believe it's justified, but it can't be argued that the valuations of several startups today defy logic. But what even is this phenomenon? Let's discuss this over a cup of coffee first.

The worth of a Starbucks coffee

I often visit the Starbucks outlet in Cyber Hub, Gurgaon and order a Venti Mocha Frappuccino. The last time I visited, I paid Rs. 350 for it. But coffee is consumed by different types of consumers for different purposes. A person looking to just get their morning caffeine hit would be happy with their homemade coffee. Someone accustomed to the *tapri* coffee served near their office would probably not pay more than Rs. 20 for a cup. But someone who likes the attention an Instagram post with a cup of coffee garners them would be happy paying a premium for it. The *value* that they derive from this experience justifies their spending.

Notice that the basic ingredients for the cup of coffee made at home, the *tapri*, and Starbucks are the same. What changes is the perceived value the consumer obtains from these experiences. The right price of the coffee, then, depends on who the consumer is and what they desire. In other words, the price depends on the consumer's *perspective.*

Startups also operate similarly. When a startup is priced and given a valuation, how the buyers - in this case, the investors - perceive its current and future prospects makes all the difference. It's this perspective that has driven the valuations of some startups beyond many people's comprehension. But saying that a startup is overpriced is similar to debating if the Starbucks coffee is rightly priced or not.

Valuation, conventionally and traditionally, does have a clear financial and business rationale to it. There are actual, mathematical methods to arrive at a valuation of a company, most of which have been used for decades.

Dr. Aswath Damodaran, a Professor of Finance at the New York University's Stern School of Business, is a globally renowned expert on valuation. He has authored several books that are studied by students around the world to learn the subject.

Using a conventional approach, in 2014, Dr. Damodaran had initially valued Uber at around USD 6 billion with the narrative of the company being a cab aggregator or a passenger transport service for the USA. This was in contrast to the valuation actually achieved by Uber, which was USD 17 billion.

The next year though, he revalued the company to around USD 23 billion by considering Uber as a logistics provider for the whole world. Clearly, the value of a logistics provider serving the entire world would be higher than a transport service for one country.

You can see how a simple change in perspective resulted in a different valuation.

It's important to note that Uber had not actually expanded to too many other countries by then, and they were still a cab aggregator service. But there was a notion that eventually, the company will expand geographically as well as functionally, thus giving it a higher valuation.

The valuation is manifested as the share price of the company. Price, as we saw in the Starbucks example, is what an individual or an entity actually pays to the seller in exchange for the overall value they derive from it. In Uber's case, there were investors who highly valued this company and its growth story, and ascribed its shares at a high price, leading to a high valuation.

At the end of the day, value is a notion. If the people who matter consider something valuable, they happily pay a high price for it.

Fundamentals of Business Valuation

Fundamentally and traditionally, valuation as a concept was only applicable to profitable businesses. It became relevant when a company was getting acquired by another player, or when it had to sell its shares in public through an Initial Public Offering (IPO) so it needed to set an initial price for those shares. A share, in other words, is simply the smallest unit of the company that can be traded. If you hold one share of a particular company, you own a small percentage of it.

If a company was operating well and generating enough profits to fulfill the objectives of its owners, there was no real need of determining its valuation. But when a company had to be sold to a larger entity, the selling and buying parties would have to agree to a price for the sale. Now unlike other daily commodities, it wasn't straightforward to calculate a company's worth. But there were several clear parameters that could be considered and analyzed to arrive at a fair price or valuation. These parameters broadly included the cashflows generated by the business in recent times, its potential to generate good cashflows for the buying entity, the assets it owned and their value, and the potential demand for the products or services that this company offered in the near future.

Also, traditionally, most businesses were highly localized and relevant only to a certain geographical market. The products offered by them were tangible in nature, and markets didn't evolve at the pace they do today. So the quantum of speculation in determining valuation was relatively low. However, things have changed significantly today. Even though the fundamentals of valuation remain intact, the nature of businesses and markets have given rise to different ways of valuing companies.

In the late 20th century, the internet brought with it possibilities that were inconceivable until that point. For a very little cost, individuals and businesses could now connect and communicate with anyone in the world. Very soon, it became an indispensable part of life for billions across the world. It set the base for businesses to become more digitally savvy, and a large chunk of operations and communication started happening through tools enabled by the internet.

The biggest fundamental change that the internet brought about was the ease of discovery and expansion. Traditionally, businesses would need to be physically present at a location to be able to serve their customers. But now, proximity was much less of a constraint. If you were worthy enough, you could be visible to millions without having any physical presence.

What this really meant was that businesses could *scale* much faster. That is, if they were truly solving a pressing problem, a large number of people could use their product or service almost immediately. The potential for such businesses to rake in super-normal revenues became incredibly high.

Valuing a business solely on the basis of current profits, then, seemed unfair. Now there were two factors startups started getting valued on: *profitability* and *scalability*.

In fact, expected profitability or future profitability would be a better representation of what matters. Current profitability, as we have seen, usually takes a back seat when valuing a startup today. The notion is that if you can scale fast and achieve a large share of the market, profitability would follow.

Products of Google, Facebook, and Amazon are used by virtually every person in the world with access to internet. These companies, when they started out, were able to create a near monopoly in the industries they functioned in. Once they gained access to a large number of customers with their first core offering, they built other products which they cross-sold in such a manner that it drove many incumbents out of the picture or shrank them to insignificance. As an example, Yahoo and Hotmail had built their email service much before Google built Gmail. But today, there's no comparison between the number of users of the former two and Gmail.

It's the idea of monopoly and how fast a startup can achieve that in their industry that drives a lot of startup founders and investors. The perspective of investors on who can create such monopolies sometimes results in seemingly exorbitant valuations. Often, these startups display one or more of the following three characteristics in their bid to disrupt a new market or industry:

- First mover - the first to disrupt a market
- Fastest - gaining market share most rapidly
- Most efficient - incurring the least costs and generating incredible returns

Although the internet and other developments did revolutionize the business ecosystem, what has truly changed in financial terms is the *nature of assets* companies started holding.

Earlier, only tangible assets would be assessed to ascribe a value to the company. Today, however, following that approach would result in highly flawed valuations for many, especially those that use technology to scale and sell.

Today, it's the people - the number of customers - that choose one brand over others that render a company more valuable. Startups look to acquire customers fast and then try to retain them with more differentiated offerings so that they keep transacting in some form.

A good example here is Byju's, the EdTech platform. Today, they offer courses right from the K12 segment to higher study preparations like IIT-JEE, CAT, GMAT, etc. If a student onboards young, they know they have the opportunity to upsell and cross-sell other products and courses as she progresses. If the child and her parents are satisfied with what they get, there's a good chance that the Lifetime Value (LTV) of this customer ends up being very high. This intangible asset - the association with a large number of customers - is today an important parameter of valuation.

Because the nature of assets has become more intangible and the business environment more dynamic, valuing a startup today often involves a high level of speculation. But if there are buyers willing to pay a certain price for a startup's shares, it's a straightforward indicator that there are enough people who find it worthy to be valued at that price. In the end, I would reiterate that value is a notion. Like they say "Beauty lies in the eyes of the beholder", value, too, lies in the eyes of the beholder.

In the subsequent sections, let's understand how different investors approach valuation.

Understanding Investor Motivations by Investor Type

Friends & Family

Your friends and family may invest in your business with the sole motive of supporting you. There's a high chance that this is their first investment in the asset class of startups. They may not want even the principal investment back. Their motivation is to propel you in your startup journey and not necessarily to generate profits.

Angel Investors

Angel investors are high-net-worth individuals who usually invest in the pre-seed or seed rounds of a startup. They typically expect to get a 2x to 3x return on their investment in the next one or two subsequent rounds. Angels prefer to take their exit by the Series A or B rounds when a marquee VC firm enters the cap table of the startup.

The context of investment by Angel Investors also plays a major role in their motivations behind investing in a startup.

Ratan Tata, the chairman emeritus of Tata Group, is a prolific investor and has made numerous investments in several startups like PayTM, Ola Electric, Lenskart, and many more. His motivation to invest is probably not to make money but to promote and support these startups. Even if his investment turns into a loss, his net worth is not affected significantly.

On the other hand, if an Angel invests 10% to 20% of their entire corpus set aside for such investments in your startup, they will expect a high return. Amateur Angel Investors who may have invested a high amount by their standards are likely to be bothersome if you are unable to generate sufficient returns in a quick time.

The motivations of Angel Investors, therefore, vary from person to person. Founders must understand the motivations of the Angels looking to invest and ensure to take money from only those whose expectations they can meet.

VC firms

The goal of any VC firm is to make money and generate returns. In spite of whatever they may claim upfront, there would be a certain pressure to generate returns in due course. This pressure varies depending on what stage of their funding lifecycle they invested in.

The lifecycle of a VC fund is generally 8 years. What this means is that they need to generate a certain multiple of the principal amount raised from their investors and give them the promised return in this period. To achieve this goal, these VCs invest in different startups across the lifecycle. Their expectations from their portfolio startups depend on how close they are to achieving their objectives.

If the VC invests money in your startup within the first two years of their cycle, the pressure won't be immense for the first 2-3 years. When the VC firm reaches the 4th year of its cycle, it needs to be in a position to at least return the principal to its investors. This is around the time when urgency starts setting in. As the VC nears its 7th or 8th year, the pressure is at its peak as they're looking to make exits. So if a VC invests in the 4th or 5th year of the fund lifecycle, they may expect quicker profits within the next two years.

I must add that this also depends on the result of the other investments of the VC firm. If some of the other startups on the portfolio of the VC have already generated significant returns for them, the VC firm will possibly be relatively relaxed in their expectations.

As a founder, you must understand and acknowledge that if you take VC funding, you have a certain obligation to generate returns to the best of your ability. A part of your business strategy must be about giving exits to your investors. However, it must be done in a fair and sustainable manner which doesn't compromise the long-term growth of the startup itself.

Strategic Investor

Strategic investors are often industry leaders who invest in startups not necessarily for quick returns, but to expand their portfolio or enter a domain inorganically. Often, such investments end up in acquisitions by the Strategic Investor at some point.

As a startup founder, if you are not comfortable with giving up control of your organization, taking a strategic investment may not be the right option for you.

Strategic Investors are primarily motivated by having a large presence. Sometimes, acquiring startups is an easier way to enter an industry and stay relevant in the fast-developing modern world than building something in which they may not have the expertise themselves. Hence, they look for control in a startup, and not necessarily monetary returns.

Incubators and Accelerators

Incubators and Accelerators set up a fund through which they invest in the startups that they support. The startup founders are expected to return at least the principal investment so that these entities can fund the next round of startups. Profits act as a bonus for these organizations as it expands their corpus and enables them to support a larger number of startups.

The primary motivation for Incubators and Accelerators is to support a large number of startups. The secondary motivation is to generate returns that enable them to support more startups going forward.

Venture Debt firms

Venture Debt firms are highly risk averse. A VC firm can write off 70% of its investments and still generate outlandish returns from high-performing portfolio startups and achieve their goals. A Venture Debt firm, however, may only be able to write off at most 25% of its portfolio as losses.

Since they offer their money at a certain interest rate, clearly their objective is to generate a fixed alpha on their investments. They are happy to forego the reward that comes with investing in high-growth startups for the stability of returns. Hence, they usually consider startups only after they have raised their Series A rounds because it somewhat establishes their capability to return the money with their equity capital. To minimize their exposure to risk, they may also take warranty measures in case things go south.

Valuation Drivers by the Stage of a Startup

Startups are valued differently at different stages. In the earlier stages, for example, the weightage is higher on the profile of the founders, but in the subsequent stages, the performance of the startup and key metrics become important. Let's go through them one by one.

Pre-seed

At the pre-seed stage, there's almost nothing tangible for a business to show. Just the idea and the team that's going to execute it. At this stage, the valuation is defined by these three factors:

i) Market Size

The startup should be playing in a large enough market, ideally worth a few billion dollars at least. When the market is large, even average ideas, when executed well, can generate good enough returns for the investor.

Market size usually refers to the total number of paying users the startup can potentially acquire. Once acquired, the startup would aim to retain them and increase their LTV, eventually resulting in higher valuations in the later rounds. It all starts with the market the startup chooses to play in, and at the pre-seed stage, becomes a critical parameter for valuation.

ii) Founding Team

In the early stages, many investors place a bet solely on the credibility and capability of the founders. Their profile, whether in terms of professional achievements or educational pedigree, acts as a strong signal for their ability to solve problems effectively. Like it or not, everything else being the same, an IIT graduate is more likely to get funded at the pre-seed stage than a tier-2 college grad.

The given chart is reason enough for investors to be bullish on IIT graduates.

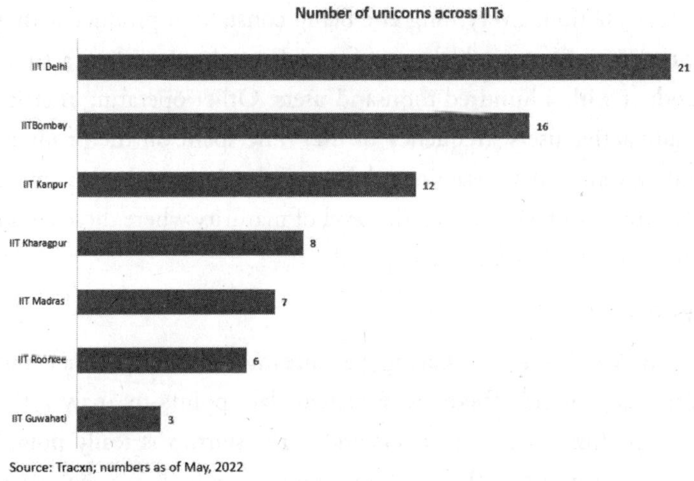

Source: News reports; numbers as of May 2022

iii) Problem and Solution

The problem identified should actually be a real one faced by a sufficiently large number of people. The founders, on their part, should be prepared with all the necessary data that points to the existence of the problem and how big it may be.

The solution proposed should also be practical and feasible, and one that cannot be easily copied by a competitor. It should be something that the target market should readily adopt, ideally at a price point that results in positive unit economics. Again, preliminary research or an MVP can go a long way in establishing its efficacy.

How a founder structures the problem and the proposed solution also helps in establishing their credibility and thereby increasing the chances of obtaining a high valuation.

Seed

At the seed stage, the valuation of the company depends primarily on the *traction*. If they have competitors in the same space, then their performance relative to other players will be closely scrutinized.

Typically, at the seed stage, the number of users is directly linked with the valuation. Everything else being constant, a product with a million active users would have a far higher valuation than a similar product with a hundred thousand users. Other operating metrics like daily active users, frequency of use, time spent on the product, referrals given, and transactions done are also important, but most startups may not have reached the level of maturity where these could be objectively analyzed and compared.

Series A

By the Series A stage, a startup has already built its product and acquired early users. There are sufficient data points to analyze the business performance and understand if the startup is really poised for long-term growth. The valuation, now, is more about the actual performance and relatively less about the promise.

When there are multiple startups operating in the same space, investors will look out for the ones who are monetizing their customers faster and more efficiently. A few metrics that can indicate this: number of customers, cost of acquiring a customer (CAC), revenue from operations, unit economics positivity, daily active users, and anything that indicates growth in a cost-effective manner.

All things aside, in many cases, the revenue can possibly be used as the main determinant of the valuation. A certain multiple to the expected annual revenue is often considered to arrive at the number. This multiple varies by industry - it is lower for non-tech, D2C startups (5-6x), while it is usually higher for tech startups (8-10x, sometimes greater). Having said that, there are always exceptions that defy this, sometimes wildly. (We'll learn more about valuation as a multiple of revenue later in this chapter.)

In an ideal world, the valuation of a Series A start-up should have been a multiple of its profits and not the revenue. However, due to intense focus on growth and extremely high marketing spending, very few startups become profitable at this stage. Hence, revenue acts as a more reliable proxy.

Series B Onwards

By Series B, the startups are expected to start generating cash flows. Profitability should either already have been achieved or should be in the near future leading up to the IPO, possibly over the next 4-5 years.

At the Series B stage, the primary valuation driver may still be the revenues, but in subsequent stages, cash flow and profits are taken into the account.

However, this idealistic approach is more an exception than a norm today. Many startups that have raised funds in Series D, E, and even more advanced rounds have no sight of profitability yet. Until the startup becomes profitable, there's obviously no way profits can be considered for calculating the valuation. Revenues continue to be the most critical factor in such cases with user growth as the second major influencer.

With startups, it's hard to predict from outside what valuation one will achieve. Different investors have different perspectives, and startup founders would obviously prefer those who put them at a premium. Although the core elements behind the valuation stay the same, how they are perceived makes all the difference.

And not just that, psychological factors like FOMO (*fear of missing out*) also play a role. It's quite common to see other VCs and Angel Investors jumping in if one credible VC believes in a startup and agrees to lead the funding round. A respected VC deciding to fund is a cue that they know something that others don't. Even if there's nothing exceptional to the information gathered by the lead VC, others still queue up behind.

When there are a large number of players interested to fund a startup, it indicates higher demand, and then a higher valuation is a straightforward economic consequence.

In the subsequent sections, let's go deeper into how valuations are actually computed for startups.

Valuation Multiples & Proxies

Traditionally, the valuation of a company depends on its financial projections. Finance professionals calculate the revenue and cash flow that the business expects to generate in the future and then discount the cash flow down to the present value. Using the discounted value, they arrive at a valuation for the company. This valuation method is popularly called the Discounted Cash Flow (DCF) Method and is covered in detail a few sections later.

The DCF method has been a fundamental technique for calculating valuation for a long time. However, making an accurate projection of a company's finances requires multiple assumptions.

Startups are inherently dynamic. Their product may often pivot in its journey. The product may be a category creator with no clear understanding of how customers may respond. Will they accept it or find it outrageous? In fact, investments also occur at seed and pre-seed stages when the product has not yet been built. Hence, it becomes extremely difficult to make financial assumptions about a business that has no certainty or clarity of a future. This brought up the need for other methods of valuation.

Valuation multiples are proxies or substitutes used to calculate the valuation of a startup, especially in the absence of other reliable metrics. They do not require the assumptions necessary for building a discounted cash flow model. In the early stages, these proxies can come in handy and simplify the process of zeroing in on a number.

EBITDA multiples, revenue multiples, and even number of users are examples of proxies used for startup valuations.

Transaction Comparables and Trading Comparables are the two common methods by which valuation multiples are calculated. These methods have been discussed in detail later in the chapter.

Dilution across Startup Lifetime

With every startup, founders have some monetary goal for themselves. How driven they are by money varies with every individual, but every founder I know wants to preserve as much stake in their startup as possible. The stake they hold directly affects their net worth. Often, founders miscalculate or disregard the stake they should dilute across funding rounds, and in a few years are left with much less than what they desired. There's a simple approach every founder can take to align their personal monetary goals with dilution across funding rounds.

Let's say you're a solo-founder building a startup that will become a unicorn in 6 years. You have calculated that you should have at least 10% stake in your company when this happens. On doing some research, you realize that unicorns in your domain took 4 rounds of funding to reach there. So how much should you dilute across your funding rounds? Let's calculate backward.

If you own 10% stake in your startup by the 4th funding round, you'd have likely set aside 10% for the ESOP pool. This means that across 4 rounds of funding, investors have acquired 80% of your startup. Simply put, the average dilution across these rounds should be 20% for you to reach your goal.

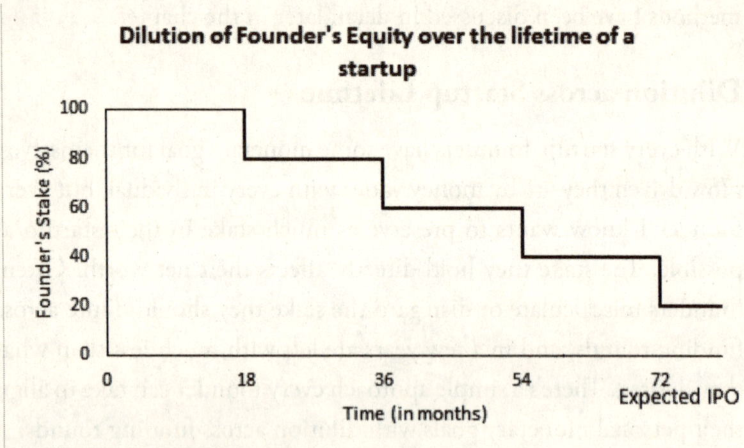

This is obviously a highly simplified take on dilution, but this approach is effective to help you stay aligned with your goals and not over-dilute in any round.

Similarly, if you found out that it takes not 4 but 5 rounds of fundraising to reach your goal, the average dilution across each round should be 16%.

Or if your goal was not to have 10% but 20% stake, and it took 5 rounds to reach there, then assuming 10% to be kept aside for ESOPs, your investors take 70% across these rounds. This means you should maintain your average dilution at around 14% in each round.

Note that the goal need not be based only on valuation. It could be purely time-based, like 10 years, or event-based, like IPO. Your reason for having a certain stake will also be a combination of monetary and control parameters. As the founder, it's for you to decide what your landmark event would be and how you'd like to be placed then. It will guide you during any dilution event.

While it may not be possible to always stick to your dilution goals, knowing the trade-offs would help you plan better for the future. Some founders may have no plan to exit. For them, a high ownership stake would mean greater control. Align your business goals with your personal ones, calculate trade-offs, and give away stake from a position of awareness rather than ignorance.

Valuation Methods

Valuing a company, in reality, is never a straightforward exercise. If two experts are left on their own to valuc the same company, there's a good chance that the numbers won't match. There are several assumptions and conjectures considered to compute the valuation which understandably leads to variability.

There are several methods, however, that help finance experts make these calculations. We shall understand them briefly one by one.

You must also know that valuation is a vast topic. There's no way I or anyone else can explain everything comprehensively in one chapter. The methods described below will help you understand the very basics of how these are used. If you're a founder, you'd become aware of the different ways investors may try to value your company, and you could use the knowledge to negotiate to your advantage. But to master the subject, I'd recommend reading Dr. Ashwath Damodaran's books or McKinsey's book on Valuation.

Discounted Cash Flows

In the traditional approach, as we discussed earlier in the chapter, businesses are usually valued on the basis of their profit-generating capability. The current performance of the business is assessed in terms of net cash inflows, assumptions are made on its ability to generate future cash flows over the next few years, and these estimates are then considered to ascribe a current value to the business. This approach, also known as the Discounted Cash Flow (DCF) method of valuation, is widely used across industries and taught in schools. Let's first take an example of how this plays out.

One of my friends had started an e-commerce business as a side hustle alongside his job. However, he eventually realized that he would be unable to invest sufficient time into the business to make it grow, and probably didn't have the conviction to quit his job and run it full-time. So he decided to sell the business. He priced it at Rs. 1 Cr and invited buyers.

Now for any buyer to consider whether this is a fair price to pay, they'll need to consider these three things:

1. The total cost of buying the business
2. The time frame in which they wish to recover this cost
3. The likelihood of the cash flows from the business to recover the cost in the desired time frame

The first point seems straightforward - the price is Rs. 1 Cr, so that should be the cost of buying the business. But if the buyer takes a loan to buy this business, the interest accrued over the duration of the loan would also get added.

The second point is subjective to the buyer. Let's say that the buyer wishes to recover this cost in 3 years. So, the total cost of business becomes 1 Cr (the asking price), and any additional costs like the interest that need to be repaid. In this case, let's assume that the buyer is considering taking a loan and the interest accrued over 3 years would amount to Rs. 30 lakhs. The total cost, then, becomes Rs. 1.3 Cr.

Some buyers may also account for inflation. For example, considering a 5% annual inflation, the real cost to be covered at the end of 3 years should be 1 Cr annually compounding by 5% for 3 years, plus the 30 lakhs interest. That would be (1.16 Cr + 30 lakhs) or Rs. 1.46 Cr for 3 years.

The third point is where the current performance and future growth assumptions are considered. Let's say the cash flow generated by the business in the last financial year was Rs. 15 lakhs. And at the present rate, it expects to generate a cash flow of 20 lakhs this year. Next year, considering certain assumptions, the expected cash flow is

30 lakhs, and then 40 lakhs the year after.

Now if the buyer wishes to recover 1.46 Cr in 3 years, the amount falls short by 56 lakhs, since the estimated future cash flows only indicate a total cash flow of 90 lakhs in the next 3 years. This buyer would then believe the company to be overpriced for them.

But the seller may not agree, as he believes that 3 years is too short a time period to recover any cost. Further, he may opine that if managed well, the business can generate much larger cash flows than the numbers estimated. In the end, both parties want to maximize their value, and an agreement on the company's worth is imperative to the sale.

Finally, after negotiations, if my friend does manage to sell his business for Rs. 1 Cr, the valuation of his company at that point is officially 1 Cr.

Traditionally, it's the *market* - buyers and sellers - that determines the price of the company. That's exactly how stock markets function as well, albeit under a different setting altogether. And this market usually considers a company's current performance and foreseeable expected performance to arrive at the price.

The DCF method assumes the net present value of future cashflows that the business expects to generate to compute its valuation. The timeframe to consider the number of years of cashflows varies, but usually falls in the 5 to 10 years range. By 'present value', it is reasonably assumed that the value of Rs. 100 today would be more than the same amount in the future on account of inflation.

In the table, the Y1, Y2, and so on represent the number of years from now, the expected cashflows for a business for these years are mentioned in the row below, and the present value of those cashflows considering an annual inflation of 5% is calculated. The valuation is simply the summation of all the Present Values.

The DCF method is still perhaps the most accepted way to compute valuations of profitable businesses.

	Y1	Y2	Y3	Y4	Y5
Cashflows (Rs.)	1200	1500	1800	2000	2400
Present Value (Rs.)	1143	1361	1555	1645	1880
Valuation (Rs.)	7584				

Transaction Comparables

The DCF method offers a mathematical approach to valuing a company. However, as stated in the section Valuation Multiples and Proxies, it does not work well for startups. Early-stage startups have a lot of uncertainty involved and cash flows can't be estimated with accuracy. Moreover, in the initial stages, even other indicators like the number of users and revenues may not draw any conclusive picture of the acceptance of the product. That's why, the need to determine a valuation independent of any assumptions or elaborate calculations developed.

Finance professionals started using proxies or substitutes of metrics for the valuation of a company. The Transaction Comparables method compares a startup to its closest competitors and ascertains a valuation primarily considering the multiples achieved by these companies.

Let's understand this with an example. Ustraa and Bombay Shaving Company (BSC) are two D2C companies that develop grooming products for men. They have a similar product range and serve the same target audience. They can be considered close competitors of each other.

The following report states their valuations in their respective funding rounds that happened within 7 months of each other.

Date	Company	Transaction Value (INR Cr)	Investors	Stake	Pre-money Valuation (INR Cr)	Revenue (INR Cr)	Revenue multiple	Remarks
Sep-20	Mcaffeine	23	Amicus, CESC Ventures	13.3%	150	n/a	n/a	
Jul-20	Ustraa	50	IIFL VC	22.7%	170	60.4	2.8x	Based on FY20 Revenue
Apr-20	Nat Habit	23.1	White-board Capital, Sequoia Capital India, Others	23.1%	76.9	n/a	n/a	
Jan-20	Mama Earth	129	Sequoia	19.3%	539.6	100	5.4x	Based on 100cr ARR Revenue
Dec-19	Mom's Co	51.3	Samaa, DSG	26.5%	142.5	n/a	n/a	
Dec-19	Bombay Shaving Company	9.1	Sixth Sense, Colgate Pal-mol-ive	4.7%	185	20	9.3x	Based on FY20E Revenue
Oct-19	PeeSafe	30	Alkemi Venture Partners	27.9%	77.4	28.5	4.2x	Based on FY20E Revenue

Source: MCA filings and news reports

Ustraa was valued at INR 170 Cr in July 2020 and Bombay Shaving Company had a valuation of INR 185 Cr in December 2019. Based on these numbers, a new D2C brand that produces men's grooming products and serves the Indian market would also fancy being valued at around INR 180 Cr.

In brief, the Transaction Comparables method compares a startup with its closest competitors with respect to product, stage, market, prices, and even founder profiles. Based on the comparison, the method values the startup at an amount that its competitors are valued at.

If we dig deeper, you may notice that there is a stark difference between the revenue multiples of the two companies. Ustraa has a revenue multiple of 2.8x. BSC had a multiple over thrice that of Ustraa, i.e. 9.3x. What could be the reason behind the difference?

One reason could be the timing of these funding rounds. Bombay Shaving Company raised a round of investment in December 2019, just before the COVID19 pandemic hit. Ustraa raised investment in July 2020, during the first wave of COVID19. The effect of the pandemic, and its influence on the macroeconomic financial markets, could have influenced the lower multiple for Ustraa.

There could be other factors at play as well. It's possible that BSC had displayed a more efficient growth curve than Ustraa and their rate of acquisition of customers was higher. Even though Ustraa had a higher revenue, if it was achieved after burning heavily on marketing spends, it wouldn't be viewed favourably by investors. Or it could have been that the investors' confidence in the founding team of BSC was higher than the respective investors' interest in Ustraa's founding team. The real reasons could be known to only those who were involved in the transaction, but as a fellow founder in the same domain, one could analyze what parameters may have been considered and prepare accordingly.

This is basically how the Transaction Comparables method works. The startup in question is compared to its closest competitors and the valuations achieved by them considering different parameters are identified. Based on this analysis, a suitable multiple is chosen to arrive at the valuation.

Let's take another example to understand better. One of my clients has built an online marketplace for jewellery and are looking to raise their first round of funding. They use the Buy Now Pay Later (BNPL) model to attract customers. I used the Transaction Comparables Method to estimate a value for their startup. This is what the analysis looked like.

Fintech Transaction Comparables				
Particulars	**Competing Fintech Startups**			
Basics	**Gold Setu**	**Rupeek**	**Ruptok**	**Simpl**
Founded	2021	2015	2020	2015
Total Amount Raised	$ 2.39 Mn	$ 144 Mn	$ 3.54 Mn	$ 83 Mn
Website	goldsetu.co	rupeek.com	ruptok.com	getsimpl.com
First Round				
Period	June 2021	Nov 2015	Jan 2021	Jun 2015
Total Amount Raised	$ 1.19 Mn	$ 88.7k	$ 1.41 Mn	$ 1.3 Mn
Valuation	$ 5.12 Mn	$ 946k	$ 4.93 Mn	$ 6.06 Mn
Dilution	23.2%	9.4%	28.6%	21.5%
Second Round				
Period	Feb 2022	Jun 2016	Oct 2021	Nov 2016
Total Amount Raised	$ 1.2 Mn	$ 346k	$ 2.13 Mn	$ 1.27 Mn
Valuation	N/A	N/A	$ 25.2 Mn	$ 7.36 Mn
Dilution	N/A	N/A	8.5%	17.3%

Original calculations by Sarthak Ahuja

The funding information pertains to the companies that are the closest competitors of my client's startup. The parameters we considered were the time when they raised their rounds of funding, the amount raised in each of those rounds, valuation at each of those rounds, and dilution of stake by the company at each round.

In the first round of investment, we found that the 4 closest competitors raised an average investment of ~$1.2Mn.

If I consider the two companies that raised funds in 2021 (closest to the present date), the average is $1.3Mn. The valuations also lie close to \$5Mn. Additionally, both these companies raised their first rounds within the first year of their operations, which is also what my client is looking to do.

Based on these numbers, raising a round of \$1Mn at a valuation of \$5Mn seems like a possibility. At the same time, they'll have to dilute 20% stake in the company if such an investment goes through.

Please note that this example is just for demonstration and the amount finally to be raised is based on the company's objectives and the milestones they want to hit over the next 12 to 18 months. The funding ask should not simply be based on what a competitor raised. But what this does provide is a proxy for what investors are comfortable with and lets you be prepared for the demand you want to make.

Trading Comparables

In the Transaction Comparables Method, one compares their startup to private, unlisted companies or startups. But the financial data of such competitors are not always available in the public domain, so comparisons would not always be possible. In such cases, we turn to listed public companies that are legally bound to publish their data and draw parallels with their metrics.

Alexander Jarvis, a UK-based Investment Banker, presented a great example of how he valued a social media company based on its competitors using the Trading Comparables Method in his blog[3]. Note that this blog was written sometime around 2017-18 and considers data from this period, so some numbers would seem outdated. However, it still does a good job at explaining the point.

Startup Name	Awesome				
MAU (M)	5				
Exit Type	Company	MAU (M)	Market Cap ($000s)	Value / MAU ($)	Awesome value @5M MAU ($M)
M&A	LinkedIn	106	26200	247	1236
Public	Facebook	2000	492619	246	1232
Public	Momo	82	8570	104	521
Public	Snapchat	300	15940	53	266
Public	Weibo	340	17220	51	253
M&A	Whatsapp	450	19000	42	211
Public	Zynga	80	3070	38	192
Public	Twitter	328	11910	36	182
M&A	MyFitnessPal	20	475	24	119
M&A	Twitch	45	970	22	108
Public	Yelp	157	3230	21	103
M&A	Instagram	50	1000	20	100
Public	YY	152	2450	16	81
	Min	5		**16**	**81**
	Mean	5		**71**	**354**
	Median	5		**38**	**192**
	Max	5		**247**	**1236**

Source: Alexander Jarvis's blog.

To explain the method, he considered a fictitious social media platform called Awesome which has 5M Monthly Active Users (MAU). In the given table, he lists 13 social media companies that went public or were merged or acquired. He also collected information on their Market Cap, and the Monthly Active Users (MAU) at the time of their IPO or acquisition.

Then he calculated the value per user for each of these companies by dividing the Valuation by the MAU count. For both Value/MAU and Valuation, he mentioned the minimum, the maximum, the mean and the median values across these 13 platforms.

The Value/MAU metric ranged from $16 to $247. Considering that Awesome has 5M MAU, the valuation range for them would lie between $80M to $1235M (or $1.23B).

The difference between the two extremities is obviously huge. At this point, Awesome's founders need to determine if they fall closer to the lower end of the spectrum or the higher end. The ones with the highest Value/MAU are LinkedIn and Facebook. The value for

LinkedIn is on the account of the revenue they generate from the users through several offerings on the platform as well as monetization through ads. Facebook's, on the other hand, is primarily driven only by advertisements which is a result of the amount of time spent by users on its platform. So if Awesome's users spend time equivalent to the average time spent by a user on Facebook, they can command a higher valuation on the account of high ad revenue potential. Or if they are monetizing a section of their existing users and observing a positive trend around the paying customer numbers, they could again command a high valuation citing LinkedIn's example. On the other hand, if there is no clarity or any proof of concept of how revenue will be generated, then chances of achieving a high valuation are slim.

To use the Trading Comparables method effectively, one must thoroughly analyze the platforms being compared to and identify why some achieved higher valuation than others. Since these will all be listed companies, they would be much advanced in their journeys and direct comparisons may be tricky. So founders must break down the metrics objectively, use their judgement, and only draw meaningful comparisons.

Scorecard Method

A marquee VC firm invests in startups based on its thesis. A thesis is essentially a set of guiding principles or parameters which the VC considers to invest in startups. Different VCs have different thesis and investment philosophies.

To enable them evaluate startups that strongly match their thesis, VCs develop a scorecard to rate different startups against the identified parameters.

Here's an example of what one such evaluation may look like:

Parameter	Total weight	Startup 1	Startup 2	Startup 3
TAM	20	18	14	10
Industry	15	12	11	12
# Users	15	10	14	12
# Paid users	15	10	12	10
CAC	10	8	9	5
ARR	10	5	6	4
MoM user growth	10	6	8	9
Churn	5	4	3	5
Total	100	73	77	67

Note that these parameters are just taken as simplified examples and every VC will have a different set of parameters they evaluate their startups against.

In the above example, if this VC firm had to pick just one startup to put their money on, they'd probably pick Startup 2 because it scored the best on their scorecard. Or if they had to invest equal money in these 3 startups, they would give a more favourable valuation to Startup 2, followed by 1 and 3 on account of the scores achieved. For VC, a lower score means higher risk, hence lower valuation.

The scorecard method is not exactly a valuation method. It is more of an insight into how VCs assess and evaluate potential startups for investment. As a startup founder, research the portfolio of a VC and assess their company against the previous investments of the firm. This exercise will give you an idea of whether you fit into their portfolio. It's only when a startup ticks all the necessary boxes defined by the thesis of a VC firm that they get considered for investment.

Valuation, as you must have understood by now, is not plain fact-based mathematics. Since many assumptions about future performance are involved, the final number really depends on who is evaluating the company and what perspectives are being considered. Each of these methods, too, works best within a certain set of scenarios. No single method can be said to be universally correct.

A founder should ideally get their valuation computed internally with all the possible methods known. That would give them a wide range of valuation figures, and they'd know exactly which one serves them most favourably. Understanding the factors behind those methods would also help them be prepared with the right information on what potentially drives their valuation down and what can increase it. This knowledge can be used to negotiate a higher valuation with investors.

IPOs and Boom & Bust Cycle

All the methods of valuation discussed apply only to unlisted private companies. They act as tools for investors and existing shareholders to price the company when there is no clear, large-scale market consensus.

All that changes post-IPO. When a startup gets listed, i.e. after its Initial Public Offering (IPO), it's the stock market that decides the share price on a daily basis. Like for all other listed stocks, the demand for each company's shares determines the share's price. Valuation, on any given day, is simply the multiplication of the share price with the total number of shares that constitute the company.

This valuation is like the ultimate judgement. It reflects the true reality of exactly how much the market values you today, and if all the preceding valuations when the company was unlisted actually made sense or not.

In the year 2021, Indian startups raised $42 billion, a 3.8x increase over the previous year, across 1583 deals[4]. This was a result of the *Bull Market* and the positive growth sentiment after the pandemic-induced slowdown in 2020. However, the trend was reversed in the 2022 'funding winter' largely originating from the Ukraine war and the domino effects it generated. People across the world were sceptical of investing in equities due to a low expectation of returns. Such phases where stock markets lose value and retail investors routinely look to sell their stocks is what we know as a *Bear Market.*

In 2021, numerous startups like PayTM, Nykaa, Zomato, and CarTrade made their Initial Public Offerings (IPOs). Businesses prefer to go for public listings during a bull market to capitalise on the positive market sentiment. All such startup IPOs in 2021 generated great initial demand, much to the delight of their promoters and investors.

2022, however, has been anything but delightful. As of writing on Aug 1, 2022, Zomato has lost over 70% of its value from its peak valuation. The share prices of PayTm, Nykaa, and CarTrade have also suffered similarly. The performance of these IPOs dissuaded a number of other startups from filing their respective IPOs this year. It makes no sense for them to do that when the market sentiment may erode their current valuation.

This *Boom & Bust Cycle* is a constant feature of public markets. You'd normally witness most companies filing for IPOs during bull markets or the Boom phase of this cycle, when the investor sentiment is positive and equities are generally in high demand. Bear markets or the Bust phase is where IPOs are rare and people are more risk averse.

Interestingly, even startup funding follows a similar trend. Startups, after all, are an equity asset class and a highly risky one at that. VCs, who are dependent on raising funds from their investors, find it harder to build their corpus when they're raising in the middle of a bear market. Their investors are less keen on putting their money in a risky asset. VCs too become more cautious in funding startups during this phase, especially the ones in growth stage, i.e. approximately Series A to Series D. Growth stage startups are usually not generating profits and need external funding to strengthen their base. Given the amount of capital involved, the exposure to risk for these VCs is extremely high. Early-stage funding requires less capital, hence the exposure to risk is relatively low.

These bull and bear markets also influence the valuation of startups in general. When the market sentiment is good, there's a higher demand for startups' equity shares, and hence are likely to be priced higher than when their demand is low. High price of a share obviously leads to a higher valuation. Since bear markets involve a larger perceived risk for investors, VCs have a higher bargaining power to negotiate a lower price for the share, and hence lower valuation.

As a startup founder looking to raise funds, it will be prudent to time your fundraising in a bull market if your situation allows you.

Valuation Inflation

A lot of startups that seem to have outrageous valuations are accused of artificially inflating them. Valuation inflation occurs when a startup achieves an abnormally high valuation without a strong enough performance to back.

This phenomenon benefits early investors the most. An inflated valuation swells up the price of the shares they hold and gives them a chance to make hefty returns on their investment. So if they can successfully create a perception of great business performance, there's a good chance they can get buyers who believe this story and purchase those shares.

Occurrences of valuation inflation happen mostly while leading up to one of these two events: IPO or acquisition. Let's understand why.

IPO

Zomato debuted on the Bombay Stock Exchange on July 23, 2021, at a listing price of Rs. 115 per share[5]. As of writing, on August 1, 2022, its shares are priced at Rs. 46.50 per unit.

CarTrade listed at Rs. 1,600 on August 20, 2021. As of writing, it's trading at Rs. 673.50[6].

Nykaa listed at Rs. 2,018, and as of writing, it's trading at Rs. 1,417.00[7].

PayTM listed at Rs. 1,955, and is today trading at Rs. 746.30[8].

The price at which they were listed on the stock exchange was much higher than the price at which they are trading today. Today's market reality suggests that these companies were significantly overvalued at the time of listing.

An IPO gives all the company's shareholders an opportunity to sell their shares in the stock market and make a return. The longer one has been a shareholder, the higher the probability of making high profits. There is a clear monetary incentive for these shareholders if their company can achieve an unexpectedly high valuation.

In the examples above, whether there were any mischievous elements at play is not for me to comment on. But what is known is that many older shareholders made an exit with the IPO by transferring their shares to the new retail buyers, and made phenomenal returns. The new shareholders who continued to hold their stocks suffered as the prices plummeted.

While it may not always be the case, it is possible for existing investors and founders to hire PR firms, oversell the growth prospects to incoming investors, and artificially create a false sense of expectation. The ones who buy this vision also buy the shares. VCs and Private Equity firms are in the business of making money from money, and it's only natural that not 100% of them are morally upright.

One example which strikes me as suspicious is that of Barbeque Nation. In January 2021, a private equity firm had invested in the company at a valuation of 1.8x of revenue. Three months later, in April 2021, Barbeque Nation went to IPO at 3.6x its revenue. The said PE firm doubled its investment value. Is it practically possible for a company to double its valuation in 3 months? I doubt.

Acquisition

The second major instance of valuation inflation can happen when existing investors and shareholders are trying to get the startup acquired by a larger company.

Since investors have an insider's knowledge of how well a startup is functioning and its true growth prospects, they may realize before others outside that the future is perhaps not encouraging. But since they are invested, they can try any means to still generate a good return from a failing investment.

One way in which this can manifest is by actually inflating valuation of the startup first, and then offering it for a sale to a larger company who may be willing to buy at that valuation. This valuation inflation can happen in the form of a funding round itself. Despite knowing the reality, the investors may put in a certain, probably smaller, amount at a valuation significantly higher than in the previous funding round. This allows them to continue selling the growth story and create a positive perception.

After some time, the startup and investors may approach other larger firms in the industry to acquire the startup at a valuation close to what was ascribed in the last round. Since a majority chunk of these investors' shares was bought in earlier rounds, even a slight devaluation would not affect their returns much.

If they successfully find a buyer who agrees to their price point, they end up making a profit from an underperforming startup just based on perceptions.

The curious case of CRED and its Valuation

Kunal Shah-founded Cred is often in the news for its fundraising rounds and ultra-high valuations. As a person who helps startups raise funds, I must admit, valuations and business performance aside, that Kunal's fundraising capability is second to none. It also reflects on the fact that he's probably different and more insightful than other founders, and VCs, who themselves constitute of extremely smart individuals, are willing to bet big on him and his startup despite the noise around.

At first look, the valuation of Cred does not make sense. In June 2022, it was reported that they raised their latest funding at a valuation of a whopping USD 6.4 billion[9]. In the financial year ending 2022, their revenues stood at Rs. 95.5 Cr, or roughly USD 12 million. Their consolidated losses were at Rs. 523.8 Cr, or roughly USD 68 million.

Their valuation, up till this point, is 533x their revenues! The 10-12x multiple that tech startups usually command is comfortably dwarfed by this figure. Why is Cred valued so highly by investors?

The reason, I feel, is the narrative about how the company plans to utilize the users on its platform. This information is not publicly available. But it surely is discussed between the founder and the investors.

Cred is building a community of credit-worthy individuals. This essentially means that these are people with a higher paying capacity and are less likely to default on payments than the average Indian. They have the capability to make high-value purchases and are a sound target group for anyone selling luxury or convenience. Cred offers such people incentives to stay and transact on their platform, collects their purchase data, and is technically well poised to offer products or services that affluent individuals will happily pay for. In 2021 itself, its user base was at 7.5 million and is likely to be higher now. No other company today has accumulated this kind of information.

This data puts them in a position to offer several things, which they are. They are now a discovery platform for niche, luxury items. They also have a peer-to-peer lending platform. They have CRED pay which allows you to make online payments seamlessly. And there's certainly a lot more brewing that we don't know about. With these offerings, they are also increasing the frequency of use of their customers as well as ramping up the number of loyal active users. While other products may also have millions of users, the ones using Cred have a much higher paying capacity. If they continue to serve them well, the LTV of each such user can be potentially extremely high. And if there are millions of such customers, the valuation would somehow start making sense.

But this is what investors believe will happen in the future. Today, the criticism Cred receives is on its inability so far to generate the revenues expected from an entity priced so high. They have been in the business for 4 years, how much more time before dreams turn into reality?

I wish I had more information to give a more informed verdict. Only time will tell how the Cred story unfolds. Most people who offer commentary on its valuation do so with incomplete information. Without full background of the facts, one can only draw conjectures and not conclusions.

Is their valuation too high? It depends on the eyes of the beholder.

How should founders think about valuation?

The precedent to this question should be "Why are you starting up?". The purpose of becoming an entrepreneur varies with every individual, and there is nothing right or wrong about it. Some do it for money, a few for impact, and others to simply follow a passion. For someone looking to make money fast, chasing a high valuation and making a successful exit would solve their purpose. How effective this approach would be, though, is something I'm not sure about.

Since this question is more personal opinion than giving an absolute right answer, my three broad suggestions to founders would be:

1. Prioritize value over valuation
2. Build to last
3. Optimize growth, but rationally

Consider these suggestions after knowing that I'm an old-school romantic when it comes to businesses. I believe businesses should be built to last till perpetuity and not simply as an object to flip for a quick buck. I know there are many who would disagree with me and I respect that.

I have briefly explained my three suggestions for founders below.

Prioritize value over valuation

It's hard to escape the valuation talk as a startup founder today, especially for the ones who are dependent on VC funds to grow and sustain. But one should remember that valuation is derived from the value you add to your users' lives. When you stop adding value, they will move away and so will the valuation.

As a founder, it's imperative that you keep doing things that add tremendous value to your users. And question everything that doesn't. Everything that adds value is essential, everything else is noise. Stay away from the noise.

Build to last

Companies become truly great when they're able to add value in a sustainable manner over a long period. HDFC, HUL, ITC, Marico, Axis Bank, and Asian Paints are great examples in the Indian context. They have delivered consistent returns to their shareholders for decades only because they could grow sustainably. Today, we don't often measure them by their valuations.

One thing common among all these companies is their incredible business fundamentals. They are all pre-VC era companies, so obviously their manner and timelines of growth have been vastly different from what startups today experience.

In my opinion, every startup must always have an eye on the traditional, core fundamentals of the business and not just the ones associated with valuation. Even though they may not perform optimally on such metrics, tracking them would ensure they don't become irreconcilable in the future. It then gives the startup a greater chance to succeed over the long term, and really build to last.

Optimize growth, but rationally

Growth is important for any company. But what separates the great from the average ones is that they draw the line between growth and growth at all costs. Many VC-funded startups have, over the years, fallen into the spiral of growing unsustainably by burning inordinate amounts of cash, only to see their customers leaving when freebies stopped.

As a startup founder today, whether you're VC-funded or not, you must always have the conviction to discourage anything that advocates irrational growth. One common symptom of such growth is an unusually high CAC. And this symptom often arises when startups raise a lot more money than they need and then proceed to splurge the surplus cash on highly ineffective activities. Bootstrapped companies never get this luxury, so they're forced to grow within their limited means which often serves them well in the long run.

You, as the founder, must know how much is too much. There's no shame in raising a smaller round if it serves your purpose. It may mean that, sometimes, you would have to sacrifice valuation for sustainability. But if I were your advisor, I'd always encourage that approach.

With this, we come to the end of this chapter on valuation.

I must, again, reiterate that the contents in this do not, even remotely, come close to covering everything about the topic. This is a highly simplified take on the subject considering the needs of startup founders. My hope and conviction are that reading this chapter thoroughly would equip you with the right mental framework to approach valuation. It will help you take decisions and manage negotiations in a more informed manner, and possibly save you from the pitfalls a few unfortunate entrepreneurs weren't lucky to avoid.

10. Creating a Pitch Deck

A pitch deck is often the first point of communication between a founder and an investor. As the first document that represents your startup, it can potentially make or break your fundraising journey, especially in the earliest rounds. So it's of utmost importance that you get it right.

I believe that a pitch deck stands for a lot more than just a set of slides talking about your company. Creating one gives the founder the chance to reflect on what they're truly building and the potential it holds.

Every slide of the pitch deck is an opportunity to build a stronger case for the startup. When prepared well, it will create the right first impression, will communicate exactly what a potential investor needs to know, and will help you take things forward with the investor.

This chapter will help you decide what to put in your pitch deck and why an investor might be interested in that information. This is, however, not a tutorial on how to design your deck or make it look beautiful. Although I do believe an aesthetic deck works in favour of the founder, the real meat is in the content itself. My primary objective here is to help you with the content.

What does an Investor want to see in a Pitch Deck?

Building a pitch deck is not a one-time job. Founders need to create decks for every funding round and even customize them for every investor they speak to. Investors look for different things in a startup depending on the stage it's in. Here, we'll focus more on the seed or pre-seed stage. However, the ideas presented can be implemented in advanced rounds as well.

In the beginning, the investor is primarily interested in the basics of your startup and they check if it matches their thesis. They want to get an overview of the problem and the solution proposed, the market you're targeting, the business model, and the team executing this. Many investors decide whether to take a conversation forward by just glancing through the deck. That's usually enough for them to know if the startup in question is building in an area or targeting a market they're bullish about.

This first version of the pitch deck is usually the briefest one, intended to communicate the main points clearly. It usually comprises just the topic headers and only the most relevant information. The idea is to give an overview to the investor without delving into the nitty-gritty.

If the investor is impressed, they may reach out to you asking for further details. This is where you need a second version of your pitch deck. It should be more detailed with data about your business and insights from the market. At this stage, investors are keen to understand how well your startup has performed in its brief existence, and if there are enough indications for future success. This deck should convey the relevant points well.

If the investor is convinced about the prospects of your startup, you may be invited for an in-person meeting for further discussions. At this point, you must be prepared with a deck that includes annexures detailing the calculations across all business aspects of your startup. This deck aims to assist a founder in answering specific questions about the current business metrics and projections under different scenarios. Do not send this deck over an email as the information is sensitive to your startup.

Also, know that no two investors will behave the same. So the example of the three different pitch decks and their use cases can vary situationally in more ways than one can imagine, but they work well as a guiding reference for your preparation.

Recommended Formats by Investors

Most marquee VCs have published and recommended formats for early-stage pitch decks. All of them essentially seek the same information but the order and terms may vary slightly.

Sequoia Capital, for example, recommends the following flow: Company Purpose, Problem, Solution, Why Now, Market Size, Competition, Product, Business Model, Team, and Financials[1].

If you notice, this flow also helps set the right narrative to build a case for their startup by a founder. They start by mentioning why the company exists in the first place and the impact they want to make in the world. They identify the problem at large and the solution they are building. Then they move on to why now is the right time and then explain their product and business model. Finally, they mention the team that's solving this problem and the financials of the company thus far.

An old recommended format by Accel Partners available on Slideshare goes like this: Team, Product, Customers, More Product Details, Market Size, Competition, Current Status, and Execution Plan[2].

If you notice, their focus is more on the team, customers, and what you have built upfront. They then move to the macro aspects of market size and competition, and how you intend to win in it.

If you speak to different investors, they all may have different preferences on the formats of pitch decks they receive. So it's fair to say that there's no one magic template that's bound to impress everyone, but in this chapter, I have recommended one which should satisfy the needs of all investors. Please note that this is considering the first version of the pitch deck that an investor checks to assess your startup, and it flows like this:

1. Title Slide
2. Problem
3. Market Size
4. Solution and Scalability
5. Earnings Model
6. Competitive Advantage
7. Competitor Analysis
8. Founders
9. Traction
10. Projections
11. Ask and Valuation

It covers all that an investor looks for in a startup with minimum fuss, and is sufficiently detailed but not overwhelming. Sometimes some of the topics may require 2 slides, but the final count shouldn't ideally exceed 15.

We'll go into the details of each of them in this chapter and then follow them up with how to present the deck to create a lasting impression.

1. Title Slide

Within the pitch deck, the title slide gives the first impression of your startup. It potentially decides whether the investor will scroll and view your complete deck or give it a pass. The title slide should act as a hook for the investor to go through the entire deck.

What should this slide have?

- **Name of the startup**

You may choose to give the name of the brand instead of the legal name. For example, Swiggy will mention 'Swiggy' and not 'Bundl Technologies Pvt Ltd' which is its legal name.

- **One-liner**

The brand name should be followed by a 5-6 word introduction of your product.

When LinkedIn was looking for investors in its infancy, its one-line description was "Your network is bigger than you think". Uber similarly stated "Next generation car service".

A good one-liner that captures the essence of your startup can be immensely impactful. It has the potential to instill anticipation in the rest of the deck, and primes the investor to view it positively.

A common way for startups to easily explain their idea is by following the "X for Y" template. As an example, DogVacay calls itself Airbnb for dogs. LinkedIn's analogy could well have been Facebook for business professionals. It should never be a forced fit though. Such analogy works only when the X of the template is easily recognizable and understood, and makes complete sense for your startup. Uber, AirBnB, Netflix, YouTube, etc. are commonly used as the X in the template. Also, be mindful that using this approach doesn't limit the scope of your product.

- **Industry**

Next, you need to indicate the industry of your startup possibly through a graphic or a colour theme. Sometimes the name itself is an indication of the industry - with BharatPe or PhonePe you could safely assume it's FinTech.

Every investor has a thesis based on which they invest in a company. When a potential investor understands within a glance that the pitch deck has been sent by a startup which serves industries of their interest, they are likely to go through the remaining slides with more attention and intent.

BuzzFeed used the image given below as its title slide. The contents are clear - the name of the company followed by a short description. BuzzFeed is a digital media company with a focus on tracking viral content. The red colour (although the colour is not visible here in the book) brings an emotion of alertness and urgency that compliments the idea.

Source: BuzzFeed's pitch deck as available on Piktochart[3]

When you build a deck that's shared with investors over email, make sure that you add the words "Confidential" or "For private circulation only" to the title slide. Your deck contains critical information about your startup. If this ends up in the hands of a competitor, you can be adversely affected. And that's just one of the ways this can go wrong.

Investors do not usually sign an NDA for a pitch deck, but mentioning 'Confidential' on the slide at least puts the thought into their minds that they are not supposed to share it. To add another layer of safety, you can write "Confidential - For the use of <Investor's name> only". This takes more effort but in case the pitch deck is leaked, you will know exactly who the culprit was. Moreover, a mention of the investor's name also develops a sense of personalization in their minds.

2. Problem Slide

The investor now has a very brief idea about your startup from the title slide, and they're probably curious about the problem you're really solving. Many startups fail because they're trying to solve something that doesn't really need solving. This slide gives the opportunity to the founder to communicate clearly that they don't fall in this bracket, and the problem is indeed a pertinent one.

Look at how Airbnb, one of the most successful startups of all time, presented the Problem slide in their pitch deck.

Problem 2

Price is an important concern for customers booking travel online.

Hotels leave you disconnected from the city and its culture.

No easy way exists to book a room with a local or become a host.

Template by PitchDeckCoach.com

Source: Airbnb's pitch deck as available on Piktochart

The 3 short and crisp sentences put the message across efficiently and effectively.

A founder may incline toward complex and wordy problem statements. They may be tempted to use long descriptions to avoid missing out on any point. Be careful to not go that route. The idea of this slide is to articulate the problem statement in the simplest way possible so that anyone can understand it in a single take. The investor reading the slide should immediately infer that you have picked a genuine problem.

Mixpanel, an advanced analytics platform, presents the two problems that it targets in two different slides. Their message is clear. The company not only measures page views but also analyzes the actions people take.

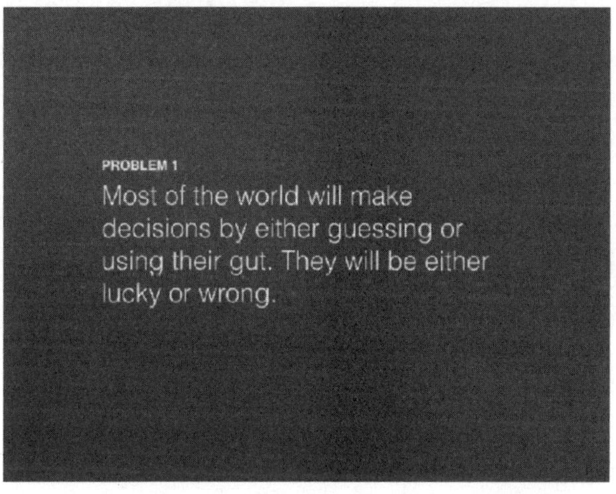

Source: Mixpanel's pitch deck as available on Piktochart

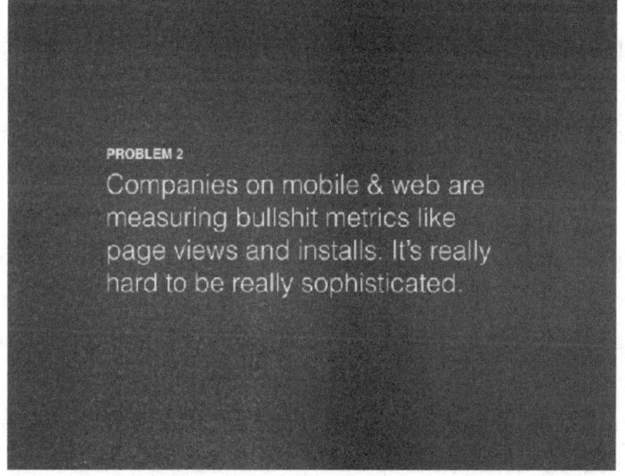

Source: Mixpanel's pitch deck as available on Piktochart

When a founder presents their pitch in front of investors, they can and should talk about their personal involvement with the problem as well. If you're a founder, chances are that this problem was faced in some form by you and you didn't find a satisfactory solution to it. Then you took it upon yourself to solve it. Narrate it effectively. It is evidence of your internal drive and motivation to solve the problem and an investor's conviction in you will go up a notch. Do not add this to the pitch deck. Use it only while presenting your pitch.

3. Market Size - TAM, SAM, SOM

The objective of every investor is to find the next big opportunity to make money. The strongest indicator of such opportunities is the Market Size.

A Market is like a river. Large, strong rivers support millions of households with their livelihoods without showing signs of distress. The reason so many civilizations developed along the banks of Ganga was her capacity to provide them with everything needed to thrive. Smaller tributaries, in comparison, can only support a limited population. Although communities build around smaller rivers too, they saturate after a point. A large, strong Market, similarly can support a much larger number of startups in the same domain than a smaller Market which may support only a few.

Think about the COVID19 pandemic. The lockdown was in effect, and the usual entertainment channels were on hold. During this period, the market for content creation grew massively because people were looking at alternate sources of entertainment as well as knowledge. The creator economy started booming and continues to grow rapidly. This is an example of a Market that is attractive.

If a startup creates even a basic product but serves a continuously growing market, many investors would want to put money into that startup. Investors realize that the market tide itself will push them forward and generate high returns as the startup grows.

That is why market size is one of the most important slides of a pitch deck and is often positioned right at the start.

Here's how Airbnb presented the market size in its pitch deck.

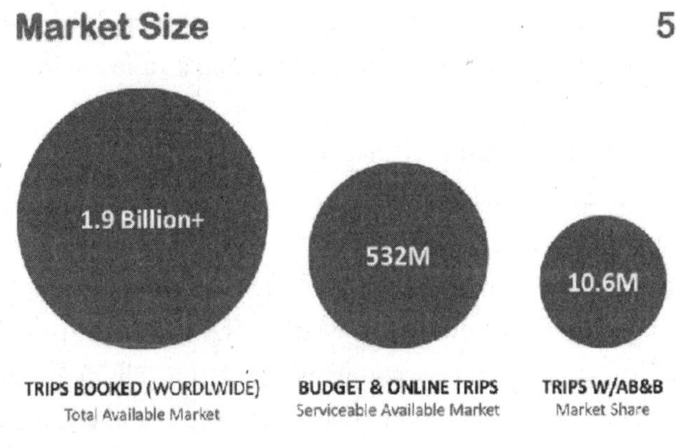

Source: Airbnb's pitch deck as available on Piktochart

We touched upon the concepts of Total Available Market (TAM), Serviceable Available Market (SAM), and Serviceable Obtainable Market (SOM) in Chapter 1, *Taking the Idea to MVP through a GTM.*

In this slide, you need to present the basic calculations of the TAM, SAM, and SOM in a bottom-up approach.

How can you calculate the TAM, SAM, and SOM of your startup? As an example, consider a D2C company that produces packaged baby foods. They have come up with a supplemental syrup for children between the ages of 2-5 years and want to ascertain the size of their market.

The syrup comes in a bottle that contains 48 teaspoons of syrup. A child is prescribed to consume 2 teaspoons per meal. The bottle is priced at Rs. 1000 each, positioning it in the premium category.

With this information, we can perform our market sizing by applying the right filters. The first is *age*.

Since the product is for kids between 2 to 5, only that section of the population can be targeted with this product.

The next filter is *income*. Since the product is a premium one, only relatively affluent consumers will be able to afford it.

Let's call the third filter *acceptance* of the product. This represents the section of people comfortable with feeding a supplement to their child.

Let's see how the numbers stack up.

Consider the population of India to be 138 crores. Applying the age filter, we can assume that 3% of the entire population comprises children between the ages of 2-5. That makes it approximately 4 crore kids. This is the Total Addressable Market (TAM) for the product.

Now, just about 2% of the country's population falls in the high-income bracket. So the total potential consumers of the syrup amount to 8 lakh. This becomes your Serviceable Addressable Market (SAM).

Out of these 8 lakh children, let's say the parents of 30% are found to be open to supplement consumption. So that makes it 2.4 lakh children who belong to a high-income group, are aged between 2-5 years, and can consume supplements.

2.4 lakh children, then, is the Serviceable Obtainable Market (SOM).

Now let's consider the market in monetary terms. If a child consumes 1 teaspoon of syrup twice a day, they require 2 spoons of syrup each day.

A bottle that contains 48 teaspoons of syrup lasts 24 days (48 divided by 2). In a year, a child consumes about 15 (365 divided by 24) such bottles in total.

For Rs. 1000 per bottle, the company potentially earns Rs. 15,000 per year from every child that consumes the syrup regularly. So, with a market of 2.4 lakh children, the SOM for the product is Rs. 360 Cr annually. Calculating the Market Size of their startup clearly demonstrates the potential an idea holds, and a large Market is often the parameter that gets highest weightage from investors.

Here's another example of how Whitehat Jr presented its market size in the pitch deck.

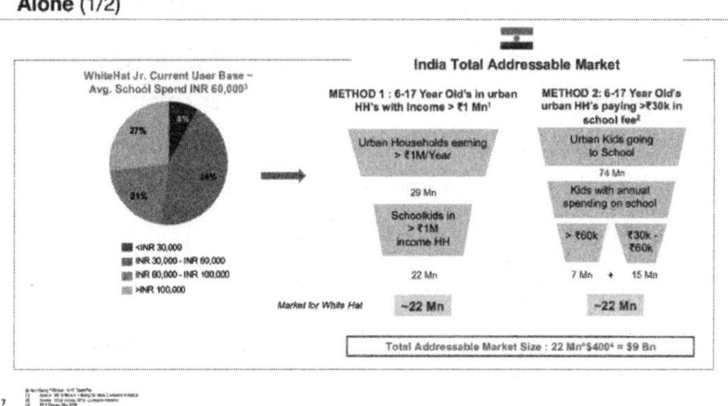

Source: Whitehat Junior's pitch deck as available on Karan Bajaj's blog[4]

They determined their Market Size just for India considering two methods. One where they calculated the number of school-going kids in urban households earning more than Rs. 10 lakh annually. In the second, they first estimated the number of school-going kids in urban areas and then divided them as per the amount they spent on schooling annually. In both approaches, the number of kids roughly numbered to 22 million. The average spending on schooling multiplied by this number gave them their India Market Size. Note that they also added the Global TAM in the footnote which is a smart way to reinforce the enormity of the market they were after.

4. Solution & Scalability

This slide presents how your startup solves the stated problem, and if it can be scaled. If addressed well, it makes your case significantly stronger.

As an example, if I need a pair of glasses with specific requirements, I, like all of us, can purchase them from a local store. This store solves a problem. But living in NCR, I can't buy glasses from a store in Bangalore unless I visit it. A single brick-and-mortar store is an example of a non-scalable solution. Lenskart scaled this solution by taking it online. They are valued at close to USD 5 billion as of June 2022.

Similar to the Problem slide, the Solution slide also needs to be effective and crisp. Avoid using technical jargon and gloating about the numerous features of your product. Instead, cover the core basis of it, how it solves the problem, and how you can scale it.

Here's how LinkedIn presented their solution in the deck they used to raise their Series B round.

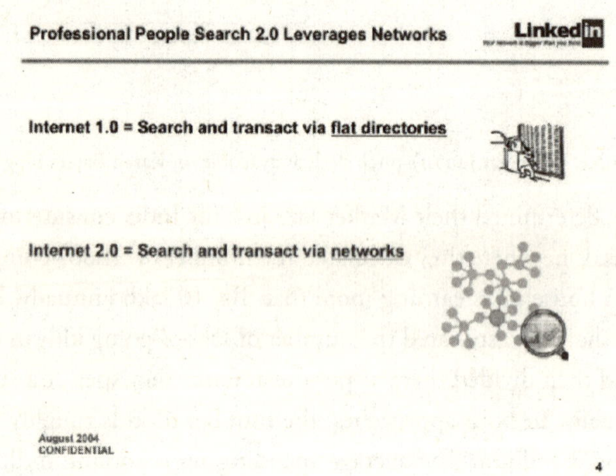

Source: LinkedIn's pitch deck as available on Piktochart

Take a look at how Copy.AI crisply presents what it offers without any unnecessary details.

Source: Copy.ai's pitch deck as available on VIP Graphics[5]

The solution slide is your opportunity to present the foundational idea of your startup. It should be easily understandable and impactful.

> Before finally sending the deck to investors, test the statement that you put out on this slide with people who have no idea about your startup, and get feedback on what they make of it. If they understood what you want them to, you're good to go. If they didn't get the point, you need to tweak your statement and test again.

5. Revenue Model & Monetization

Every investor invests in a startup with the expectation (or hope) of generating extraordinary returns in the future. The returns, however, are generated only if a startup thrives over a considerably long period (at least a few years). And only those with strong business fundamentals are eventually able to. Strong fundamentals start with a solid revenue model. This slide elucidates how you will generate revenue and if your unit economics is healthy enough.

If you consider a social media platform like Instagram, the video streaming and discovery platform YouTube, or the search engine Google, the earnings model of each of these companies is almost completely based on advertisements. In a way, these are advertising platforms that collect user data and assist brands in targeted advertising. For Google, the search engine is just an enabler to collect this data which is eventually monetized through ads. That's their revenue model.

Companies like Uber or Zomato follow the commission model, where they take a percentage of the ticket size of orders on their platform.

SaaS companies work on subscription models, where users pay a fixed periodical fee to use their softwares.

Take a look at how Bliss, a collaboration platform for coders, presented the revenue model slide.

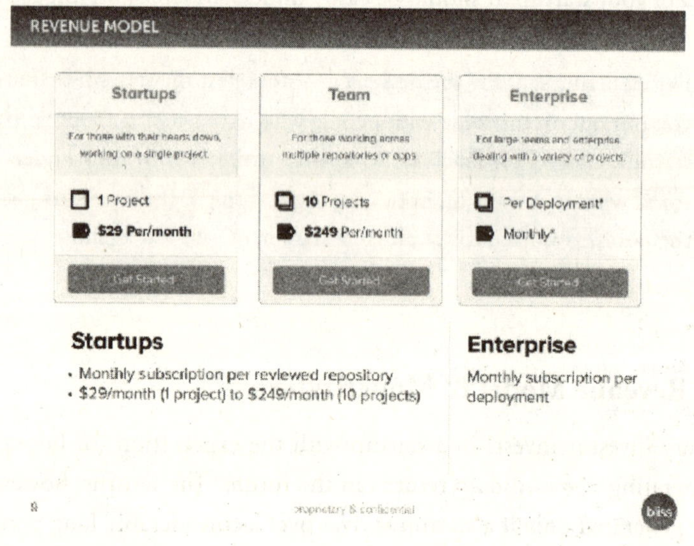

Source: Bliss' pitch deck as available on Piktochart

The company evidently followed a subscription-based monetization model.

In this slide, the founder needs to mention the earnings model of their current product and also hint on how the pricing can pivot going forward. In some cases, achieving a certain set of metrics like the number of users, engagement rate, etc. are imperative for the startup before they're able to generate revenue. They must then present how monetization can happen in phases and how they foresee earnings between certain milestones. This will give the investors an idea that even if the product doesn't directly generate revenue in the present, the founder has thought through the avenues that eventually will make them money.

The Revenue Model slide should clearly indicate a positive unit economics model, either in the present or at least a path towards that in the future. Chances of finding an investor willing to invest in a business that loses money on every sale are close to nil.

BuzzFeed, a digital media startup, listed its revenue streams in the freemium model they offer.

Source: BuzzFeed's pitch deck as available on Piktochart

Like BuzzFeed, you also don't need to delve into the minute details of your earning model. A brief overview of how you plan to monetize your product with an indication of unit economics positivity serves the purpose.

6. Competitive Advantage or Moat

When castles were built, they were surrounded by a deep trench of water to protect them against enemies and unwanted intrusions. This trench is called a *moat.*

In the start-up world, the word "moat" is now popularly used to imply a key competitive advantage that sets a company apart from its competitors. This is what you convey in the Competitive Advantage slide.

To figure out the moat of your business, I find it handy to use Porter's Five Forces framework, popularized by renowned strategy expert and former Harvard professor Michael Porter. The five forces are:

1. **Industry rivalry:** The larger the number of competitors vying for market share, the lesser the power of a company, especially a new one. If you can build a monopoly or duopoly, you can set the terms as per your convenience and charge higher prices.
2. **Threat of new entrants:** Lesser the time and money it costs for a competitor to enter a company's market, the more a company's position could be significantly weakened in the future.
3. **Bargaining power of suppliers:** Fewer the number of suppliers to the industry, the more a company would depend on one or a limited number of suppliers. In this scenario, your supplier has more power and can favour your competitor at any point, resulting in your loss.
4. **Bargaining power of buyers:** A company that has many independent customers, compared to those with a smaller client base, will have an easier time charging higher prices to increase profitability. If your business is dependent on just a handful of clients, you always run a risk of losing a large volume of business even if one of them defects to a competitor.
5. **Threat of substitutes:** Companies that produce goods or services for which there are no close substitutes will have more

power to increase prices and lock in favourable terms. To date, no company has been able to match Apple in terms of user experience. That's why the company enjoys an extremely loyal customer base and became a trillion-dollar business at one point.

Note that the framework is for you to understand and assess your startup's competitive advantages and not to paste it on the slide.

The next picture shows how LinkedIn presented the barriers of entry to its business in the pitch used to raise the Series B round.

LinkedIn's Market-Leading Position Creates Strong Barriers to Entry

- Inherently viral product design with tipping point effects
  Promotes ongoing market leadership
- Reputation system and network of relationships between users
  Enables very strong network effects and user trust
- 2 key patents in viral marketing and "social networking"
  1 granted, 1 pending with 1999 priority date

August 2004
CONFIDENTIAL

18

Source: LinkedIn's pitch deck as available on Piktochart

The moat of a company can take various forms.

- If you sell a good quality product at the lowest cost in the market and can do that sustainably and profitably, then the cost acts as your moat.
- When you have a patent for a particular technology that no one else can replicate, this intellectual property (IP) acts as your moat.

- If you're an old, renowned player in an industry with a loyal customer base, your brand value acts as a moat. There are numerous cola drinks available in the market, and many smaller players have tried to venture into the domain. But none of them ever seriously challenged Coca-Cola, even if they had equally good or better products. That's the power of a brand.
- If a business requires high capital to set up, then this initial capital requirement acts as s barrier to entry into the industry. For example, only individuals like Elon Musk and Jeff Bezos have the resources to start a space flight company (SpaceX and Blue Origin respectively).
- Exclusive contracts with distributor channels, vendors or suppliers can also act as a moat.

Take a look at how Mixpanel talked about its competitive advantage.

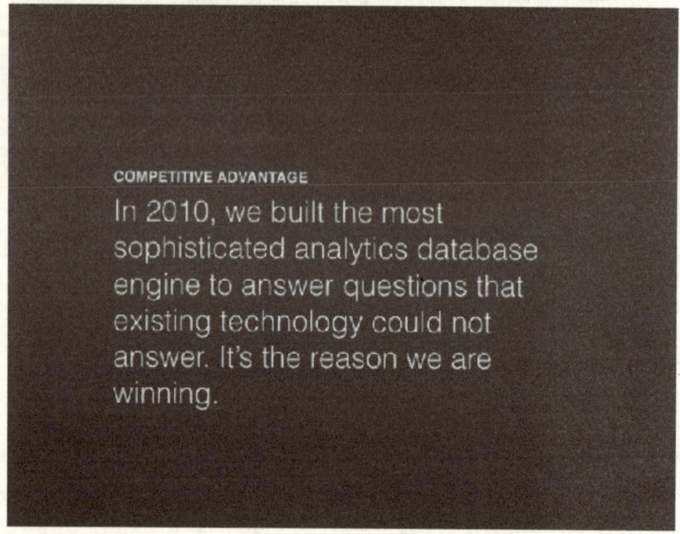

Source: Mixpanel's pitch deck as available on Piktochart

The presentation of this slide, yet again, needs to be similar to that of the Problem and Solution slides. Refrain from using technical jargon and write crisp, effective sentences. Use short bullet points if there are clear, multiple advantages over your competitors. Support them with icons or images if they help emphasize your points better.

7. Competitor Analysis

After you have established how you stand out through the Competitive Advantage or Moat slide, you compare your product against competitors to reinforce exactly why customers will choose you over them. A startup cannot hope to succeed (or raise funds) without customers willing to pay for its products or services. Through this slide, the investor should realize that your product is indeed better than incumbents and will acquire a large number of paying users.

A traditional method of presenting the competition is to create a 2x2 matrix. The two axes represent two competitive advantages and you place your startup and its competitors in different quadrants.

Here's how Airbnb used the four-quadrant system to create their competition slide.

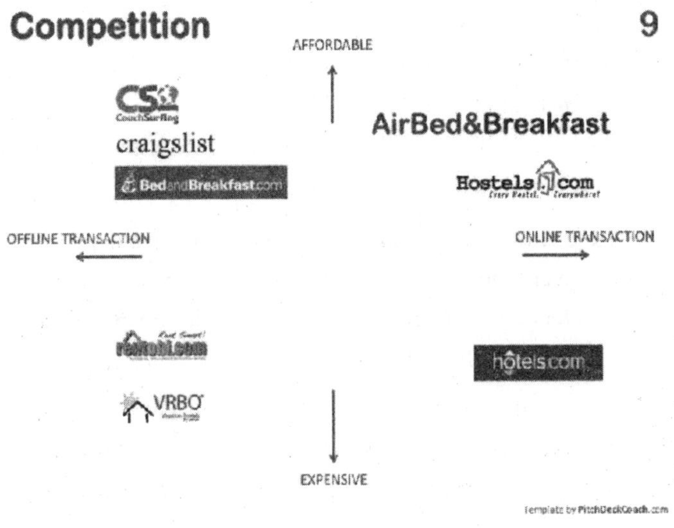

Source: Airbnb's pitch deck as available on Piktochart

However, you can only consider two advantages of your startup through this method. That's why a more efficient way is to probably use a grid.

- Build a table where the first column lists the benefits, and the others list your competitors.
- Keep the first column to your own startup, go right in decreasing order of priority.
- The rows define the benefits you deliver and not the features. For example, a chatbot is a feature that any competitor can build into their product easily. A benefit or advantage can be a massive amount of customer data that may be used to offer a personalized product.
- Start with your biggest value proposition as the top row and go down in preferential order.
- Fill in the grid with quantitative data and not qualitative description. For example, if your delivery time is the fastest, quantify how fast it is and show that others are slower through actual data of average time.
- Leave the field blank if the benefit doesn't apply to a competitor instead of mentioning N.A. or 0 or X.
- Consider benefits under heads of product, distribution strategy, pricing, stickiness, and usage frequency.

The table shown is an example of how you could present your superiority over your competition[6]. Google can simply enlist the benefits it offers over its competitors on the relevant parameters that search engines are evaluated on and compare.

	Google	Bing	Baidu	Yahoo	Yandex
Shows most relevant results	Y				
Load time <1s	Y	Y	Y	Y	Y
Shows >8 file types	Y	Y	Y		
Largest Ad inventory volume	Y				
Owns mobile operating system	Y				

Ensure that the Competition slide is self-explanatory and impactful. Do not hide obvious shortcomings just to project yourself well. That indicates immaturity and ignorance. It's ok to mention where your competitors may have an edge and mention how you can tide over this drawback. It also shows that you know your competition well.

8. Founding Team

When an investor looks at the Founders slide of a pitch deck, they are mainly looking for 3 qualities:

1. **The ability to execute:** Is this founder truly someone who can take the startup to success? Can they put their words into action?
2. **Commitment:** Startups are difficult. A founder should have skin in the game and be committed for the long run. Do they demonstrate it in some manner?
3. **Team capability:** A founder, even if driven, may not be capable to build a successful startup alone. How capable is their team? Do they have the right mix of individuals to run this business?

The objective of this slide is to establish credibility in the eyes of the investor. Founders sometimes also mention the names of Advisors on this slide. It can add to the credibility if the Advisors are highly accomplished folks in the startup's domain. But if the founders have good profiles themselves, mentioning Advisors may not be necessary.

LaunchRock, a startup that helps businesses build landing pages, dedicated one complete slide to their investors and advisors.

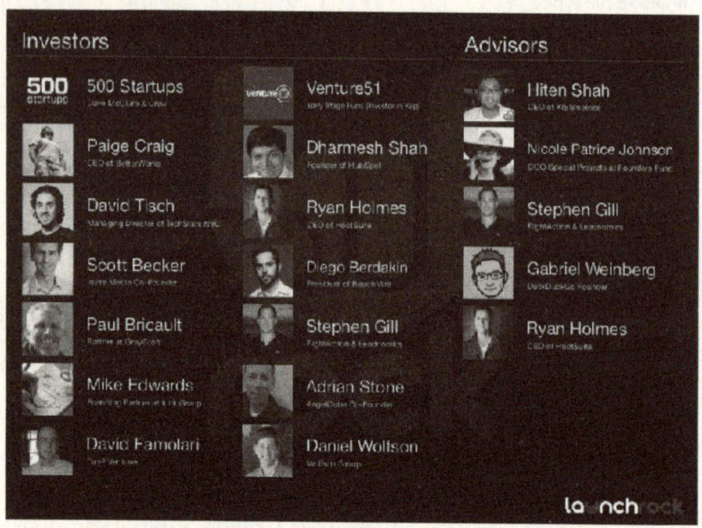

Source: LaunchRock's pitch deck as available on Piktochart

Admittedly, so much information feels like an overkill in a pitch deck, but you get the point.

Here are the elements that you must mention in the Founders slide of your pitch deck:

1. Name
2. Picture
3. Your position at the startup (CEO, CTO, CFO, etc.)
4. Some form of achievement.

Create a minimal but effective slide. Bliss offers a great example.

TEAM

Brian York
CEO
Self-funded 3 businesses to profitability. Most recently Encore.io $500k revenue in first year.

Ian Connor
CTO
Previously CTO/Co-founder at Pubget (acquired by Copyright Clearance Center).

Advisors

11 proprietary & confidential

Source: Bliss' pitch deck as available on Piktochart

You can observe how they have added their achievements which add credibility to their profiles.

9. Traction - Performance & Achievements

The traction slide is where you describe what your startup has accomplished to date in terms of business metrics. Every investor would need details about your performance so far before putting money into your venture. Traction metrics are an indicator of the execution capabilities of the founding team, and also helps signal if the startup can succeed in the future.

The metrics to be put in this slide vary depending on the stage your company is in. The following table can be used as a reference to pick what's relevant.

Note that you need not mention all the relevant metrics. Only put those that indicate the health of your startup the best.

Pre-product	Pre-Revenue	Post-revenue
1. No. of customer meetings 2. No. of interested design partners 3. No. of people willing to try or buy the product 4. No. of early access signups 5. Do you have a patent? If you have applied for one, what is the status of the application?	1. No. of pilots run and their results 2. Number of signups and downloads (for a B2C company) 3. Engagement metrics 4. CAC 5. Do you need any regulatory approval for your business? If yes, what is the status?	1. MRR and ARR 2. LTV to CAC ratio 3. Number of customers 4. User retention 5. Customer engagement rate

This is how SteadyBudget, a budget management software, presented their traction details.

Client Traction

- 35+ PPC agencies actively using the app
- $4,400,000+ in monthly ad spend under management
- 15,000+ campaigns tracking
- 1,500+ budgets created
- Customers committed to "Premium" version - May 2015

SteadyBudget

Source: SteadyBudget's pitch deck as available on Piktochart

Here is how Copy.ai presented their MRR and ARR in a slide to emphasize their growth potential.

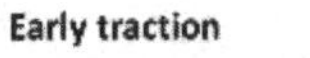

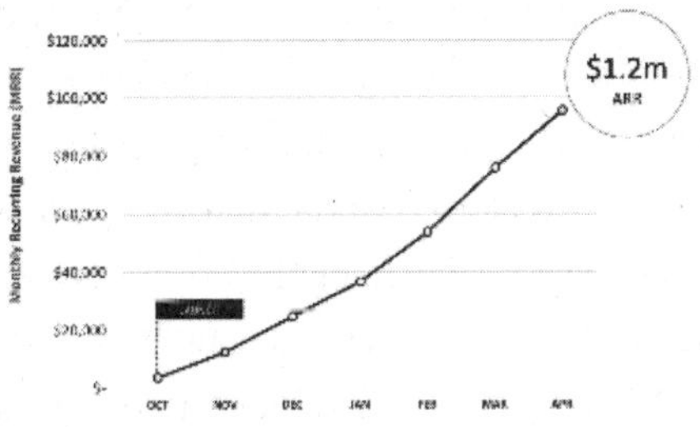

Source: Copy.ai's pitch deck as available on VIP Graphics

Be honest while showing your traction numbers. I have seen founders contemplating showing inflated figures to create an impression, but they invariably get found out at some stage and founders lose all their credibility. Think of long-term consequences before giving in to these ploys.

10. Financial Projections

Investors understand that no one can accurately predict the future. They will inherently consider your projections with a pinch of salt. What they want to understand through these projections is whether your goals and approach are practical for the industry you function in.

Let's say I want to start an e-commerce business for gold jewellery. I expect the Average Transaction Value to lie between Rs. 15 to 20 thousand. In my calculations, I have projected my profits on the basis of a Customer Acquisition Cost (CAC) of Rs. 400. But the industry average for the CAC in jewellery e-commerce may be much higher, about Rs. 4000. Any investor would want to understand the logic behind my assumed CAC. Unless I have solid reasoning, I cannot expect to impress the investors. They would be interested to know what different I'd do to reduce the CAC. If they figure it's a number I've randomly pulled up, I'm certain to be shown the door.

In the deck, you don't need to present the detailed reasoning behind your projections. As long as the numbers are not outrageous, they won't raise eyebrows. But you must be prepared with the detailed calculations on how you arrived at the figures. There would certainly be questions around the rationale behind those projections and how you intend to achieve them in later discussions.

In this slide, an investor essentially wants to understand two things:

1. Your vision for your startup in the financial sense
2. Basic logic and assumptions behind the vision

Here's how Whitehat Jr presented the projections of Gross Bookings from the years 2020 to 2024.

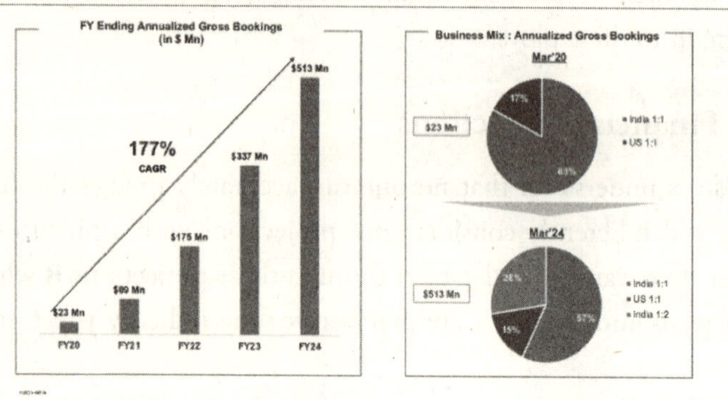

Source: Whitehat Junior's pitch deck as available on Karan Bajaj's blog[4]

They have also estimated the growth of various other metrics for the same period.

Similar to how they did it, you can use graphs to show the growth trajectory of your business. Pick the most important metrics and present your calculations in an easily consumable format. Ensure not to over-analyze or reveal more than what's necessary.

Significantly **Improved Unit Economics** from 1:2 and US Scaling

Mar'20

In $	India 1:1 (86%)	US 1:1 (14%)	Blended
ARPU net of Taxes	337	541	366
Direct Cost	186	164	183
Gross Margin	150	377	183
Gross Margin %	**45%**	**70%**	**50%**
Ops Cost	14	30	16
Contribution Margin	136	347	166
Contribution Margin%	**40%**	**64%**	**45%**
LTV	477	1,144	569
CAC[1]	119	117	119
LTV: CAC Ratio	**4.0x**	**9.8x**	**4.8x**

Mar'24

In $	India 1:1 (62%)	US 1:1 (12%)	India 1:2 (26%)	Blended
ARPU net of Taxes	389	537	253	**370**
Direct Cost	186	147	127	**166**
Gross Margin	202	390	126	**204**
Gross Margin %	**52%**	**73%**	**50%**	**55%**
Ops Cost	16	9	12	**14**
Contribution Margin	186	381	114	**190**
Contribution Margin%	**48%**	**71%**	**45%**	**51%**
LTV	652	1,258	400	**657**
CAC[1]	120	216	60	**115**
LTV: CAC Ratio	**5.4x**	**5.8x**	**6.7x**	**5.7x**

(1) Includes all performance, sales and trial costs. Excludes Branding and Long-Term Testing Expenses.
(2) Contribution Margin LTV = Contribution Margin based on actual renewal rates.
(3) 1 USD = INR 74

19

Source: Whitehat Junior's pitch deck as available on Karan Bajaj's blog[4]

11. Ask & Valuation

In this slide, you state your funding requirement and the valuation you seek.

There are 3 main points that need to be conveyed.

1. The fundraising amount - how much you want to raise
2. The runway - the period you will need these funds for.
3. The use of funds - how you plan to utilize these funds and what goals or milestones you're targeting.

This is how Fittr, a Pune-based fitness startup, presented their ask and utilization of funds.

RAISING
$250,000

INVESTMENT GOAL

- SEO Campaign
- Targeted Advertising
- Server Costs
- Create nutitional plans
- Hire developer for future features
- Sporting team workout databasing
- Android App
- Profitibility within 1 year

TYLER PERKINS
TYLER@FITTR.COM

INVESTING

Source: Fittr's pitch deck as available on Piktochart

If you already have other investors on board who have agreed to invest in the ongoing round, you must mention the committed amounts by these investors and the balance left to be raised. It also helps build further credibility for the startup and you're more likely to get the benefit of doubts, if any.

Similarly, you can also mention your past investors in a separate slide.

In the next image, observe how Mixpanel added the details of all their previous rounds in their pitch deck.

Financing history

2009	2009	2011	2012
$15K	$500K	$1.25M	$10.25M
Seed	Seed	Seed	Series A
Y Combinator	Max Levchin, Michael Birch	Sequoia Capital, Keith Rabois, Max Levchin, Michael Birch	Andreessen Horowitz, Marc Benioff, David Sacks

Source: Mixpanel's pitch deck as available on Piktochart

This brings us to the end of the 11-slide pitch deck structure. Some additional points that you can use to design your pitch deck are as follows:

1. Use 2 font styles - one for the header and another for the body of the slide.
2. Maintain a colour theme - use 2 at the most. You can search for the emotions or ideas that colours usually represent and pick accordingly, or simply stick to the brand colours you already have.
3. Maintain clarity. Avoid clutter by leaving a considerable amount of white space.
4. Treat numbers and data points as a tool to emphasize your potential. Add them only where they add significant value.
5. Mention the sources of your research in the footnote of each slide.
6. Do not add Excel charts to your pitch deck. Create visually appealing charts and graphics. Any detailed calculations should not be added in the initial deck, and only presented in

the appendix or in meetings.

Every investor goes through multiple pitch decks daily. Understandably, their bandwidth to consume and process information is low. So make your deck as easy to read as possible while ensuring that your startup's propositions are not compromised. It's a fine line and needs iterations, feedback, and some practice to perfect.

One-page Pitch Deck & Elevator Pitch

You may create an efficient pitch deck, but it's not always feasible to present in a restricted environment. Say, you attend a startup networking event where you intend to meet with investors and create an impression. You can't just open your laptop and start pitching in that interaction. Anything that looks desperate doesn't send great signals. But a one-page pitch deck or the elevator pitch may be the right tool to use in such situations.

An elevator pitch is a heavily (but smartly) abridged version of the formal pitch deck. It is usually developed with the assistance of a communication design professional and presents only the most relevant details of your startup.

You can remove details like financial projections and the funding ask with goals and only retain the points that cover what you really do. If possible, include the market size, and if it builds a good case for you, include some traction details. Adding a QR code or a link to your product would be a smart idea. Do not forget to mention your communication details.

A founder can share this one-page pitch with investors and whoever is ready to listen to their story. If the product interests them, they can easily reach out to you asking for a meeting or more details. Having a physical one-pager also increases the recall value, similar to how visiting cards work but with more information.

I have shared a link for the one-page elevator pitch examples compiled on the Slide Team website (slideteam.net) in Annexure 10.1. You can also refer to the Business Model Canvas proposed by Alexander Osterwalder (Annexure 10.2) to create one.

Presenting the Pitch

You must understand any audience before you address them. Yours will be a set of individuals who are both very smart and very busy and have seen countless pitches in their life. It's easy for them to get bored and lose attention if you do just the bare minimum. To stand out, you must make them feel that their time spent listening to you is worth it. And the most effective way to do that is by telling a story!

While you may have all the information in your slides, it won't be effective until it tells a compelling story. As the presenter, your chances of garnering the attention of anyone go up if you build a powerful narrative and smoothly let your listeners absorb the point. In fact, a good story can even cover other shortcomings you may have as an orator.

Can you recall the pitch by Jugaadu Kamlesh on Shark Tank India? He wasn't the suavest of contestants on the show and didn't have any charming presence on first look. But he had an emotional plea, humour, authenticity, struggle, and everything that one wants from a good story. And all through, he never veered from his main point of raising funds for his startup, which he believed would make the lives of farmers much easier. The reason that it garnered so much publicity was because of the story he built and then how the last Shark remaining, Peyush Bansal, offered to fund him after all others had refused. That made for a great emotional watch, didn't it? You can watch it on YouTube by accessing this link: https://rb.gy/is1c0x[7].

A story, as we saw in Kamlesh's case, effectively hooks the audience with the speaker and makes the content more palatable for them. Andy Raskins, who helps build strategic narratives for CEOs and business leaders, suggests a wonderful story-telling framework in a Medium article[8]. It is, in fact, inspired by Elon Musk's keynote address on Tesla Powerwall in 2015. The framework suggested is as follows:

1. **Name the Enemy:** Do not start a pitch talking about yourself,

your team, product, or market. Start with the biggest impediment to the customer's happiness in the current scenario. If possible, try to paint an emotional picture of how the lives of the people you target are being impacted because of this.

2. **Answer "Why Now":** Explain why the timing is perfect to change the status quo. Investors always want to be sure if "now" is the right time to invest. Drive the point through effectively with an eye on how painful the process or existing solution has been and will continue to be for the people who matter.
3. **Show the promised land before explaining how you'll get there:** Almost like giving away the punchline, explain what a better world would like for the people. Raskins says in his blog post, "Before describing anything about batteries, Musk describes his version of happily-ever-after." Don't just mention the functional benefits yet, show the outcome of those benefits first.
4. **Identify obstacles and how you propose to overcome them:** How does your product get through these obstacles, or how are you proposing to solve these problems through your product? Steep obstacles invite the audience's interest. No one likes a story where the hero fights a weak, weaponless villain.
5. **Present evidence to show your capability:** To finally convince your audience that whatever you have said so far is not plucked out of thin air, you demonstrate what you have built and the results that you have attained at whatever scale you're operating. If there's a live, physical product, bring it along. If it's a tech product, show a working demo.

A walk-through demo of the product is often the best option for SaaS and E-commerce businesses. You can also add images or videos to the pitch deck for good effect. If your product is still in the idea stage, you can get a sketch or clean wireframes created by a designer, or a 3D model if it's a physical product in works.

The image shows how Canvas, a startup that replaces paper-based processes with affordable and easy-to-use mobile apps and forms, added images of their product to the pitch deck.

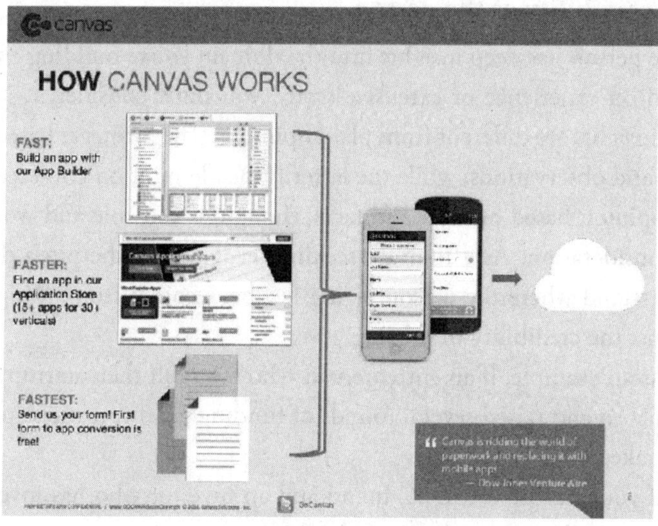

Source: Canvas's pitch deck as available on Piktochart

Use the information in the pitch deck to support your story. When you simply explain facts, you lose the listener much faster than when you use facts to emphasize the relevance of your story. The information in the deck is the supporting actor here, your story is the hero.

Ideally, the CEO of a startup should pitch to investors, but all the founders should ideally be present in the room. At times, you may find one of the co-founders, other than the CEO, more suited to pitch due to better communication skills or personality. In such a case, that co-founder can pitch the idea.

Understanding Feedback & Improvements

Once you create your deck, it's natural to show it around and seek feedback. As much as constructive and meaningful feedback helps, I have also seen founders approaching too many people from different backgrounds for it and only ending up confused.

Consider the following two factors when seeking and considering feedback.

The credibility of the person

If the person has deep insights into the domain you're building either based on experience or extensive study, you must consider it. Note that insights are different from plain opinions. The former is based on data and observations, while the latter is mostly built on conjectures. An opinion based on data and facts, though, is valuable and worthy of consideration. As a founder seeking feedback on the pitch deck, understand where the person giving feedback comes from. Weigh it against the credibility they bring.

As an example, if an entrepreneur who has built their startup into a unicorn and raised several rounds of funding gives you suggestions, you take it.

If your startup is a D2C brand and an investor who has invested in many such startups gives you feedback, you take it.

If a regular corporate employee who has never built or invested in a startup gives feedback, think before taking it. That largely depends on how highly you rate that person and their advice, so apply the right filters.

The most common suggestions

It's possible that when you show your deck to many people, some points of feedback turn up more frequently than others. This means there are certain aspects that many feel are missing in your deck and may be worth looking into.

All said, use your judgment to decide how you want to make the changes in your pitch deck. Create mental filters, and consider feedback on their merit.

Any pitch deck's primary job is to make the prospective investors interested and curious to know more about the company. It acts like an effective ad campaign that creates recall value for the product by highlighting its benefits in a compelling manner. But whether you become a long-term customer of the product truly depends on the product itself and how well it serves you. Similarly, a great pitch deck does open more doors, but getting an investor to invest is a function of all the factors that make a business great. That said, the more the number of doors you can enter, the higher the chances of you getting funded.

11. Building a Financial Model

The pitch deck and the first 2-3 conversations determine if prospective investors find your idea interesting enough to probe further. If they do, they'd want to dig deeper into the startup's performance so far and the way forward. A well-prepared financial model helps clarify these for investors to a great extent.

The term 'financial model', though, is something that many founders dread, especially the ones without a background in finance. Part of the reason is the very traditional financial modelling spreadsheets going around in the startup ecosystem. Even I find them cumbersome to study.

If it's hard for the founder to comprehend, it would be even more arduous for the investor to analyze. While a heavy excel sheet inundated with formulae and numbers may appear professional and smart, it doesn't really serve the purpose. The objective of this financial model is to help investors understand the current business health and future projections better, and it should be done as simply and easily as possible. In this chapter, we'll see how to approach building one with a few easy examples.

What does an Investor want to see in a Financial Model?

Investors become interested in a startup's financial model only after they like the pitch deck and the idea matches their thesis. At this point, they already have a basic understanding of what's being built, and now want to delve deeper. The financial model helps answer more specific questions about the performance so far and projections for the future.

Interestingly, this model also gives investors a peek into the mind of the founder. A simple, well-made document with all the numbers based on sound logic and assumptions indicates clarity of thought. There's a perception among some founders that one should show inflated numbers in projections because only then will they become interested. I detest this approach and strongly advise against it. It signals immaturity and would ensure the deal falls flat.

In this chapter, I have explained how to prepare your startup's financial model through the examples of two startups - a D2C company and a gaming company. You'd find the approach simple for you to learn and for investors to consume.

Broadly, a financial model in Excel would consist of the following sheets:

1. Introduction
2. Dashboard/Cashflow/Financial Plan
3. User Acquisition and Marketing Channels
4. Revenue
5. Unit Level Economics (for D2C startups)
6. Fixed Costs/Manpower

Depending on the nature of your business and the industry you operate in, you may need to tweak some of the things I explain here. But regardless of it, this would give you a good template to work with.

For your reference, I have presented an Excel screenshot of each of the sheets explained. These have been taken from actual working financial models which I created for two of the startups I worked with. The numbers are dummy but indicative. Let's understand the model sheet by sheet.

Step 1: Distribution Channels & User Acquisition

This sheet aims to segregate the different user acquisition channels and clearly demonstrate how many users/customers can be won relative to the amount spent across them.

In the following image, you'll notice that the sheet has been named "Digital Ad Funnel". Since the main sources of acquiring users for any D2C business are online ads, this sheet has been accordingly named.

This startup runs ads on Facebook, Google, and third-party apps. They have spent a total of Rs. 14 lakhs across the three channels. Notice how this ad spend has been used to progressively calculate the number of impressions achieved on that channel, number of clicks, additions to cart, and finally orders.

If you move further across, you can multiply the sale orders with the average order value (AOV) to get total monthly sales (calculated under Sales (Rs.)).

CTR, which stands for click-through rate, is the percentage of users that convert to customers after they see the ad. In this example though, I have calculated it as the % of customers won relative to every rupee invested. For example, on the FB channels, an investment of Rs. 4,00,000 is giving me 3,750 sale orders, which is a 0.94% conversion on the amount invested. The same number is 1.13% for Google because a Rs. 7,50,000 investment is yielding 8,438 sale orders. You can choose to define this metric yourself, but make sure it's easy to understand.

The Blended CTR is the total number of sale orders being generated relative to the total ad spend done across the three channels.

The cells with a darker shade are where you input values based on the actual performance or industry standards, as in the case of impressions, click rate, cart additions, and cart-to-order conversions. If you consider a figure other than the industry benchmark, you should have proper reasoning to back it.

Monthly Spend on Digital Ads

Digital Ad Campaigns	Ad Spend	Impressions	Click	Website / Cart	Sale Orders	AOV	Sales (Rs.)	CTR	Weight	
Facebook (FB, IG, WA)	₹ 4,00,000	6,00,000	75,000	7,500	3,750	₹ 750	28,12,500			
		150%	12.5%	10%	50%			0.94%	4.00	3.75%
Google	₹ 7,50,000	9,37,500	1,40,625	21,094	8,438	₹ 600	50,62,500			
		125%	15%	15%	40%			1.13%	7.50	8.44%
Third Party Apps	₹ 2,50,000	2,50,000	25,000	2,500	1,500	₹ 600	9,00,000			
		100%	10%	10%	60%			0.60%	2.50	1.50%
									14.00	**0.98% Blended CTR**

Marketing Spend	No.	Monthly Rate	Monthly Spend	Starting from
Agency Fees	1	5%	70,000	Q1
Influencer Costs	5	17,000	85,000	Q1
Branding Spends	1	25,000	25,000	Q1

Similarly, the marketing spends on agencies, influencers, and branding of the startup have also been specified in the section below. In essence, all the expenses incurred on user acquisition should feature on this sheet.

Let's analyze the user acquisition model for a gaming app now.

The two images shared next elaborate upon the same principles that we talked about for the D2C startup.

A gaming startup relies heavily on influencers, referrals, and digital ads to acquire more users. If you observe, the model has used a top-down approach to arrive at the number of weekly active users (WAU) each of the three channels can bring. As in the D2C example, actual data points have been considered for absolute values like cost per influencer, and industry standards have been considered for the different metrics for digital ad conversions.

Irrespective of the industry your startup is in, this sheet should clearly map out your user acquisition channels and how exactly you expect the spending done to convert to users or customers. Every assumption should be justified, and every number should be derived logically from what it's dependent on.

Gaming Company Pvt. Ltd.										
User Acquisition Model		**Actual**	**Q1**	**Q2**	**Q3**	**Q4**	**Q5**	**Q6**	**Q7**	**Q8**
New Acquisitions										
Total Downloads		2,00,000								
Total Users	80%	1,60,000								
Total WAU Acquired	45%	72,000	83,100	85,377	3,62,372	3,09,231	2,64,061	9,24,075	6,95,756	5,24,517
Total DAU Acquired	15%	10,800	12,465	12,807	54,356	46,385	39,609	1,38,611	1,04,363	78,678
Cumulative Users										
Total WAU (Net of Churn)	85%		83,100	1,56,012	4,94,982	7,29,965	8,84,532	16,75,927	21,20,294	23,26,767
Total DAU (Net of Churn)	70%		12,465	21,532	69,428	94,984	1,06,098	2,12,880	2,53,379	2,56,043
Distribution Channels										
1 YouTube Influencers										
- No. of Influencers		4			12			36		
- Total Following of Influencers		4,50,000			27,00,000			81,00,000		
- Avg. Following per Influencer		1,12,500			2,25,000			2,25,000		
- Total Influencer Cost p.m.		2,25,000			27,00,000			1,08,00,000		
- Avg. Payout per Influencer		56,250			2,25,000			3,00,000		
- Total Events held per month		6			18			54		
- No. of Events per Influencer p.m.		2			2			2		
- New Users acquired p.m.	12%	55,000	55,000	56,650	2,80,500	2,38,425	2,02,661	7,42,500	5,56,875	4,17,656
- Growth through new partnerships	3%				-15%			-25%		
Operating Metrics for Channel										
- Conversion Rate of Users to WAU	40%	22,000	22,000	22,660	1,12,200	95,370	81,065	2,97,000	2,22,750	1,67,063
- CAC per WAU		10			24			36		
2 Referral Model										
- Total WAUs - New		22,000								
- No. of WAUs Actively Referring	15%	3,300			7.5%			5%		
- No. of Users Acquired per R-WAU		5			3.5			2.5		
- Total Users Acquired from Referral		16,500	16,500	16,995	29,453	25,035	21,279	37,125	27,844	20,883
- Total Payout for Referrals		50,000			5,00,000			7,50,000		
Operating Metrics for Channel										
- Conversion Rate of Users to WAU	20%	3,300	3,300	3,399	5,891	5,007	4,256	7,425	5,569	4,177
- CAC per WAU		15			85			101		

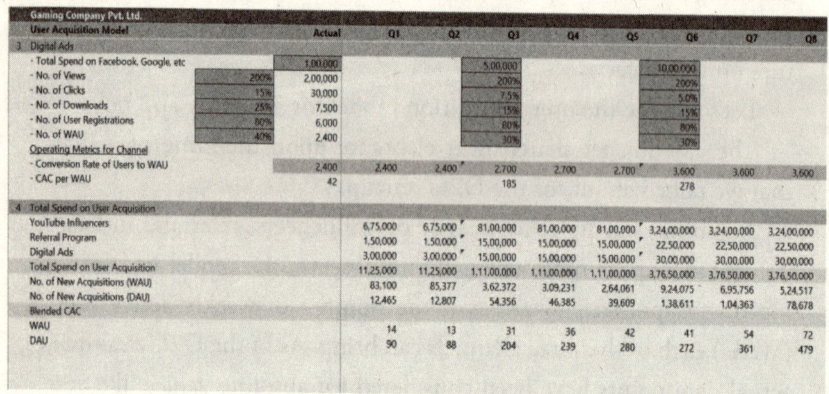

Gaming Company Pvt. Ltd.										
User Acquisition Model		**Actual**	**Q1**	**Q2**	**Q3**	**Q4**	**Q5**	**Q6**	**Q7**	**Q8**
3 Digital Ads										
- Total Spend on Facebook, Google, etc		1,00,000			5,00,000			10,00,000		
- No. of Views	200%	2,00,000			200%			200%		
- No. of Clicks	15%	30,000			7.5%			5.0%		
- No. of Downloads	25%	7,500			15%			15%		
- No. of User Registrations	80%	6,000			80%			80%		
- No. of WAU	40%	2,400			30%			30%		
Operating Metrics for Channel										
- Conversion Rate of Users to WAU		2,400	2,400	2,400	2,700	2,700	2,700	3,600	3,600	3,600
- CAC per WAU		42			185			278		
4 Total Spend on User Acquisition										
YouTube Influencers			6,75,000	6,75,000	81,00,000	81,00,000	81,00,000	3,24,00,000	3,24,00,000	3,24,00,000
Referral Program			1,50,000	1,50,000	15,00,000	15,00,000	15,00,000	22,50,000	22,50,000	22,50,000
Digital Ads			3,00,000	3,00,000	15,00,000	15,00,000	15,00,000	30,00,000	30,00,000	30,00,000
Total Spend on User Acquisition			11,25,000	11,25,000	1,11,00,000	1,11,00,000	1,11,00,000	3,76,50,000	3,76,50,000	3,76,50,000
No. of New Acquisitions (WAU)			83,100	85,377	3,62,372	3,09,231	2,64,061	9,24,075	6,95,756	5,24,517
No. of New Acquisitions (DAU)			12,465	12,807	54,356	46,385	39,609	1,38,611	1,04,363	78,678
Blended CAC										
WAU			14	13	31	36	42	41	54	72
DAU			90	88	204	239	280	272	361	479

Step 2: Active Users & Revenue

This sheet calculates the projected revenues the startup expects from all the different streams.

In the next image, we see all the revenue streams that the D2C startup has - Modern Trade, Amazon/Flipkart/Nykaa, and Performance Marketing. Performance Marketing here refers to the sales made from the direct channel with the help of ads run, as we saw in the last section on user acquisition.

If you note the line items under each of the revenue streams, you'll notice how the final number is being projected based on a bottom-up approach. We have extrapolated the number of orders one modern trade store can achieve monthly, then multiplied it across all the stores the startup expects to have, and also account for the growth rate to achieve a reasonable figure for each quarter. A similar approach has been taken for the e-commerce channels.

For the gaming startup, the revenue streams are completely different. They have classified their users into four categories - free, Class A, Class B, and Class C. These categories are all derived from the active user base which is mentioned in the top section, and then the revenues generated from the three paid categories are estimated.

Finally, revenues for the company are calculated after accounting for the payout done to the users, transaction fees, and the GST. This is actually the money that the company finally has at its disposal.

Again, you may not be able to use these two templates exactly for your startup to prepare this sheet. But you can refer to these to understand how each revenue stream is broken down and how the values are estimated based on logical assumptions. Ensure to include all possible revenue streams, and calculate the net revenues only after accounting for all transactional expenses.

Sales Channel & Revenue Projections		Q1	Q2	Q3	Q4	Q5	Q6	Q7	Q8	Total
A *Modern Trade*										
No. of Modern Trade Chains contracted	0			1			1			
No. of Stores per Chain	8			8			8			
No. of Orders per Store per Month	200			200			260			
Avg. Order Value	500			500			500			
Quarterly Growth Rate	0%			2%			2.5%			
Projected Revenues from Modern Trade		₹ 0	₹ 0	₹ 24,00,000	₹ 24,48,000	₹ 24,96,960	₹ 24,00,000	₹ 24,60,000	₹ 25,21,500	**₹ 1,47,26,460**
B *Amazon / Flipkart / Nykaa*										
No. of Websites listed on	2			2			2			
Avg. # Orders per Website per Month	500			500			500			
Avg. Order Value	450			450			450			
Quarterly Growth Rate	0%			5%			7.5%			
Projected Revenues from Marketplaces		₹ 13,50,000	₹ 13,50,000	₹ 14,17,500	₹ 14,88,375	₹ 15,62,794	₹ 16,00,003	₹ 17,20,003	₹ 18,49,004	**₹ 1,23,37,679**
C *Performance Marketing*										
Ad Spend per Month	14,00,000									
CTR	0.98%									
No. of Orders	17,688									
CAC per Order	102									
Projected Revenues from Performance Mktg		₹ 2,63,25,000	₹ 2,63,25,000	₹ 2,63,25,000	₹ 2,63,25,000	₹ 2,63,25,000	₹ 2,63,25,000	₹ 2,63,25,000	₹ 2,63,25,000	**₹ 21,06,00,000**
Total Revenues		₹ 2,76,75,000	₹ 2,76,75,000	₹ 3,01,42,500	₹ 3,02,61,375	₹ 3,03,84,754	₹ 3,03,25,003	₹ 3,05,05,003	₹ 3,06,95,504	₹ 23,76,64,139
Sales from Modern Trade	6%	₹ 0	₹ 0	₹ 24,00,000	₹ 24,48,000	₹ 24,96,960	₹ 24,00,000	₹ 24,60,000	₹ 25,21,500	₹ 1,47,26,460
Sales from Marketplaces - Organic	5%	₹ 13,50,000	₹ 13,50,000	₹ 14,17,500	₹ 14,88,375	₹ 15,62,794	₹ 16,00,003	₹ 17,20,003	₹ 18,49,004	₹ 1,23,37,679
Sales from Performance Marketing	89%	₹ 2,63,25,000	₹ 2,63,25,000	₹ 2,63,25,000	₹ 2,63,25,000	₹ 2,63,25,000	₹ 2,63,25,000	₹ 2,63,25,000	₹ 2,63,25,000	₹ 21,06,00,000

Gaming Company Pvt. Ltd.										
Revenue Model			**Q1**	**Q2**	**Q3**	**Q4**	**Q5**	**Q6**	**Q7**	**Q8**
Cumulative Users										
Total MAU (Net of Churn)			83,100	1,56,012	4,94,982	7,29,965	8,84,532	16,75,927	21,20,294	23,26,767
Total DAU (Net of Churn)			12,465	21,532	69,428	94,984	1,06,098	2,12,880	2,53,379	2,56,043
Classification of DAUs										
Free Players	91%		11,343	19,594	63,180	86,436	96,549	1,93,721	2,30,575	2,32,999
Paid Users - Class A	1%		125	215	694	950	1,061	2,129	2,534	2,560
Paid Users - Class B	3%		374	646	2,083	2,850	3,183	6,386	7,601	7,681
Paid Users - Class C	5%		623	1,077	3,471	4,749	5,305	10,644	12,669	12,802
Revenue Channels										
Commissions on Paid Games	Stake/Game	Games/Day								
Paid Users - Class A	100	3	37,395	64,596	2,08,284	2,84,953	3,18,295	6,38,640	7,60,138	7,68,130
Paid Users - Class B	30	10	1,12,185	1,93,788	6,24,853	8,54,859	9,54,884	19,15,920	22,80,415	23,04,389
Paid Users - Class C	5	15	46,744	80,745	2,60,356	3,56,191	3,97,868	7,98,300	9,50,173	9,60,162
Gaming Company Pvt. Ltd. Rake on Total Pool	25%		49,081	84,782	2,73,373	3,74,001	4,17,762	8,38,215	9,97,682	10,08,170
Revenues										
Revenues (Net of Payout)			44,17,284	76,30,420	2,46,03,604	3,36,60,071	3,75,98,551	7,54,39,347	8,97,91,338	9,07,35,302
Less: Transaction Fees	4%		7,06,766	12,20,867	39,36,577	53,85,611	60,15,768	1,20,70,296	1,43,66,614	1,45,17,648
Less: GST @ 18%			6,73,823	11,63,962	37,53,092	51,34,587	57,35,372	1,15,07,697	1,36,96,984	1,38,40,978
Revenues (Net of Trsc. Fees + GST)			**30,36,696**	**52,45,591**	**1,69,13,935**	**2,31,39,873**	**2,58,47,411**	**5,18,61,355**	**6,17,27,739**	**6,23,76,676**

Step 3: Unit Economics - Gross Margins, Contribution Margins

The purpose of this sheet is to clearly show the margins you make on every sale done. A high unit-economics positivity is one of the most sought after signals for investors to consider a startup for investment. It indicates that the business, when scaled, has the potential to be highly profitable and is worth an investment today.

In the next image, notice the first section is again mentioning the total sales done. The numbers here are derived from the previous sheets on revenues.

The next section mentions the costs expected to be incurred as a percentage of the final sale value. These percentages are used to specify the different costs in absolute terms, and calculate the Gross Margin and Contribution Margins 1 & 2.

Contribution Margin 2 is the amount that the business earns after incurring all the operational costs. This is the number that every business wants to maximize.

Unit-level economics does not exactly pertain to a gaming startup. They do not sell a tangible product per se. That is why it's not included in their financial model. It would be the same for any business offering a completely digital offering, like a SaaS product.

Unit Level Economics			Q1	Q2	Q3	Q4	Q5	Q6	Q7	Q8
Total Sales			2,76,75,000	2,76,75,000	3,01,42,500	3,02,61,375	3,03,94,754	3,03,25,003	3,05,05,003	3,06,55,504
Avg. Order Value			719	719	719	719	719	719	719	719
Avg. Price per Item			250	250	250	250	250	250	250	250
No. of Items per Order			2.88	2.88	2.88	2.88	2.88	2.88	2.88	2.88
Total No. of Items Sold			1,10,700	1,10,700	1,20,570	1,21,046	1,21,539	1,21,300	1,22,020	1,22,782
No. of Units										
Procurement Units (Current + Next 45 Days)			1,66,050	1,15,635	1,20,808	1,21,292	1,21,420	1,21,660	1,22,401	1,22,782
Material Cost	20%									
Packing Cost	2%									
Logistics Cost	10%									
Marketplace Commission	15%									
Modern Trade Commission	35%									
Total Procurement Cost (Material + Packaging)			₹91,32,750	₹63,59,925	₹66,44,426	₹66,71,074	₹66,78,075	₹66,91,301	₹67,32,056	₹67,53,011
Gross Margin		67%	₹1,85,42,250	₹2,13,15,075	₹2,34,96,074	₹2,35,90,301	₹2,37,06,680	₹2,36,33,702	₹2,37,72,948	₹2,39,42,493
Logistics Cost			₹27,67,500	₹27,67,500	₹30,14,250	₹30,26,138	₹30,38,475	₹30,32,500	₹30,50,500	₹30,69,550
Marketplace Commission			₹41,51,250	₹41,51,250	₹41,61,375	₹41,72,006	₹41,83,169	₹41,88,750	₹42,06,751	₹42,26,101
Modern Trade Commission			₹0	₹0	₹8,40,000	₹8,56,800	₹8,73,936	₹8,40,000	₹8,61,000	₹8,82,525
Contribution Margin 1		42%	₹1,16,23,500	₹1,43,96,325	₹1,54,82,449	₹1,55,35,351	₹1,56,11,100	₹1,55,72,452	₹1,56,54,697	₹1,57,64,317
Digital Ad Spend			₹42,00,000	₹42,00,000	₹42,00,000	₹42,00,000	₹42,00,000	₹42,00,000	₹42,00,000	₹42,00,000
Contribution Margin 2		27%	₹74,23,500	₹1,01,96,325	₹1,12,82,449	₹1,13,35,351	₹1,14,11,100	₹1,13,72,452	₹1,14,54,697	₹1,15,64,317

Step 4: Fixed Costs & Overheads

In this sheet, you list down all the non-operational fixed costs that the startup incurs and expects to incur - employees, rent, overheads, tech subscriptions, and any other fixed costs you could think of. Including these help the investors (and you) understand the true extent of investments needed. Even if the unit economics is excellent, a very high fixed cost would plant seeds of doubt. Higher the fixed costs, longer the road to profitability.

For a D2C startup, the list of items is quite straightforward as you can see in the next image.

For a gaming startup, you'd notice in the next image that the contribution of technology-related fixed costs is significantly high, in addition to the regular manpower and admin expenses that any company would incur.

Manpower & Other Expenses			Q1	Q2	Q3	Q4	Q5	Q6	Q7	Q8
Manpower Requirement	Monthly Pay	Units								
CEO Co-Founder	₹1,50,000	1	₹4,50,000	₹4,50,000	₹4,50,000	₹4,50,000	₹4,50,000	₹4,50,000	₹4,50,000	₹4,50,000
CMO Co-Founder	₹1,50,000	1	₹4,50,000	₹4,50,000	₹4,50,000	₹4,50,000	₹4,50,000	₹4,50,000	₹4,50,000	₹4,50,000
Data Analyst	₹75,000	1	₹2,25,000	₹2,25,000	₹2,25,000	₹2,25,000	₹2,25,000	₹2,25,000	₹2,25,000	₹2,25,000
Designer	₹40,000	2	₹2,40,000	₹2,40,000	₹2,40,000	₹2,40,000	₹2,40,000	₹2,40,000	₹2,40,000	₹2,40,000
Customer Care	₹18,000	2	₹1,08,000	₹1,08,000	₹1,08,000	₹1,08,000	₹1,08,000	₹1,08,000	₹1,08,000	₹1,08,000
Community Managers	₹10,000	3	₹90,000	₹90,000	₹90,000	₹90,000	₹90,000	₹90,000	₹90,000	₹90,000
Sr. Accountant	₹45,000	1	₹1,35,000	₹1,35,000	₹1,35,000	₹1,35,000	₹1,35,000	₹1,35,000	₹1,35,000	₹1,35,000
Virtual CFO	₹15,000	1	₹45,000	₹45,000	₹45,000	₹45,000	₹45,000	₹45,000	₹45,000	₹45,000
Storekeepers / Guards	₹15,000	2	₹90,000	₹90,000	₹90,000	₹90,000	₹90,000	₹90,000	₹90,000	₹90,000
Runner & Housekeeping	₹18,000	1	₹54,000	₹54,000	₹54,000	₹54,000	₹54,000	₹54,000	₹54,000	₹54,000
Other Administrative Expenses										
Shopify & Subscriptions	₹5,000	1	₹15,000	₹15,000	₹15,000	₹15,000	₹15,000	₹15,000	₹15,000	₹15,000
Rent - Office & Warehouse	₹75,000	1	₹2,25,000	₹2,25,000	₹2,25,000	₹2,25,000	₹2,25,000	₹2,25,000	₹2,25,000	₹2,25,000
Legal & Professional	₹15,000	1	₹45,000	₹45,000	₹45,000	₹45,000	₹45,000	₹45,000	₹45,000	₹45,000
Other Admin Expenses	₹40,000	1	₹1,20,000	₹1,20,000	₹1,20,000	₹1,20,000	₹1,20,000	₹1,20,000	₹1,20,000	₹1,20,000

	Gaming Company Pvt. Ltd.										
	Fixed Costs	Rate/Month	Nos.	Q1	Q2	Q3	Q4	Q5	Q6	Q7	Q8
1	**Tech Development Costs**										
	Server Space (AWS & Cloud)	3,50,000		10,50,000	10,50,000	10,50,000	10,50,000	21,00,000	21,00,000	21,00,000	21,00,000
	Troubleshooting AMC	30,000		90,000	90,000	90,000	90,000	90,000	90,000	90,000	90,000
	Software Subscriptions										
	- Data Analytics	15,000		45,000	45,000	45,000	45,000	45,000	45,000	45,000	45,000
	- CRM & Bots	25,000		75,000	75,000	75,000	75,000	75,000	75,000	75,000	75,000
	- G Suite, Slack, Communication	15,000		45,000	45,000	45,000	45,000	45,000	45,000	45,000	45,000
	- Anti-Virus, Data Security	20,000		60,000	60,000	60,000	60,000	60,000	60,000	60,000	60,000
	Outsourced Coding Costs				25,00,000		65,00,000			85,00,000	
				13,65,000	38,65,000	13,65,000	78,65,000	24,15,000	24,15,000	1,09,15,000	24,15,000
2	**Manpower Costs**										
	CEO	2,00,000	1	6,00,000	6,00,000	6,00,000	6,00,000	6,00,000	6,00,000	6,00,000	6,00,000
	COO/CTO	4,00,000	1	12,00,000	12,00,000	12,00,000	12,00,000	12,00,000	12,00,000	12,00,000	12,00,000
	CMO	2,00,000	1	6,00,000	6,00,000	6,00,000	6,00,000	6,00,000	6,00,000	6,00,000	6,00,000
	Coders & API Managers	1,15,000	3	10,35,000	10,35,000	10,35,000	10,35,000	10,35,000	10,35,000	10,35,000	10,35,000
	Testers & Data Managers	1,75,000	2	10,50,000	10,50,000	10,50,000	10,50,000	10,50,000	10,50,000	10,50,000	10,50,000
	Brand Manager & Partnerships	85,000	2	5,10,000	5,10,000	5,10,000	5,10,000	5,10,000	5,10,000	5,10,000	5,10,000
	Graphics Designer	75,000	2	4,50,000	4,50,000	4,50,000	4,50,000	4,50,000	4,50,000	4,50,000	4,50,000
	Virtual CFO	95,000	1	2,85,000	2,85,000	2,85,000	2,85,000	2,85,000	2,85,000	2,85,000	2,85,000
	Accounts Manager	75,000	1	2,25,000	2,25,000	2,25,000	2,25,000	2,25,000	2,25,000	2,25,000	2,25,000
	Accounts Clerk	35,000	1	1,05,000	1,05,000	1,05,000	1,05,000	1,05,000	1,05,000	1,05,000	1,05,000
	Runner & Housekeeper	20,000	1	60,000	60,000	60,000	60,000	60,000	60,000	60,000	60,000
				61,20,000	61,20,000	61,20,000	61,20,000	61,20,000	61,20,000	61,20,000	61,20,000
3	**Admin Costs**										
	Rent & Utilities	1,50,000	1	4,50,000	4,50,000	4,50,000	4,50,000	4,50,000	4,50,000	4,50,000	4,50,000
	Compliance & Legal Costs	60,000	1	1,80,000	1,80,000	1,80,000	1,80,000	1,80,000	1,80,000	1,80,000	1,80,000
	Traveling, Conveyance, Staff Welfare	2,75,000	1	8,25,000	8,25,000	8,25,000	8,25,000	8,25,000	8,25,000	8,25,000	8,25,000
	Office Supplies	35,000	1	1,05,000	1,05,000	1,05,000	1,05,000	1,05,000	1,05,000	1,05,000	1,05,000
	Other Miscellaneous	35,000	1	1,05,000	1,05,000	1,05,000	1,05,000	1,05,000	1,05,000	1,05,000	1,05,000
	Fixed Assets / Computers				20,00,000		10,00,000		10,00,000		
				16,65,000	36,65,000	16,65,000	26,65,000	16,65,000	26,65,000	16,65,000	16,65,000

Step 5: Cash Flow and P&L

The next sheet presents a summary of the business projections for the next two years or eight quarters. The usual runway that investments are raised for is 18 to 24 months. I usually advise startups to consider the higher end of the runway for calculations, hence the period considered.

The image shared of this sheet below gives an overview of the cash flow of a D2C startup. The different heads of inflows (Revenues) and outflows (Variable Costs and Other Expenses) are further divided into streams relevant to this specific startup. The difference between Revenues and Expenses gives the Net Burn. These figures are projected for the next 8 quarters.

It must be noted that all the figures in this sheet are the results of calculations in the subsequent sheets, where each line item has been elaborated upon and calculated. It serves the purpose of providing quick information on the revenues a startup expects and the expenses it will incur. The total net burn also gives an idea of the funding that the business may be looking for.

The next image presents a similar set of information for a gaming startup. A gaming business functions very differently from a D2C one. It is reflected in how this sheet (and other sheets) is prepared for them.

As you can observe, the sheet starts with the North Star Metrics - WAU and DAU. Gross Burn is the summation of the total CAC (calculated below in the sheet) and Tech, Manpower & Admin Costs. The Net Burn is calculated as the difference between Net Revenue and Gross Burn.

The figures in this sheet are also the results of calculations of the subsequent sheets.

Cash Flows	Q1	Q2	Q3	Q4	Q5	Q6	Q7	Q8	Total
Revenues									
- Modern Trade	₹ 0	₹ 0	₹ 24,00,000	₹ 24,48,000	₹ 24,96,960	₹ 24,00,000	₹ 24,60,000	₹ 25,21,500	**₹ 1,47,26,460**
- Amazon/Flipkart/Nykaa	₹ 13,50,000	₹ 13,50,000	₹ 14,17,500	₹ 14,88,375	₹ 15,62,794	₹ 16,00,003	₹ 17,20,003	₹ 18,49,004	**₹ 1,23,37,679**
- Performance Marketing	₹ 2,63,25,000	₹ 2,63,25,000	₹ 2,63,25,000	₹ 2,63,25,000	₹ 2,63,25,000	₹ 2,63,25,000	₹ 2,63,25,000	₹ 2,63,25,000	**₹ 21,06,00,000**
GMV	₹ 2,76,75,000	₹ 2,76,75,000	₹ 3,01,42,500	₹ 3,02,61,375	₹ 3,03,84,754	₹ 3,03,25,003	₹ 3,05,05,003	₹ 3,06,95,504	**₹ 23,76,64,139**
Less: GST @18%	₹ 42,21,610	₹ 42,21,610	₹ 45,98,008	₹ 46,16,142	₹ 46,34,962	₹ 46,25,848	₹ 46,53,306	₹ 46,82,365	**₹ 3,62,53,852**
Revenue Net of GST	₹ 2,34,53,390	₹ 2,34,53,390	₹ 2,55,44,492	₹ 2,56,45,233	₹ 2,57,49,791	₹ 2,56,99,155	₹ 2,58,51,698	₹ 2,60,13,139	**₹ 20,14,10,287**
Variable Costs									
Material & Packaging	₹ 91,32,750	₹ 63,59,925	₹ 66,44,426	₹ 66,71,074	₹ 66,78,073	₹ 66,91,301	₹ 67,32,056	₹ 67,53,011	**₹ 5,56,62,616**
Logistics	₹ 27,67,500	₹ 27,67,500	₹ 30,14,250	₹ 30,26,138	₹ 30,38,475	₹ 30,32,500	₹ 30,50,500	₹ 30,69,550	**₹ 2,37,66,414**
Commissions	₹ 41,51,250	₹ 41,51,250	₹ 50,01,375	₹ 50,28,806	₹ 50,57,105	₹ 50,28,750	₹ 50,67,751	₹ 51,08,626	**₹ 3,85,94,913**
Performance Marketing	₹ 42,00,000	₹ 42,00,000	₹ 42,00,000	₹ 42,00,000	₹ 42,00,000	₹ 42,00,000	₹ 42,00,000	₹ 42,00,000	**₹ 3,36,00,000**
Other Expenses									
Marketing Costs	₹ 5,40,000	₹ 5,40,000	₹ 5,40,000	₹ 5,40,000	₹ 5,40,000	₹ 5,40,000	₹ 5,40,000	₹ 5,40,000	**₹ 43,20,000**
Salaries & Manpower	₹ 18,87,000	₹ 18,87,000	₹ 18,87,000	₹ 18,87,000	₹ 18,87,000	₹ 18,87,000	₹ 18,87,000	₹ 18,87,000	**₹ 1,50,96,000**
Other Office Expenses	₹ 4,05,000	₹ 4,05,000	₹ 4,05,000	₹ 4,05,000	₹ 4,05,000	₹ 4,05,000	₹ 4,05,000	₹ 4,05,000	**₹ 32,40,000**
Net Profit/Burn	**₹ 3,69,890**	**₹ 31,42,715**	**₹ 30,52,440**	**₹ 38,87,215**	**₹ 39,44,138**	**₹ 39,14,604**	**₹ 39,69,391**	**₹ 40,49,952**	**₹ 2,71,30,345**

Gaming Company Pvt. Ltd.										
Dashboard - Financial Plan	Q1	Q2	Q3	Q4	Q5	Q6	Q7	Q8		
North Star Metrics										
WAU	83,100	1,56,012	4,94,982	7,29,965	8,84,532	16,75,927	21,20,294	23,26,767		
DAU	12,465	21,532	69,428	94,984	1,06,098	2,12,880	2,57,379	2,56,043		
Blended CAC (WAU)	14	13	31	36	42	41	54	72		
Gross Burn	1,02,75,000	1,47,75,000	2,02,50,000	2,77,50,000	2,13,00,000	4,88,50,000	5,63,50,000	4,76,50,000	**24,74,00,000**	**100%**
Net Burn	72,38,304	95,29,409	33,36,065	46,10,127	-45,47,411	-30,11,355	-53,77,739	-1,45,26,676	**-27,49,274**	
Revenues										
Rake from Money Pool	44,17,284	76,30,420	2,46,03,604	3,36,60,071	3,75,98,551	7,54,39,347	8,97,91,336	9,07,35,302		
Less: GST	-6,73,823	-11,63,962	-37,53,092	-51,34,587	-57,35,372	-1,15,07,697	-1,36,96,984	-1,38,40,978		
Gross Revenue	37,43,461	64,66,458	2,08,50,512	2,85,25,484	3,18,63,179	6,39,31,650	7,60,94,353	7,68,94,324	**30,83,69,421**	
Less: Transaction Fees	-7,06,766	-12,20,867	-39,36,577	-53,85,611	-60,15,768	-1,20,70,296	-1,43,66,614	-1,45,17,648	**5,82,20,147**	
Net Revenue	30,36,696	52,45,591	1,69,13,935	2,31,39,873	2,58,47,411	5,18,61,355	6,17,27,739	6,23,76,676	**25,01,49,274**	
Customer Acquisition Cost (CAC)										
YouTube Influencers	6,75,000	6,75,000	81,00,000	81,00,000	81,00,000	3,24,00,000	3,24,00,000	3,24,00,000		
Referral Program	1,50,000	1,50,000	15,00,000	15,00,000	15,00,000	22,50,000	22,50,000	22,50,000		
Digital Ads	3,00,000	3,00,000	15,00,000	15,00,000	15,00,000	30,00,000	30,00,000	30,00,000		
	11,25,000	11,25,000	1,11,00,000	1,11,00,000	1,11,00,000	3,76,50,000	3,76,50,000	3,76,50,000	**14,85,00,000**	**60%**
Tech, Manpower & Admin Costs										
Tech Development & Maintenance	13,65,000	38,65,000	13,65,000	78,65,000	24,15,000	24,15,000	1,09,15,000	24,15,000	**3,26,20,000**	**13%**
Manpower Costs	61,20,000	61,20,000	61,20,000	61,20,000	61,20,000	61,20,000	61,20,000	61,20,000	**4,89,60,000**	**20%**
Admin Costs	16,65,000	36,65,000	16,65,000	26,65,000	16,65,000	26,65,000	16,65,000	16,65,000	**1,73,20,000**	**7%**
	91,50,000	1,36,50,000	91,50,000	1,66,50,000	1,02,00,000	1,12,00,000	1,87,00,000	1,02,00,000	**9,89,00,000**	

Step 6: Dashboard with Investor Summary

For startups with fewer complexities in their business models, e.g. limited revenue streams and cost heads, the Cash Flow sheet adequately represents everything that an investor seeks on the first look. However, for startups with more nuanced business processes, complex streams of revenues, and cost items occupying over 25 rows in your Excel sheet, it's better to summarize the most important metrics and present them in a separate Dashboard. This comes at the beginning.

The objective is to help the investor understand the business performance using broader, most relevant metrics without overwhelming them with details. The details can be easily viewed in the subsequent sheets for further clarity.

As an example, if you have an employee strength of 80 working across 8 different departments at different positions, instead of sharing the exhaustive list, the Dashboard can just show an overall expense figure by the department. In fact, if there are 5 or more big cost heads, only the manpower cost can be mentioned separately along with the other larger expense items. The idea is to show only the important metrics that give just enough idea to the investor about the health of the company.

Insights and Points to Remember

- A financial model is simply your business metrics presented in a well-structured manner. You can easily build it by yourself.
- Don't make things overly complex. Conventional financial models are hard to read for everyone. Even if your model is complex and needs breaking down, don't go beyond the top 4 factors. It's just harder to process. Follow the KISS principle - keep it simple, stupid.
- Colour code your cells. The ones that require input and the ones that shouldn't be altered should be separately coded. It makes things easier for you as well as the person studying it.
- Try to keep the number of input variables at a minimum. More number of variables indicates a higher probability of uncertainty, and a tendency to lose focus.
- This is almost silly advice, but use colours to make your document more palatable and remove gridlines. I colour my Excel sheets light gray, and denote major heads in different colours.

12. Fundraising Instruments & Mechanics

Contrary to what many believe, the instruments through which a founder can raise funds for their startups are numerous. Not all types of funding require the company founders to part away with their ownership. Startups at different stages may have different funding needs, and if founders can pick the best instruments available, they may end up protecting a large chunk of their equity while still fulfilling the business goals. In this chapter, we'll understand all the different investment instruments and how they function.

Understanding Shares - Equity and Preference

To begin with, shares are the units of equity ownership in a company. The value and the ownership stake of any individual or entity in a company depend on the number of shares they hold and the price of each share. All shares, when put together, comprise 100% of the company ownership. In the beginning, when a startup is just incorporated, the founders hold all these shares among themselves. Gradually, with external investors and more employees joining, the shareholding gets distributed among different stakeholders.

There are primarily two types of shares - *equity* and *preference*. Let's understand each of them briefly.

Equity shares

Equity shares, also known as ordinary shares, are normally the shares held by founders and employees of the company.

When you hold shares of any company in the stock market, if the company does well, its share price increases and you can opt to sell your shares to make a profit. These equity shares are, evidently, valuable assets that show up in your financial portfolio. But you obtain a monetary benefit only when they are sold and encashed, or the company you hold the shares of decides to pay a dividend.

Holding equity shares works well when they belong to publicly listed companies. They are highly liquid assets in that case and can be encashed at any time. With startups, however, equity shares or any type of shares cannot be traded publicly. These are relatively illiquid and instances of sale of shares occur under very controlled settings. However, if the company does get acquired for a large amount, these equity shareholders enjoy the upside that comes with it.

Since equity investing in startups is inherently risky, there are ways through which investors safeguard their interests. One of them is through preference shares.

Preference shares

Preference shares are now the standard route through which investors pump money into startups. It gives them the first right to cash, or a preference over the equity shareholders, in a liquidation event. A liquidation event, in most cases, refers to an acquisition by a larger organization or a private purchase of a company's shares by another investor. But the explanation is not that straightforward.

Traditionally and conventionally, preference shares are a medium to prioritize the dividend payout for such shareholders. That is, if a company creates an annual dividend pool, it's the holders of preference shares that get the dividend first. When such shares are allotted, this dividend rate is capped. For example, issuing 10% preference shares means the shareholder is entitled to annually receive a 10% dividend on the face value of the shares they hold, and this payout will be prioritized over the dividends of the equity shareholders.

Investors invest in startups through an instrument called Compulsorily Convertible Preference Shares (CCPS) which gives them the benefit of both - protection of their principal as well as a stake in surplus profits. We'll understand how it's executed later in the section on CCPS.

Can an Investor Invest without a Valuation?

These days, startups often get funded at stages where there's no clear indication of how the business would shape. The earlier the stage, the more the uncertainty, and the higher the chances of funding being done on shaky grounds. Usually, it's just the founders' profiles, the market, and investors' conviction in their abilities on the basis of which such investments happen.

Valuation, though, normally requires at least a few key metrics to be calculated with some reasonability. Without them, both investors and founders may have widely varying points of view and the chances of them aligning may be slim. Without a solution, either the deal may go off or one of the parties ends up compromising significantly leading to undesirable consequences.

Unvalued rounds provide a good middle ground for such deals where ascertaining a valuation may be tricky, but both parties are interested in the fundraise. In such cases, the valuation is deferred to a later stage after the startup generates enough traction or gets sufficient time to hit certain milestones. So any subsequent round of funding happens with a proper valuation with possibly marquee VCs involved. Investors who invested in the unvalued round get the benefit of a *valuation discount* or a *valuation cap*.

A valuation discount means that the early investors would get a pre-determined discount on the share price finalized after valuation. For example, if an investor put in Rs. 1 crore in the unvalued round, and after the valued round the valuation was determined to be Rs. 20 crores, then without a discount this investor would receive 5% of the company (1/20). But considering a valuation discount of, say, 20%, the stake awarded is based on not 20 crores, but 16 crores, after factoring in the discount. So this investor actually gets 6.67% (1/16) of the company ownership.

Another way to calculate this is based on the share price. Assuming that the company has a total pool of 200,000 shares after the latest funding, it means each share is priced at Rs. 1000 for a 20 Cr valuation. Without the discount, a 1 Cr investment would have fetched this investor 10,000 shares, which is 5% of the company (1000/200,000). But a discount of 20% means they get these shares at Rs. 800, which gives them ownership of 12,500 shares. This is equivalent to 6.67% of the company (12,500/200,000).

A valuation cap is a mechanism which guarantees a minimum stake to the early investor. In the above example, if there was a valuation cap of Rs. 10 crores offered instead of a discount, then the early investor would end up holding 10% of the company. But if the final valuation was calculated to be Rs. 8 crores, they would end up holding 12.5% (1/8). The valuation cap is the highest valuation at which shares will be allocated to such early investors. If the actual value of the company comes out to be under this figure, then shares are allocated as done for any other investors. But if it exceeds, then this valuation cap is used as the marker to award them shares. Founders obviously try to push this cap as high as possible to avoid any additional dilution in case their company does command a higher than expected valuation in the next round.

Valued vs Unvalued Rounds

Unvalued rounds have emerged as a great means to ensure the conclusion of funding for many early-stage startups when the future is still uncertain. They also get completed much faster than valued rounds. However, this may not necessarily be the ideal route.

If you raise a large amount in an unvalued round but are unable to secure a high valuation later for whatever reasons, you stand to lose a much higher share of equity than desired. Suppose you raised $2M in an unvalued round confident of hitting a $20M valuation by the next fundraise. A 20% valuation discount would mean these investors would get a 12.5% stake at $20M valuation, apart from whatever the new incoming investors are owed. But either due to your own poor performance or any macroeconomic events like a pandemic or a war, if the situation suddenly turns grim right when you need funds, you would be left with little option but to compromise on valuation. If you then raise funds at a reduced valuation of, say, $8M, then the early investors end up obtaining 31.25% of your company after accounting for the discount. This is outside of what the new investors take.

Unvalued rounds are more typical of early-stage investments like pre-seed, seed, or pre-Series A rounds. Marquee VCs that usually invest in Series A and beyond don't prefer unvalued rounds.

Unless absolutely critical, I usually advise my clients to opt for a valued round primarily because of the potential downside an unvalued one brings. Things often go wrong early in startups' journeys, and terms for unvalued rounds are crafted with a bias for success, which can be perilous.

The table below gives a quick comparison between valued and unvalued rounds. Note that the points are reflective of the more conventional fundraising instances and there will be startups that don't adhere to one or more of these.

(Note: Convertible Note (CN), Compulsorily Convertible Preference Shares (CCPS), and Compulsorily Convertible Debentures (CCDs) have been explained in the next section.)

Parameters	Valued	Unvalued
Stage of investment	Series A and later	Pre-seed and seed
Amount of investment	Upwards of USD 500K	USD 100K - 1 Mn
Type of investor	Marquee VC firms	Angel Investors, Incubators, Accelerators, Micro VC firms
Use of funds	To scale the product and generate revenue	To build an MVP and get the initial users
Instruments used	CCPS, Equity	SAFE, CN, CCD
Time to conclude	3-6 months	1-2 months

Convertible Securities

A convertible security is an investment instrument that can be changed from one form to another based on certain conditions. An investment through convertible security starts out in the form of debt and gets converted to equity, either at a *conversion event* or when the *maturity period* is over.

A conversion event is defined as the point in time when the investment turns into equity. It is defined in the agreement signed by the startup and the investors. An example of the definition of a conversion event may look like this:

The convertible security of Rs. 1 crore will convert to equity when the startup raises an investment of at least Rs. 10 crores at a valuation of at most Rs. 100 crores in a future round.

In case the startup does not raise any future rounds, the investment will mandatorily convert to equity at the end of the maturity period, at the then current valuation of the startup. This duration is generally taken as 3-5 years.

The *floor* is the minimum future valuation at which the convertible security will convert to equity, and the *cap* is the corresponding maximum valuation. These numbers depend on the expected fundraising amount in the subsequent rounds.

Convertible securities often include a *discount* on the conversion. It is a method to reward early investors of the business for the higher risk they took on their investment. Instead of allocating them shares at the current fair price, they are given those at a discount to that value, thus giving them a relatively larger portion of the company compared to other investors who come in late. So at a 20% discount, at the time of conversion, a share with a face value of Rs. 100 is offered to them at Rs. 80. The other investors who do not receive a discount will get the shares at a value of Rs. 100. The examples shared in the previous sections also demonstrate this.

20% is the standard rate of discount offered in convertible securities.

The law dictates that investors charge interest on their investment for the time it exists as a debt. Investors may opt for a nominal interest rate of 0.01% to comply with the law. In case an investor does charge interest, the startup can choose to not pay but accumulate it. At the conversion event, they can convert the total sum of the principal investment and the interest into equity.

Based on the features and uses, convertible securities can be categorized into three types:

1. Convertible Note (CN)
2. Compulsorily Convertible Preference Shares (CCPS)
3. Compulsorily Convertible Debentures (CCD)

Convertible Notes (CN)

Convertible Note (CN) is a debt instrument issued in the form of a simple loan agreement and to equity typically in a subsequent valued financing round. It is often used by startups in the seed or pre-seed stages when valuing the company may not be straightforward. It's also executed in a relatively shorter time making it favourable for early-stage founders. The entire process can be in fewer than two weeks.

Since Convertible Notes are mainly employed by early investors of a startup, their investment is into shares at a discounted rate to reward them for the higher risk that they took. The discount can be given either flatly on the shares, like a 20% discount on the price, or as a valuation cap as demonstrated earlier.

Convertible Notes require minimum investment of Rs. 25 lakhs the startup being invested in should be on the Startup India website.

Compulsorily Convertible Preference Shares (CCPS)

CCPS are the preference shares allotted to investors that must convert to equity shares after a pre-determined period or on achieving pre-defined milestones. Usually, this conversion happens when the investor wants an exit after making a substantial profit on their investment.

CCPS allows the investor to have the preference in a liquidation event over the equity shareholders, as well as claim a stake in the profits.

CCPS are usually allotted in valued rounds. For the amount invested, investors get the commensurate number of shares based on the share price. These are issued as preference shares. Additionally, they can be given a certain liquidation preference, e.g. 1x, 1.5x, 2x, etc. This means that during a liquidation event, these shareholders will have the first right to encash a certain multiple of the principal invested. In a 2x liquidation preference, preference shareholders have the right to claim double the principal they invested before the surplus gets shared among the equity shareholders.

There's also the concept of *participating* and *non-participating* liquidation preference. Let's understand these through an example.

Example 1: 10% CCPS at 1x participating liquidity preference

Assume a startup has raised a seed round in equity funding. An investor invests Rs. 2 crores in the startup at a valuation of Rs. 10 crores for a 20% stake. The investor has been allotted CCPS with a dividend cap of 10% and a 1x participating liquidation preference.

At the end of year 1, the investors are entitled to receive Rs. 20 lakhs (10% of Rs. 2 crores) as a dividend.

At the end of year 2, they receive an additional Rs. 20 lakhs as stipulated. The dividends can either be paid out every year or continue accumulating each year as returns until they hold these shares.

This means that at the end of year 2, their investment of Rs. 2 crores has grown to Rs. 2.4 crores through dividends.

Let's say the startup gets an acquisition offer of Rs. 15 crores at this point.

Since the investors hold preference shares and have a 1x liquidation preference, they get the first right to encash their investment in the company. The investors will receive Rs. 2.4 crores out of the total Rs. 15 crores as a return on their investment.

Now, since they have a 'participating' liquidation preference, it means that the investors can participate in the residual profits as well. Apart from claiming the 1x liquidation as preference shareholders, they can also convert these to equity shares and partake in the surplus profits left after pocketing their 2.4 crores, which is 12.6 crores.

After converting their preference shares to equity shares, since they hold a 20% stake in the company, they are entitled to receive 20% of Rs.12.6 crores, i.e. Rs. 2.52 crores.

So finally, the investors receive a total of (2.4+2.52) crores, or Rs. 4.92 crores.

It's easy to see how this arrangement is lopsided in favour of such investors. While they had only a 20% stake, they ended up taking over 32% of the final acquisition value owing to the liquidity preference and the participating nature of CCPS.

Example 2: 10% CCPS at 2x participating liquidity preference

In this same example, if the investors had a 2x liquidity preference, they would be first entitled to 2x their principal+dividends, i.e. 4.8 Cr. Then, they would also claim 20% of the 10.2 Cr surplus remaining, i.e. 2.04 Cr, finally earning 6.84 Cr.

It's clear that with investors having CCPS with participating liquidity preference greater than 1x, equity shareholders stand to gain substantially only when they're able to generate multifold returns. The larger the valuation, the smaller the significance of liquidity preference.

Example 3: 0.01% CCPS at 1x non-participating liquidity preference

A non-participating liquidity preference bars the preference shareholders from claiming both their liquidation preference as well as participating in the surplus profits. They can either walk away with the principal+dividend or convert their preference shares to equity shares and obtain the same benefits as other equity shareholders.

Continuing with the same example where the investor put in 2 Cr for a 20% stake, if they had 1x non-participating liquidation preference, they wouldn't get a share of the surplus left after receiving their principal and dividends.

In this case, at the end of 2 years, they have negligible dividend accumulated since the rate is only 0.01%. If the acquisition happens at 15 Cr and the investor chooses to convert the preference shares to equity shares, they simply get 20% of the acquisition value, i.e. 3 Cr.

Alternatively, if they chose to not convert to equity shares, they would have the option to exit with their principal of 2 Cr and Rs. 4000 accumulated as dividends. The 'non-participating' clause ensures only one of the two can be exercised.

In such cases where investors have non-participating liquidity preference, they choose to not convert their preference shares to equity if the acquisition happens at a valuation lower than what they invested at. Converting to equity would result in a loss on the principal invested. Holding and exercising their preference shares protects them from such a loss.

However, when the valuation is greater than when they invested, they convert to equity and enjoy the upside along with other equity shareholders.

I advise founders to always negotiate for a 1x non-participating liquidity preference when issuing CCPS. As we saw in the examples above, a participating liquidity preference is heavily partial towards investors and leaves the founders with relatively little if the startup doesn't do well. If the startup does well, even with a non-participating liquidity preference, the investors anyway get their rightful claim to the upside.

CCPS with 1x non-participating liquidity preference is gradually becoming a standard because of its fairness to all stakeholders. But remember that an investor's lawyers may not set terms this way, so use this 'standard' as an anchor to negotiate. There can be scenarios built around liquidity preference which protects every party's interest fairly.

Also, at times, investors may prefer Optionally Convertible Redeemable Preference Shares (OCRPS) if they're not fully confident of the founders' ability or willingness to raise further rounds of funding. For investors, an optionally convertible instrument like OCRPS helps their right to redeem their principal and seek it back at any time. They usually set pre-defined milestones on achievement of which these options convert to shares. Again, this instrument too weighs heavily in the interest of investors, and I usually discourage founders from accepting any terms that are fraught with uncertainty.

Compulsorily Convertible Debentures (CCD)

A Compulsorily Convertible Debenture (CCD) is a bond that must convert to preference or equity shares on maturity. They typically start off and act as debt with a regular servicing of interest to the holders before converting to shares on the maturity date.

The paperwork for obtaining CCD is similar in length to CCPS. There is minimum limit for an investment an investor can make through CCDs.

Optionally Convertible Debentures (OCDs) provide similar protection to investors as in the case of Optionally Convertible Redeemable Preference Shares (OCRPS).

As a founder, you would prefer CCPS or CCD so that the investor's money compulsorily converts to equity shares at some stage.

SAFE/KISS - Applicability of Western Ideas in India

SAFE and iSAFE

Y Combinator developed SAFE back in 2013 as a type of Convertible Note. SAFE stands for Simple Agreement for Future Equity and is a type of convertible security issued by early-stage start-ups to raise funds in their initial round.

SAFE notes can be converted to equity shares at the next valuation round at a discount. They are simple and fast to execute. A startup can raise funds through SAFE in less than a month at a cost of approximately Rs. 30,000 in professional fees.

SAFE is not an instrument available to startups incorporated in India. Here, 100X.VC popularized iSAFE, or India SAFE, as an Indian equivalent of SAFE. The iSAFE document can be downloaded from the 100X.VC website.

KISS

KISS stands for Keep It Simple Security, which is type of Convertible Note instrument proposed by 500 Startups, a California-based early-stage VC, a year after Y Combinator released its SAFE documents.

KISS aims to achieve the same objective of early-stage startups raise funds quickly by deferring the negotiation on valuation to the next round of financing. It keeps the simplicity and user-friendliness of a SAFE but offers some of the investor protections found in Convertible Notes.

KISS tries and plugs the following gaps which are missing (purposely) from the SAFE:

1. KISS is converted automatically on maturity date if there is no equity round raised within the term.
2. If there is no equity round raised and the startup exits through an acquisition before the maturity period, the KISS investor receives the same returns that an equity investor would receive.

Thus, KISS is a little more detailed than SAFE.

Regardless, in the Indian context, you should use these terms to fundraise very cautiously only after consulting a CA or a lawyer who has worked with them before.

Venture Debt

Equity, contrary to what is generally perceived, is a more expensive source of capital than debt. In debt financing, once you repay the principal and the interest amount to the lender, the deal is done. The lender does not have any say in how you run the business or what you do with the money.

In equity financing, you give away part ownership of your company. The shareholder not only gets extraordinary returns in case of success but also some form of control over the business in many cases.

A startup founder may not wish to give away equity to fund short-term, operational expenses where returns are foreseeable. In such cases, it makes more sense to raise funds through debt. The loan can be repaid once the purpose of the funding is fulfilled.

When one needs a loan, the first institution that comes to mind is a bank. However, banks are often unwilling to fund startups due to the high risk of failure. They also usually offer secured debts. Since startups do not always have tangible assets to offer as collateral, chances of obtaining a loan from the bank become minimal.

Venture debt is offered as a form of debt financing by registered Non-Banking Financial Corporations (NBFC) without taking any collateral. Such firms are also called Venture Debt firms.

Since Venture Debt firms offer unsecured loans that have a higher risk, their interest rates are generally higher, usually around 15% annually, and may go up to 24%. They also do not prefer to invest in the early stages of a startup. They favour the ones who have already found their product-market fit and have earned or raised enough capital to be able to repay their debt in case things go south. Hence, they generally finance startups after the Series A round.

Ecommerce and D2C startups may look towards venture debt firms to fund short-term operational expenses related to working capital, or slightly longer duration requirements like the expansion of offline stores. Both these purposes require upfront capital but there's usually a foreseeable timeframe within which they can be recovered through operational revenues. Venture debt is preferred by founders to cover such short-term expenses of a company. It is cheaper, faster, and comes with no additional liabilities except purely financial ones.

Venture debt firms may sometimes keep the option of converting their debt into equity at a later stage open. If they find that the startup is growing fast, they may want to benefit from the upside. They might keep a clause in the agreement that gives them the option of converting a certain portion, usually 30-40%, and in some rare cases even 100% of the debt into equity in the future.

Banks, on the other hand, still follow the traditional approach of lending money and are usually too rigid in their approach to suit startups.

Revenue Based Financing

Certain business models are inherently scalable and may not need a constant influx of capital.

SaaS products, for example, need capital mainly for product development and to acquire their early users. Once the product is built and deployed, and if the response is good, then additional capital is not really needed to scale the product. Revenues from operations are usually enough to manage the operational expenses thereafter and recover the upfront costs as well in due course. Additional capital from operations is used to reinvest into the business and improve the product further.

D2C businesses too need not raise money through equity funding if they can be operationally profitable. Typically, they would need initial capital to get the first batch of products ready and acquire the first set of users through marketing and advertising. If the product is well received, it may organically receive good traffic and nominal marketing spend after that may be sufficient to drive sales.

For such founders, raising money through equity financing may not be ideal because of the additional liabilities they bring. Revenue-based financing is a better instrument to cater to the needs of such founders. In this, the investors get a percentage of future revenues in return for the money invested. There's no equity given away by the company.

The founder can use this investment to enable more sales, make profits, and then use the profits to reinvest into the business, improve the product, and then generate even more sales. Since the repayment is done from the revenues generated, there's no undue pressure to repay quickly.

Such investors can end up making 15-30% over the money invested in the company. Klub, Getvantage, Velocity, Credavenue, and Creditnable are some investment firms that finance startups on a revenue basis.

Director's Loan

Founders face the choice of investing money into their company either in the form of capital or debt. One can start a company with a capital of Rs. 1 Lakh or more. However, to build a complete product and acquire customers, this amount may not be enough. The founder can invest more in the form of equity, but that means that they now need to make a secretarial filing to increase the authorized capital, allot more shares to themselves, and do more paperwork. Instead, the amount of investment can be booked as a liability or a loan towards the founder or Director. This is called the founder's loan or Director's loan ("Loan from Directors" as per the Companies Act 2013). If an individual formally appointed as Director but is not a founder, puts in money, it can be categorized as Director's loan.

The first level of Angel Investors may not allow the repayment of the founder's loan through the amount invested by them. It usually happens at the Series A stage when a marquee VC firm decides to invest.

The founders or directors usually do not charge any interest on their loans, since it was used for their own startup.

The Companies Act also allows relatives of directors to extend loans to the company. To avoid malpractice, the term "Relatives of

Directors" is also well-defined in the Act and not up to interpretation.

Community Stock Options (CSOPs)

Community Stock Options or CSOPs are similar to ESOPs but different in the sense that they get offered to consumers and not employees as in the case of ESOPs. Consumers can be offered certain terms under which they can invest an amount and buy the company's stock options. It is seen as a method to reward a company's customers for their belief in their services and contribution to their growth. In India though, the laws are still not very clear about their legal prevalence. In August 2021, AltF CoWorking was reported to introduce CSOP to their customers[1].

13. Reaching Out to Investors

Every investor is in the business of making money from money. Their job is to invest money in startups that have the potential to grow and generate sky-high returns for them. They look for signals and estimate which ones can scale and become successful.

Since only a small portion of startups eventually succeed, they are cautious with their choices of investments. They are answerable to their investors whom they have pooled the money from and are responsible for their returns. If a founder, after a point, is unable to grow their startup and achieve higher valuations, their investors will cease to support them in subsequent fundraising efforts.

Sometime in January 2022, a founder approached me to guide him in raising funds for his startup. During a conversation, he made an interesting comment. "Investors want to make profits, but they seem to instantly reject most of the startups that approach them. How do they understand what will work if they reject so quickly?" I understood where that came from. I asked him if he knew the acceptance rate of Y Combinator. He made a close guess of 2%. It does lie between 1.5%-2%.

There's an extraordinarily large number of applications for every batch of the renowned accelerator. The situation is similar for all good investors. Every week, between 60 to 100 startups email any well-known VC firm with their pitch deck. Out of them, the firm may choose to meet 5 or 6 and finally invest in 1 or 2.

In fact, the first season of Shark Tank India received 62,000 applications, out of which 198 businesses were selected to pitch their ideas[1]. Out of the 198 pitches in the show, 67 businesses got deals in the first season. 67 out of a total of 62,000 - that's just slightly better than 0.1%!

Although these statistics are discouraging, the fact is that investors too are on a perpetual hunt for the next great idea. VCs compete amongst themselves to invest in promising startups because that's the only way to achieve their business goals. They have their methods to screen and shortlist efficiently. All probabilities aside, a founder building a useful product poised to scale fast need not worry. Money, either in the form of investors or business success, will surely arrive, sooner or later.

Initial Screening & Creation of a Wishlist

Most founders, when they start reaching out to investors, take a haphazard approach. They try to connect with anyone and everyone they can and miss out on the more probable opportunities due to poor planning or lack of preparedness. I understand this hustle mindset, but founders can ill-afford to waste precious time. Inefficiencies lead to longer times to completion, which in turn cost more money. Money is precisely what fund-seeking founders don't have. A well-planned approach is imperative to start this journey.

The first step is to create a list of all possible investors. If you have been following the startup space, you'd probably be able to name a few VCs at the drop of a hat. Create a list of all such investors - VCs, micro VCs, Angel Investors, Angel Syndicates, and even Accelerators and Incubators. For your reference, I have compiled a list of VCs, Angel Syndicates, Accelerators, and Incubators in the Annexure 13.1. Note that it's nowhere close to being a comprehensive list and there are many outside of it. Include as many of them as possible in your database.

I'll suggest an effective method to screen and plan your outreach in the next section, but broadly, the parameters that contribute to an investor's interest in your startup constitute of the following:

1. **Funding activity**: If an investor hasn't invested in any startup in the last 12 months, chances are that they are inactive presently and are unlikely to be interested.
2. **Industry preference:** Often, investors prefer a few sectors over the others while picking startups. Their past investments clearly indicate any such preferences.
3. **Stage preference:** Angel Investors and Micro VCs such as 100X.VC and Titan Capital are likely to invest in early-stage startups upto a maximum of Series A round, in most cases. Marquee VCs usually come in at Series A and beyond, and Private Equity players come in even later. For every investor, check if they actively fund startups in similar stage as yours.
4. **Competitors funded**: If an investor has funded a direct competitor of yours, chances are that they won't invest in yours. However, exceptions exist.
5. **Geography preference**: This becomes relevant if you're targeting international investors. Check if their past investments indicate an interest in India (or wherever you're building), or if they have made any media statements suggesting an increased interest in your geography.

Other factors include the market conditions and the fund status of the investor.

Investors are more cautious in deploying funds into startups in bear markets. They become more rigorous with screening and valuations since the perceived risk of investing in these times is higher than usual. We have seen in 2022 that there was a significant decline in funding activity over the previous year on global cues.

VCs also have a limit to the funds they can invest. If they have already deployed most of their available funds, they may not be left with enough to invest in your company, even if everything else works in your favour. This may be hard to figure if they operate in relative stealth.

In the next section, let's understand how to plan your outreach.

Investor - Market - Product - Stage Fit

We discussed the various parameters which contribute to the probability of an investor being interested in your startup. Here, I have considered 4 variables that you can easily identify for every investor. For each of these variables, you can give them a score of 0, 0.5, or 1 depending on how closely they match your startup. If there's a perfect match, it's a 1, and on no match, you give it 0.

'Industry match' considers how active or bullish an investor is about the industry you operate in. 'Stage match' considers how actively an investor invests in the stage of your startup. 'Activity match' is simply about how active the investor has been in general with funding startups. 'Priority group' indicates how aspirational a particular investor is for you. If you are keen to associate with someone, you give them a 1, and if you're indifferent about their involvement, you probably give them a 0.

Also, this is just one suggestion on how you could score. You can customize it as per your needs, and probably give scores as 0, 0.25, 0.5, 0.75, and 1. Smaller the interval, more precise your judgement.

The table given is a simple example of how you can plan. The final score gives an indication of the investors you probably want in your cap table. The closer this number is to 4, the higher should it rank in your priority.

S.No.	Investor	Industry match	Stage match	Activity match	Priority group	Final priority score
1	Sequoia	1	0	0.5	1	2.5
2	Blume	0.5	1	1	1	3.5
3	Elevation	0.5	0.5	0.5	1	2.5
4	Accel	1	0.5	1	1	3.5
5	Titan	1	1	1	1	4
6	Better	0	0	1	1	2
7	Angel 1	1	0.5	1	0.5	3
8	Angel 2	0.5	1	0.5	0.5	2.5
9	Angel 3	0	1	1	0.5	2.5
10	Angel Syndicate 1	1	0.5	0	0	1.5
11	Angel Syndicate 2	0.5	1	1	0	2.5
12	Angel Syndicate 3	1	1	0	0.5	2.5

The next step is to find a way to contact a decision-maker at all these places. The best case and the most improbable scenario is that you know the decision-maker yourself. In such a case, you can reach out to them directly as there's already a level of credibility established. In most cases, try to find a warm connection who could introduce you to the right person. It could be through someone you know who's working with that firm, any founder you know who was invested in by them, or through any other credible acquaintance willing to put in a good word.

If you're relatively young and inexperienced, and it's your first startup, it might be a good idea to reach out to a junior employee at the VC firms first. They would also be more likely to have a chat at this stage. If they are impressed, they'll refer you to the senior folks and then you could make your mark.

A cold outreach should be the absolute last resort. Chances of response are the lowest with them. We'll discuss more on how to maximize your outcomes with it later in this chapter. Either way, you must get the contact details - at least the email - for all the investors you can. Maintain an Excel file with these details.

With the list now ready, arrange them in the reverse order of priority - scores arranged in ascending order. This is the priority order of your outreach. If there are investors with the same score, the one that scores lower on 'Priority group' parameter should be positioned higher in this list, i.e. lower on overall priority.

Before we get into how to manage cold outreach and get warm introductions, one topic that is often discussed is the 'founder-investor' fit. We know that a good working relationship between co-founders is critical to minimize the risk of a conflict that may hamper the startup. It works similarly, albeit to a lower extent, with founders and investors. It's difficult to have a prior working relationship with an investor or a VC firm for first-time founders, but there are certain aspects you can optimise to ensure good professional relationship with your investors.

Two factors founders can check for in investors are their domain expertise and their financial strength. Investors who have put money into other startups in your domain are likely to have deeper insights than the ones who haven't. These can be helpful in your quest to succeed.

VCs that are strong financially have the capacity to fund subsequent rounds and also bring in more investors with their influence. That greatly reduces your efforts in scouting for a new set of investors every time you raise funds. Another benefit of having deep pocketed VCs is that they have likely put in a relatively tiny amount in your startup. If you do well, they stand to make impressive gains, but even if things go south, they are much less likely to give you grief over the lost money because of the relatively low impact on their records.

A good way to assess professionalism of VCs is how they treat the portfolio startups that failed after raising funds. If they get an endorsement from founders of such startups, it's a clear indicator of a highly professional firm.

Warm Intros vs Cold Outreach

As we discussed in the previous section, investors can either be reached through a warm introduction or a cold outreach. While there's little doubt that warm intros work better than cold outreach, let's understand each of them and see how we can maximize our efficiency in both.

Warm Intros

Firstly, regardless of how you get introduced, always try to connect with the low-priority investors first. Use these interactions as practice for improvement. Since they are low priority, your stakes are lower if they don't invest. This ensures that by the time you reach out to your high-priority investors, you are habituated to the process, have received enough feedback on your pitch, and are better prepared to impress the ones that matter.

As explained in the previous section, for every investor you map, find someone who can introduce you to the decision-maker or an employee who could lead to them. Prefer to be introduced by someone who himself or herself has high credibility with this person. Fellow founders who have been invested in by them are one example. Colleagues, whether current or former, a common professional acquaintance, or a fellow alum of your alma mater are other ways to get introduced. Keep in mind that your first impression will somehow be connected with this person making the introduction. So if it's not someone you regard, it's probably better to explore other ways. This rigour increases as you move up the priority order.

Warm introductions are known to be a lot more effective in eliciting a response than a cold email. The reasons are intuitive and obvious. If the person making the introduction is regarded highly by the investors themselves, the probability of a response increases further. In fact, I know about investors who have only funded startups that were introduced to them by someone credible.

If you don't boast of a robust network, then it might be prudent to build one through startup networking events. Meeting someone in person is often more impactful than emailing them. If you can impress someone influential with your idea and performance so far, there's a chance they agree to introduce you to the right people.

Advice for people taking this approach is to not appear desperate. It indicates a lack of confidence which is sure to rub off on anyone you meet. Meet others as an equal, with a belief that you're indeed building something great. Have conversations but don't forcefully pitch. Let the conversation unearth what you're building and how.

Although this doesn't fall under the ambit of 'warm intros', another way to attract interest is through social media activity. Post about what you do and your progress, and share insights. You are more likely to be spotted by an investor or an analyst working at any of the VC firms if you're consistent. However, ensure that your personal branding is consistent with your startup's. If you post derogatory or cringe-worthy content, you'll get eyeballs at the expense of your brand. It will do more harm than good.

When you get discovered by an employee at any of the VC firms through this route, they'll likely ask you for a meeting. This is an opportunity to make an impression and get a meeting with the decision-makers.

Other mediums to similarly grab attention are AngelList - list your startup here and post updates, job openings, etc.; Tracxn - get them to list your startup on their portal; and publications in credible media platforms like YourStory, Inc42, Economic Times, Mint, and the like.

Cold Outreach

Getting a response from cold outreaches is, admittedly, challenging. Marquee investors sometimes receive hundreds of emails weekly. It's humanly impossible for an already busy individual to read or even skim through all of them. There is an element of luck, of course - if they don't even see your email, they'll obviously not read it. But you can work through the probability and do what's in your control to maximize your chances.

In your control is writing an email that's effective. Allie Janoch, founder of a SaaS startup called Mapistry, shared in a Medium post about her first failed attempt to get the attention of investor Jason Lemkin from SaaStr. The email she shot is shared here[2].

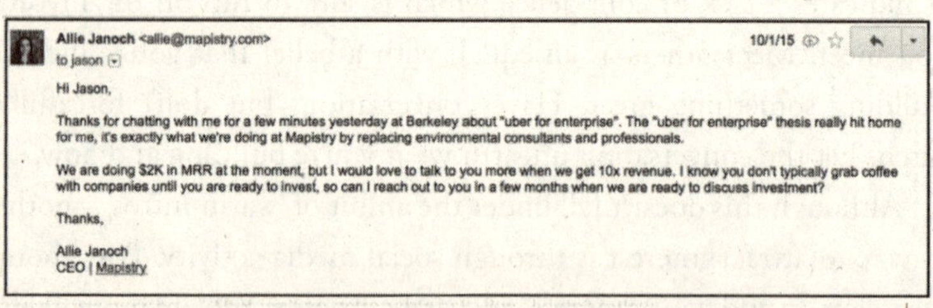

Allie Janoch <allie@mapistry.com> 10/1/15
to jason

Hi Jason,

Thanks for chatting with me for a few minutes yesterday at Berkeley about "uber for enterprise". The "uber for enterprise" thesis really hit home for me, it's exactly what we're doing at Mapistry by replacing environmental consultants and professionals.

We are doing $2K in MRR at the moment, but I would love to talk to you more when we get 10x revenue. I know you don't typically grab coffee with companies until you are ready to invest, so can I reach out to you in a few months when we are ready to discuss investment?

Thanks,

Allie Janoch
CEO | Mapistry

Source: Alice Janoch's article on Medium

About this outreach, she writes:

> *I made the email somewhat personal and mentioned something that he had talked about during the event.* ***But a lot is missing****. Didn't explain what Mapistry does, I alluded to it, but didn't provide a clear explanation. In the second paragraph, I was pretty self-deprecating, which looking back at, I hate. I didn't brag about our progress; I mentioned our MRR but essentially said* ***"our traction is pretty lame, and I'm sure you wouldn't want to talk to me now,"*** *might be true, but why did I say it? Finally, my ask is awful. "Can I reach out to you in a few months…"* ***That isn't an actionable ask.*** *Plus, I didn't follow up in a few months! Overall the email comes off as unconfident and vague.*

Two years later, however, she claims she was more ready and confident and adopted an approach that eventually worked. She shot an email to the same investor and got a response within a few hours.

Date: Thu, Oct 19, 2017 at 5:50 PM
Subject: Mapistry -- SaaS for environmental regulations -- Fortune 500 Customers -- Seed

Hi Jason,

My name is Allie, and I am the CEO of Mapistry. Mapistry is a SaaS application for environmental regulations at industrial facilities. Environmental regulations are notoriously confusing and complicated, yet the technology used to manage them is usually no more sophisticated than excel spreadsheets and email. This system leaves manufacturing companies vulnerable to multi-million dollar lawsuits and severe damage to their brand.

Traction & numbers:

- **customers include Fortune 500 companies like 3M, Republic Services, Tesla and Procter & Gamble**
- growing 15% month over month
- September revenue: $67K
- fully ramped, our existing customer base corresponds to a $4M run rate.
- United States TAM: $3.7B ($1T environmental market globally)

You can check out more details about Mapistry in a short deck here.

I am raising a seed round of funding for Mapistry to maximize on our recent momentum, expand our product to other environmental domains (focused on stormwater to date), and continue to develop software that automates services traditionally provided by environmental consultants.

I've been following SaaStr for a while. In particular, I saw your talk with Veeva from the SaaStr conference and I'd love to talk to you about how we fit into this trend of vertical SaaS. One of the reasons so few companies are using software for environmental compliance is that the only tools available are so unspecific and horizontal that the customizations required are so immense, they become unrealistic.

I liked what Peter had to say about services. We also feel very strongly that we have great people and we aren't going to give their time away for free. We like to think of our environmental services as being paid for sales and/or customer success. In fact, I just did a quick, back of the envelope calculation, and looks like we've been doing about 35% profit margins on our services for 2017, which has been a nice source of revenue for the rest of the company while we get off the ground.

I'd love to schedule a time for a 30-minute phone call or coffee. Do you have any time the week after next?

Allie Janoch
CEO | Mapistry

Source: Alice Janoch's article on Medium

She writes:

> *For each investor I emailed, whether it was an intro or cold, I modified the template to personalize it for them. For Jason, who was my number one choice for an investor, I spent a couple of hours researching and putting together the later part of the email.*

Apparently, the recipient, Jason Lemkin, said this about the email[3]:

"It does a good job of summarizing the opportunity, early customers and traction, growth profile, and market size. Perhaps just as importantly, it is truly personalized.

"Also for me at least, it's low drama. 'Do you have any time the week after next?' The confident and relatively data-rich but low drama emails work best. Knowing there's little time it is much less risky to meet a founder you've barely met before and dig in."

However, you must take into account that every individual has their own preference, and one's views won't apply to all. It usually takes time to perfect your cold-emailing template to receive maximum responses. Since it's bound to take a few hits and misses, that's another reason to practice these with low-priority investors. When they start getting you meetings, you can then move up the order with a refined approach.

Karan Bajaj, founder of WhiteHat Jr, stated in his blog that he approached investors only through cold outreaches on LinkedIn[4]. He shared an example of the template that he claimed got 6 out of 10 VCs to respond. In this, Anup Gupta of Nexus Venture Partners responded almost immediately.

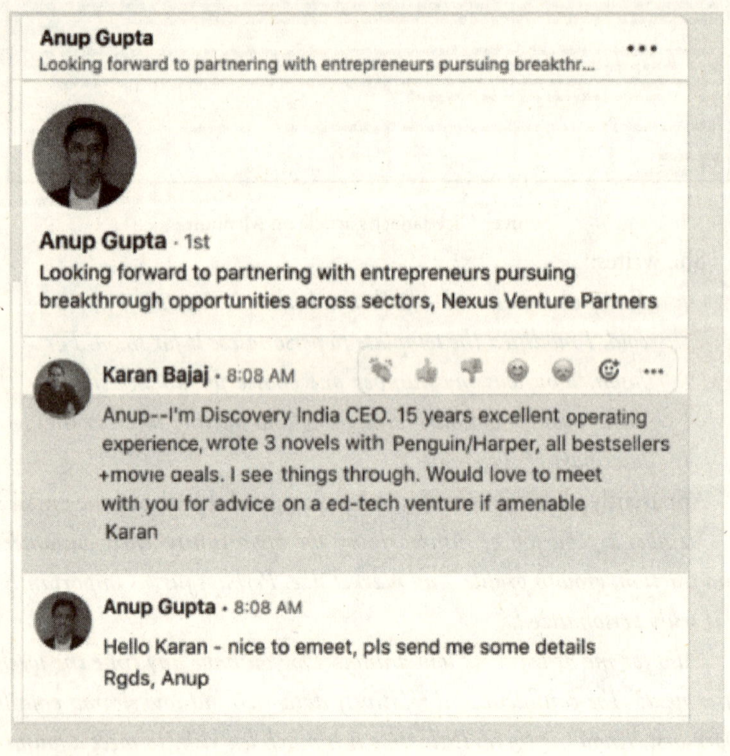

Source: Karan Bajaj's blog post "How to Raise Startup Funding with No Product"

He further writes: *"Contrary to public perception, I found almost all Indian venture capitalists extremely responsive and courteous, both in their acceptance and rejection."*

This is obviously an encouraging statement for founders. But know that this comes from someone who wrote good cold messages, and was already a highly distinguished professional when he started out.

His credentials allowed him to reach out to decision-makers directly and request for a meeting. For someone less experienced, it may not be the greatest idea especially if you haven't tested the waters and received interest from other low-priority investors.

Alice Janoch elaborated her cold email template in the same blog, which I have slightly modified and summarized in the pointers below.

- A crisp subject line that quickly but effectively explains the purpose of the email; also helps if you name the investor here
- Explain the problem you're solving as easily and simply as possible
- Mention the most important traction numbers and other impressive facts (e.g. stellar team, product demo link) as bullet points
- A clear reason for raising money and what you intend to achieve with it
- End with a clear request for a 30-minute call or a meeting and give enough time so that the recipient doesn't feel rushed
- Attach your deck with the email
- Some additional pointers:
- Make the email personal - it should never feel like a copy-pasted template
- Be brief - minimize the usage of words and make information more palatable by using bullet points and numbers
- When you send emails, send to 5-6 investors on the same day to increase the probability of securing at least one meeting in the next few days

Many VCs have shared their versions of the perfect cold emailing template. While you can refer to them, understand that every individual responds and acts differently. Also, know that business behaviour varies geographically. If you're raising funds in India, I'd suggest giving Indian investors' suggestions higher weightage.

Finally, you should feel confident about your email. How you write reflects how clearly you think. Make sure that the flow feels natural to you. Again, as crude as it may sound, use the low-priority investors as your practice ground to gain confidence.

Investors will probably not respond to your first cold outreach. In such cases, wait for about 3-4 days before politely sending a follow-up. If you have any new information to add, use this email as the opportunity to share it. You can consider sharing a line about your startup again as a quick reminder of what you're building. It makes it easier for the investor to grasp the idea than plainly asking them to 'refer to the trailing mail'. The chances of responses to follow-up emails are higher, especially when asked politely and professionally. It also somewhat indicates the tenacity of the founder. But again, ensure there's a clear line between tenacity and desperation. Don't follow up in intervals shorter than 3 days, and don't be too repetitive if there's no response.

How many pitches and meetings does it take?

In 2015, Brian Chesky, the co-founder and CEO of Airbnb published an article on Medium titled 7 Rejections[5].

> *"On June 26, 2008, our friend Michael Seibel introduced us to 7 prominent investors in Silicon Valley. We were attempting to raise $150,000 at a $1.5M valuation. That means for $150,000 you could have bought 10% of Airbnb. Below you will see 5 rejections. The other 2 did not reply.*
>
> *"The investors that rejected us were smart people, and I am sure we didn't look very impressive at the time. Next time*

you have an idea and it gets rejected, I want you to think of these emails."

to Brian, Joe, Nathan 7/16/08

Thank you for the introduction. Brian good to meet you -- while this sounds interesting it is not something we would do here -- not in our area of focus, do wish you best of luck

8/1/08

to Brian, Joe, Nathan

Hi Brian,

Apologies for the delayed response. We've had a chance to discuss internally, and unfortunately don't think that it's the right opportunity for from an investment perspective. The potential market opportunity did not seem large enough for our required model.

to Brian 7/30/08

Brian:

I ran this by my partner. First, it's not in one of our prime 5 target markets so it's a long shot for our involvement. Also, since it's not an area where we are currently investing, getting us involved doesn't give you the expertise that would be best for your company.

My recommendation is to keep us posted. If you get to the point of a Series A investment please let us know and we'll take a look.

9/2/08

to Brian, Joe, Nathan

Brian

Thanks for the follow up. I was unavailable to get on the call today as I'll be out of town through end of day Thursday. I really like the progress you guys have made, but between issues outstanding with ABB and my current time commitments to other projects, specifically existing investments, I'm not going to be able to proceed with an investment at this point. My biggest remaining concerns are:
- significant ramp up in traction post the DNC and RNC
- technical staffing
- investment syndicate

10/28/08

to Brian

Brian

We decided yesterday to not take this to the next level

We've always struggled with travel as a category

We recognize its one of the top e-commerce categories but for some reason, we've not been able to get excited about travel related businesses

Source: Brian Chesky's article on Medium titled "7 Rejections"

Any investor who may have taken the chance and invested $150,000 in Airbnb at that time would have been worth billions of dollars today.

Notice that two of these emails are over 3 months apart, so you know it may take months of convincing and the outcome may still not be in your favour. You can look at these emails and get either inspired or dejected, but as a founder looking to raise funds, you must have a thick skin to absorb such rejections and continue improving. Statistically, you will have to pitch to at least 30-40 investors to get the first term sheet. However, the process becomes smoother after that as the first one helps you attract more willing investors to take the bet.

You can make the process efficient by tracking your efforts and outcomes with different investors. An example of such a tracker is given here.

Investor	Priority score	Contact identified	Email 1	Email 2	Meeting 1	MIS shared	Valuation	Term sheet
Investor 1	1.5							
Investor 2	1.5							
Investor 3	2							
Investor 4	2							

Each cell can contain remarks on learnings or feedback you obtained at different points of communication. This will help you improve your approach with every new investor you get in touch with.

The number of meetings and pitches it takes varies with the investor as well as your idea and product. If you have carefully applied the filters suggested in the section on Investor-Market-Product-Stage Fit and are still repeatedly getting rejected, it's likely that either the idea lacks merit or is not investable as a VC business. **Getting feedback at the end of every such discussion by simply asking "Do you think this is an investable business idea?" can help you obtain clarity early. If they think it's not, then you can follow up with "What do you think can make this idea investable?" If you get similar suggestions from all the investors you speak with, see if any of those can be implemented in your business to make it more investable.** However, do it only if it makes proper business sense to you and is aligned with why you started out.

If an investor asks you to get back in a few months or even if they express unwillingness to invest, you can continue sharing quarterly updates about your progress on email. The ones who have refused may be suited for future rounds if not the first one.

Finally, understand the different ways of refusal. Some investors would give a direct 'No' which is clear and allows you to move on immediately. Others give some variation of "not now". And then there are a few who give no response or ghost you. If a few follow-ups don't elicit any response, consider it a refusal to invest and move on. However, you can continue keeping them in loop with your progress updates, especially the more desirable ones.

It's hard to accurately estimate how many meetings it might take to conclude a round. But designing small and effective feedback loops helps you become efficient in the process, and allows you to refine the approach faster, and hopefully close the deal within your target date.

How much time does it take?

Founders often underestimate the time it takes to conclude a funding round and have the money in the account. Broadly, getting the first term sheet is the most unpredictable part of the process and can take anywhere between 1 month (if you're extremely lucky) to 4-5 months. If it's taken over 3 months and there's not even an indication of interest from any VC, introspect if external funding is even the right strategy. Or if the idea has enough weight to compete in the market.

Once you get the term sheet, it takes another 1 to 1.5 months for all the due diligence. The more advanced the stage, the longer this process takes.

Finally, it takes another 1-1.5 months at least to complete all the compliance related paperwork. These are sequential in nature, and many filings can happen only after the previous one has concluded. If any part of the process becomes a bottleneck, it elongates the conclusion further.

You can safely assume that it would take 3 months or more for the money to hit the bank account after receiving the term sheet. If there are any irregularities found between your claims and actuals, the process may take much longer. However, if it's an unvalued round, the process may be concluded in about a month from the date you receive the term sheet.

To be diligent and efficient, keep track of these processes in an Excel sheet and have target deadlines for each. When you see slow movement at any stage, you could interject and expedite anything that's in your control.

Should you get an Investment Banker?

To execute a fundraising round, you basically need three types of people. A CFO or a CFO-equivalent who can take charge of the entire process on the startup's behalf. A financial advisor, usually a CA experienced in this industry and on such deals, who helps ascertain a valuation. Then there's someone to manage the legal compliances and paperwork, usually a CS or a lawyer experienced in this domain.

In the early stages, the requirements are lower. Since there's not a lot of data or history to study, due diligence is faster. As long as there's a representative from the company (could be one of the founders) to assist in basic requirements, the process can be concluded smoothly even without an investment banker. However, I do advise getting a startup legal expert (not any legal expert) to help founders study the term sheet and avoid any unnecessary pitfalls. Incubators and accelerators usually provide their startups with such assistance in executing the round.

Having said this, fundraising is indeed a time-consuming process and many founders would prefer to spend it working on the core business. If there's a CFO on the team, they can undertake this responsibility, but if not, getting an investment banker will help them save a lot of time and effort.

In the later stages though, getting an investment banker becomes a necessity. Unless you have a highly capable CFO experienced in executing funding rounds earlier, it would be incredibly hard to do it without one.

Additional Help Investors Provide

Every investor wants to see their portfolio startups succeed. Apart from the monetary investment, they add further value in the form of resources, networks, mentorship, etc. to ensure the growth of the startup. A few ways in which they help are given below.

1. Network

If you watched the episodes of Shark Tank India, you may have observed Namita Thapar, one of the sharks on the show, offer her vast network in the pharma industry as a benefit to the founders who were building a product in the healthcare space.

Established investors have a huge network that comprises other investors, lawyers, industry experts, and entrepreneurs. A relationship with an investor opens this network to you. These connections can help you in different ways to grow your business - strategic advice, mentorship, support for non-core company items, hiring for key positions, etc.

An attachment of the investor's name with your startup also adds credibility. Every startup that gets selected by YCombinator gets ahead of the pack in every respect, thanks to YC's credibility. Similarly, startups funded by major VC firms and angel networks instantly grab eyeballs through press coverage.

2. Mentorship

Investors often help startups get the right mentoring they need. The people running the VC firms are extremely smart and competent and act as great sounding boards for any business plans. Good VCs are known to help founders navigate their problems smoothly.

3. Access to free resources

At times, investors have deals with SaaS platforms, software companies, etc. and their portfolio founders get free access to all these tools to help build their business.

They also host sessions with industry experts and general industry meet-ups where the founders can get personalized counselling.

4. Hiring

At any given point, at least a few of a VC's portfolio startups would be hiring. A number of times, great candidates are passed over for different reasons. Such candidates could be referred to the VC who can then connect them to another portfolio company that may be a great fit for them.

Also, if there is a startup that is shutting down, the employees of that company can then be referred to other portfolio companies for quicker placement.

5. *Jugaad*

Investors, especially the ones who have been around for a long time, know many vendors, services, and, in general, people. They can help you find the right services at the cheapest prices. They can also help you find the solutions to specific problems by getting you in touch with a founder who may have solved a similar issue in the past.

In all of these ways, an experienced investor adds significant value to a startup. Ensure that you make the best use of them whenever you can.

Part III
Getting the Deal Through

14. Incorporating Your Startup

Sometime in January 2021, I caught up with a college friend and he told me all about his startup. He had conceived a product idea in the D2C food-tech space. Some of his office colleagues liked his concept and joined him as co-founders. They quickly got their company registered and were getting started on their MVP.

When I met him again in 2022, the situation was different from what I had hoped. There had been a fallout between the co-founders. Since they could not agree on a common vision, they decided to cease operations and shut down the company. But shutting down isn't that easy. My friend was now stuck in a compliance quicksand and discovered how slow and complicated the process is. As of writing this book in August 2022, the company has still not officially shut down and my friend pays around Rs. 20,000 annually to maintain an entity whose business is non-existent.

Many aspiring founders similarly rush to register their company immediately after getting an idea and finding willing partners. It's understandable that having a company in one's name lends a sense of accomplishment. It's like a milestone achieved, and they officially become founders. But they don't realize how elaborate and painful the shutting down process could be. I always suggest startup founders test the waters properly before investing their time and money (and even peace of mind, in many cases) in the registration of a business entity.

The subsequent sections cover the business entities of a Proprietorship, Partnership, LLP, OPC, and Pvt. Ltd. Within each entity, I have covered the basic characteristics of the entity, who should consider registering it, the process of registration and shutting down, and a comparison of pros and cons for each of them. Following that, we talk about the different countries where you may register your startup. Please feel free to skip the sections you find irrelevant. However, if you haven't registered your entity yet, I'd urge you to go through the entire chapter carefully to make an informed decision.

What kind of company to register?

Founders are intuitively inclined to register a Private Limited because that's what is most visible. However, many would be better off registering a different entity depending on the type of business and the stage they are in. Let's understand the options available in India.

Proprietorship

Proprietorship works best if you are a solopreneur or work in a small team, and have a predominantly service-based model. Freelancers of all types can operate as sole proprietors under a business name to lend themselves more credibility. Essentially, it's the founder operating with just a business name officially allotted.

It must be noted that a Proprietorship brings unlimited liability to the founders. It means that anything attributed to the business - complaints, financial irregularities, etc. - makes the founder directly responsible for it. Unlike a Private Limited, Proprietorship is not considered an entity separate from the founder. Some Proprietors take professional indemnity insurance to mitigate the risk. It is a scheme that protects one from professional negligence or cases where you can be sued by your client for unsatisfactory service. The insurance covers the cost. But it has its limitations concerning the total coverage, so any such insurance scheme must be thoroughly inspected before signing up.

Overall, Proprietorship is a great means to start a business officially for its ease of compliance and even shutting down. It also allows complete secrecy of the business financials which is not the case with a Private Limited. Even taxes are paid as per your individual income slab, whereas in a Private Limited a flat 30% of profits is paid as taxes

Registration

- No separate registration is required to work as a proprietorship. You may require a GST if revenues cross the threshold.
- You may have to open a current account with any bank with your personal details and ID proofs. This account, accounts for the business receipts, and savings for salary incomes, etc.
- For the tradename, you have to file a UDYAM registration under the MSME act. The process of this registration is easy and can be completed online within 10 minutes.
- You may also require a Shop and Establishment registration and a CA certificate of the ownership of the tradename.

The registration of a proprietorship generally costs less than Rs. 5000. This cost (and the ones mentioned for the other entities) is exclusive of the income tax and GST compliances.

Shutting Down

To shut down a proprietorship, there's barely any cost. You just need to close the bank account, surrender GSTIN and file the business income and expense details in your personal ITR.

Partnership

A partnership, very simply put, is a Proprietorship but with multiple business partners. A simple agreement is done between the business owners or Partners on all the different terms of business - functional responsibilities, decision-making powers, profit split, salaries, etc. All other functional parameters, and benefits and disadvantages are almost the same as in a Proprietorship.

Registration

- The partners mention the terms on which they plan to run the business in a partnership deed and print it on stamp paper. The stamp duty varies from state to state, but a general stamp paper of INR 500 works.
- After the partnership deed is printed, they apply for a PAN.
- Once they receive their PAN, they can open a bank account and commence business activities.

A partnership may also need a Shops & Establishment Registration and GSTIN to open a bank account. The registration of a partnership generally costs around Rs. 5-10K.

The Indian Partnership Act defines two different types of partnerships.

Registered Partnership	Unregistered Partnership
The partnership deed is registered at the local registrar of the firm's office in the appropriate jurisdiction.	No such registration.
Can sue a third party as it is a registered entity in the eyes of the law.	In this case, only the partners can sue each other but not any third party because the contract is only between them.

Shutting Down

To shut down a partnership, the founders need to file ITR, surrender GSTIN, and make a dissolution deed by which they distribute assets and liabilities between themselves.

There's a minimal cost of doing the paperwork of dissolving a partnership and takes about 2 months. The process is much easier if the necessary agreements have been done between the partners.

LLP (Limited Liability Partnership)

LLP as an entity was introduced in the Limited Liability Partnership Act of 2008. The objective was to solve the problem of unlimited liability that came with a Proprietorship or Partnership. While Private Limited was still an option for such businesses, the delta between this and a Partnership was huge in terms of compliances and ease of setting up and shutting down. Moreover, such businesses didn't need many of the key provisions offered by Private Limited, like raising external funds or granting ESOPs to their employees. The issue was mainly of unlimited liability which could potentially create unnecessary problems for the founders, especially after the business grew and comprised different moving parts.

Limited Liability Partnership (LLP) was introduced mainly to enable multiple partners belonging to the same profession to set up an entity with limited liability. A team of lawyers, for example, could come together and start a legal consultancy business under an LLP. Similarly, a group of architects could join hands and start an architecture firm. The nature of these professions is such that if something goes wrong, an unlimited liability on the personal assets of a partner can be unjustifiably high. For example, if an architect designs a house for an individual, and later after its construction, some faults are discovered, it may not necessarily have been the architect's wrongdoing. In such a case, if the individual sues the architect, there's an unnecessary liability on them personally.

LLPs were incepted mainly to give limited liability to a Partnership, to avoid cases like the one mentioned above. A Private Limited could also have been an option, but such firms don't need external funding or need to give away ESOPs, and they don't intend to lose the secrecy of their financials, so it would have been unnecessary.

In an LLP, if two partners have invested Rs. 1 lakh each, and the company makes a profit of Rs. 3 lakhs over time, the total capital of the LLP amounts to 5 lakhs. If anyone sues the LLP, the liability will be limited to the value of asset or money, which is Rs. 5 lakhs in this example. Any legal case or suit for recovery beyond this amount will be invalid as the LLP does not have that much money. So the partners are insulated from the risk of having to liquidate their personal assets to pay for damages.

LLP thus provides a good middle ground between a Partnership and a Private Limited.

Registration

- A partnership deed, containing the terms of execution of the business, is printed on a stamp paper and signed by all the partners.
- The LLP then needs to be registered on the MCA portal with the Ministry of Corporate Affairs.
- The name of the LLP needs to be approved by the MCA. The name needs to be representative of the industry the LLP will function in and will be followed by the suffix "LLP".
- An LLP also has certain filing requirements. If the capital contribution in the partnership is more than Rs. 25 lakhs or the total turnover of the business for a year is more than Rs. 40 lakhs, then a statutory audit by a CA on an annual basis is mandatory.
- An LLP has to ensure a mandatory annual filing with the MCA, in addition to ITR filing and GST filing.
- The director's KYC needs to be done online on the MCA portal every year.

The registration of an LLP generally costs around Rs. 7.5-15K.

Shutting down

Shutting down an LLP has a higher effort of executing the paperwork and filing it on the MCA portal compared to a Partnership, but easier than Pvt Ltd.

It can only be shut with all filings done and approval obtained from the Ministry of Corporate Affairs (MCA), which can take about 6 to 12 months to complete.

Private Limited (Pvt. Ltd.)

Private Limited allows a business to run as a full-fledged business entity with no liability to the founders, allows it to raise external funds and grant ESOPs to employees, and gives it a professional look. If you plan to build a company with multiple such stakeholders in the business, it's best to register as a Pvt. Ltd. under the Companies Act 2013.

Registration

Every Pvt. Ltd. entity needs to have a Memorandum of Association (MOA), Articles of Association (AOA) and Certificate of Incorporation (COI).

- The first step in the registration is the name approval.
- A Pvt. Ltd. entity needs to have a minimum of two shareholders and directors. Solo founders often enlist a family member as the second shareholder and director.
- A Pvt. Ltd. is required to have at least four board meetings in a financial year and the difference between two board meetings cannot be more than 120 days. At least one director of the company has to be in India for more than 182 days in a year.
- An annual audit by a CA is mandatory for a Pvt. Ltd. The financial statements, balance sheet and P&L statement, audit report, etc. have to be filed on the MCA portal. Moreover, these documents are publicly available at a nominal price.

The registration of a Pvt. Ltd. generally costs less than INR 15 to 30 thousand. It can vary based on the amount of initial capital invested, the number of directors and shareholders.

Shutting Down

- Shutting down a Pvt. Ltd. is the most arduous among all entities.
- You can shut down a Pvt. Ltd. only after approval from the MCA or Registrar of Companies (ROC).
- You need to get a "No Objection" from the GST department, the Income Tax department, and other relevant departments to ensure that the entity does not have any external liabilities.
- The directors and shareholders need to give indemnities to the government so that if any liability arises in the future, the directors will be personally liable for it.
- There has to be no business for a minimum period of two years if you have the run business for a couple of years or more.

Certain schemes are offered from time to time that expedite the process of shutting down. But if no such scheme is in place, then the process is time-consuming. It costs at least Rs. 20,000 to shut one down, and can take 1-2 years or even more.

One Person Company (OPC)

OPC was introduced as a concept in the Companies Act 2013 to help plug some gaps that a Pvt. Ltd. or an LLP alone couldn't provide. For example, if a single person wanted to register a Pvt. Ltd., he or she needed to bring along another Director just to show it on paper as it was mandatory to have 2 Directors. This created obstacles, and unnecessary liability for the silent Director. The name of the company should mandatorily end with "(OPC) Pvt Ltd."

OPC removed these hurdles and allowed a single person to be named Director, with just a nominee added in case the Director expired during the tenure. Earlier, the OPC provision was capped at Rs. 2 Cr annual revenue after which it had to mandatorily convert to a Pvt. Ltd., but now the limits have been removed.

However, an OPC can't raise external funds, give ESOPs, or have any other shareholders. They'd need to be converted into a Pvt. Ltd. to enable these.

So OPC is great for a solo founder who wants to register their business professionally but maintain limited liability. In other words, it's a more secure form of Proprietorship for them.

Registration

The registration takes place with the MCA and there is only one person who acts as the shareholder and the Director. The process otherwise is similar to a Pvt. Ltd.

Shutting Down

The process, again, is similar to a Pvt. Ltd. but can be slightly easier since there's just one shareholder and Director which reduces the compliance needs.

The following table can be referred for a good summary of all these entities.

Entity	Who should consider	Pros	Cons
Proprietorship	Solopreneur/ Freelancer	- Low registration cost - Ease of registering - Ease of shutting down - Secrecy of financials - Potentially lower taxes	- Unlimited liability - Can't accept external equity funds - Can't offer ESOPs - Can't have official business partners
Partnership	Two or more co-founders building a service business, or just testing the waters before a larger foray	- Can have multiple co-founders - Low cost of registration - Relative ease of registering and shutting down	- Unlimited liability on founders - Can't accept external funds - Can't offer ESOPs

Entity	Who should consider	Pros	Cons
Limited Liability Partnership (LLP)	Group of professionals providing a service prone to liability - doctors, lawyers, architects, CAs, etc.	- Liability to partners limited to the total value of assets in LLP - Secrecy of financials - Low cost of registration - Gives a more professional outlook than Proprietorship or Partnership - Can be converted to Pvt Ltd any time	- Higher cost of maintenance than Proprietorship/Partnership - Can't accept external equity funds - Can't offer ESOPs
Private Limited (Pvt. Ltd.)	Anyone looking to build a large company and have multiple shareholders in the form of investors and employees	- Liability to founders is limited - Allows external funding - Easy transferability of shares - Different categories of shareholders can be created - Succession planning is easiest	- Highest maintenance cost - Shutting down can take painfully long and cost the most - Company financials can be accessed by competitors
One Person Company (OPC)	Solo founder seeking limited liability	- Protection against unlimited liability - No requirement of a silent Director or shareholder	- Can't accept external equity funds - Long drawn shutting down process

People often complain about the painful shutting down processes of most entities due to administrative reasons. I have myself seen cases where it lasted beyond 2 years.

Should you register in India or outside?

In recent times, founders have shifted the incorporation of their businesses to the global startup hubs of Singapore, Dubai, Delaware, and Estonia.

The decision of the location of incorporation of a startup should be based on two factors: the *go-to-market* and the *largest market*. You will need an entity in the location where you will be hiring your first employees and testing the product on initial users.

Don't consider incorporating in a country only to save taxes or other compliance costs. The Indian tax laws will anyway find a way to tax you, and the administrative charges to run the entity will also be huge.

Here, I have listed the advantages of setting up a business entity in four international locations popular with Indians.

1. Dubai

- No income tax or corporate tax. VAT (like the GST) is at a minimal rate of up to ~5%. However, a corporate tax of 9% may start in 2023.
- Profits are 100% repatriable to other countries.
- You can set up a business entity in less than a week.
- A flourishing startup culture with multiple incubators, accelerators, and investors.
- 100% foreign ownership is allowed in Free Zones, where it might be mandatory for one to take their services of renting office space.

2. Singapore

- The corporate tax rate is at 17% compared to India's 25-30%.
- Capital Gains Tax is 0% compared to India's 15-20%.
- Foreign Investment norms are more liberal in Singapore than in India.
- Intellectual Property (IP) protection laws in Singapore are more mature and robust.
- Investor funds are plenty in Singapore and access to VCs easier due to it being a finance-focused island nation.

3. Estonia

- Corporate Tax, Personal Tax and VAT (if annual turnover > EUR 40,000) all at 20%.
- No tax if profits are retained and not distributed by a com-

pany.

- Company setup time is less than a day.
- No dividend tax, so no double taxation of profits
- Only fixed monthly expense paid to the government is in the form of a PF, which constitutes a few subheads such as Unemployment Tax, Social Tax and Pension Fund.

4. Delaware

- Company setup time is less than a day.
- No need to pay the state tax of 9% if you generate income in a different location.
- Investor secrecy and friendliness.
- The legal library of the court pronouncements and judgements is exhaustive and leads to most efficient dispute resolution.

15. Understanding & Negotiating a Term Sheet

The Term Sheet is seen as the Holy Grail for founders seeking investment. Securing one is perceived as the end of the fundraising journey for a particular round. However, it's only partially true. In this chapter, we'll understand the Term Sheet in detail and cover everything it is and isn't. In the subsequent chapters, we'll understand the steps to be completed even after a Term Sheet is obtained which clarifies the actual fundraising process further.

What is a Term Sheet, and what is it not?

A Term Sheet is a legal document Investors share with the Founders after they have agreed to invest in their startup. It is usually 5-6 pages long and outlines the details of the association between the investor and the startup. It is the first point of understanding between the two parties and a skeleton for the terms and conditions based on which the investment in the startup will take place. The Term Sheet is negotiated upon and finally, when the investor and the startup both agree on the details of the investment, it gets signed.

However, it is not a guarantee or a promise to invest a particular amount of money at the valuation agreed. The final investment is subject to the thorough due diligence of the business, and any discrepancies could potentially lead to a change in valuation or even withdrawal of investors from the process.

A Term Sheet is a handshake agreement stating the terms at which an investor is putting money into a startup. But **it is not legally binding on either the investor or the startup**. Any of them can back out from the transaction until the Definitive Agreements (Shareholder's Agreement, Share Subscription Agreement, Share Purchase Agreement - covered in Chapter 16) are signed.

However, some of the clauses of a Term Sheet can be binding and you should be cautious about them. These clauses are usually related to confidentiality and no-shop and have been explained further along in the chapter. It basically safeguards the details of conversations between the two parties from being put out in the public or shared with a competitor to benefit the startup at the investor's expense.

An investor has the right to cancel an offered Term Sheet when serious discrepancies emerge in the performance of the startup during due diligence. A founder too can back out of a Term Sheet if they get a better offer of investment from a different investor.

Control Terms vs Economic Terms

The terms in a Term Sheet can broadly be classified into two: Economic and Control terms.

Economic terms denote the clauses that impact the value of the business or the investors or the founders. They affect the valuation and dilution of the shareholding and returns of the business.

Control terms refer to the clauses that pertain to decision-making powers in the company.

Economic Terms	Control Terms
Valuation	Board of Directors
ESOP	Drag-Along Rights
Liquidation Preference	Info Rights
Promoter's Lock-In and Vesting	Reserved Matters
Antidilution Protection	Restriction of Transfer
	Right of First Offer (ROFO)
	Right of First Refusal (ROFR)

Term Sheet Clauses & Negotiation Tips

In this section, we have laid out the Term Sheet with all their clauses as available on the Startup India website and prepared by LetsVenture[1]. I have made explanations and mentioned points that could be used during negotiations wherever relevant.

1.0 Transaction Details

The "Business" term simply states the description of the business.

1.1	**Business**	The Company is currently engaged in the business of [•].

Ensure that this description is the same as that given in the Memorandum of Association of the company. Startups often pivot in their initial stages. It may happen that the product that you are raising funds for is not what the MoA mentions. Before you raise funds, ensure the details are aligned.

1.2	**Promoter(s)**	The Company is currently controlled by [•] and [•].

1.3	**Current Capital Structure**	The current paid up and issued share capital of the Company comprises of [•] equity shares with a face value of INR [•] per share and [•] preference shares with a face value of INR [•] per share. The Promoters hold [•] % in the current paid up and issued share capital of the Company. The shareholding pattern of the Company as on the Effective Date is as set forth in Schedule 1 hereto.

This clause details the cap table of the startup.

A startup has 3 categories of shareholders in this respect - founders who hold equity, investors who hold equity, and investors who hold convertible securities that have not yet been converted into shares. A founder needs to ensure that they **add the fully diluted cap table here**, taking into consideration the securities that will be converted at a future date.

Details on the fully diluted cap table before the investment takes place are added to a document called Schedule 1.

1.4	**Instruments**	Equity shares having a face value of INR [•] each at a price of [•] per share ("Equity Shares"). "Definitive Documentation" shall have the meaning ascribedto it under Clause 3.1 of this Term Sheet.

Instruments denote the instrument through which the investment will take place. It can be equity shares, preference shares, CCPS, CCDs, Convertible Notes, etc.

1.5	**Valuation**	For the purpose of the Proposed Transaction, the pre-money valuation of the Company is INR [•].

The **pre-money valuation** of the startup at which the investor puts money into the business is stated in this section.

A point that a founder needs to clarify with the investor is whether they have considered the pre-money or the post-money valuation for the investment.

Normally, **pre-money valuation + investment = post-money valuation**

But if the discussion between the founders and investors is being based on valuation, without specifying if it's pre-money or post-money, it may lead to confusion and delay.

> Assume that the pre-money valuation of your startup is Rs. 75 crores. With an investment of Rs. 25 crores, the post-money valuation will amount to Rs. 100 crores. If the investor calculates their shareholding using the post-money valuation, they own a 25% stake in the company. But if there was a miscommunication and the investors meant the 75 Cr to be the post-money valuation after their investment of 25 Cr, their shareholding becomes 25/75, or 33% of the company. There's an evident mismatch.

1.6	**Proposed Transaction**	(i) Subject to applicable law, the Investor, along with certain other persons as set forth in the Definitive Documentation (collectively, "Investors") proposes to make an investment of up to INR [•] (the "Investment Amount") into the Company such that the post-investment shareholding structure of the Company shall be in the manner set out in Schedule 2 hereunder. It is agreed by the Parties that the Investment Amount may be subject to change at any time subsequent to the execution of this Term Sheet but prior to the execution of the Definitive Documentation, and in the event of the same, the post-money valuation and shareholding pattern of the Company shall be accordingly revised. (ii) The Parties will work towards achieving completion of the Proposed Transaction, including but not limited to the remittance of the Investment Amount and issue of corresponding Equity Shares ("Closing") within the timeframe specified in the SSSHA. (iii) The shareholding pattern of the Company, immediately upon Closing shall be as set forth in Schedule 2 hereunder.

This clause states the amounts that each investor will put into the startup. It may not give the complete list of all the individual investors of an angel syndicate but may state the lead.

The shareholding structure of the business post-investment is detailed in Schedule 2. A founder should make sure that the two schedules, Schedule 1 and 2, are clarified and agreed upon during the negotiations to avoid any confusion in the future.

This section also states that the valuation of the company may change during the due diligence, and hence, the shareholding pattern may have to be revised. During due diligence, the investor may find some metrics to be worse than what was initially believed and may insist on reducing the company's valuation on that basis. Hence, they add this statement in their interest.

1.7	**Advisory Equity**	The Company agrees to issue at the time of Closing, to [•], Equity Shares ("Advisory Equity") equivalent to [•]% of [•] in value, in consideration of the advisory and mentoring services to be rendered by [•] on an ongoing basis, subject to the terms set forth in the Definitive Documentation. [LV Note: This is an optional clause and is to be included if an investor is getting advisory equity.]

Advisor equity details the pool of equity set aside for advisors of the startup and is an optional clause.

> Investors generally want founders to issue advisor shares from their own shares so that investors' holding is not diluted.

2.0 Key Considerations

This is a control term and refers to the demand of investors to appoint a Director and/or a Board Observer.

Investors can have two types of controls as Board Members - positive and negative.

2.1	**Board Composition And Incidental Matters**	The Company is currently engaged in the business of [•].The Board of Directors of the Company (the "Board") immediately upon Closing shall comprise of [•] directors, of which the Investors shall be entitled to nominate 1 (one) director ("Investor Director") and the other directors shall be nominated by the Promoters. In the event of any increase or decrease in the number of directors, the number of directors so nominated by the Investors and the Promoters shall be proportionately increased or decreased. The Investors shall be entitled to nominated 1 (one) person as the observer of the proceedings of the Board ("Board Observer").

Positive Control is the investor's ability to vote as a Director in the board meetings and shareholders' meetings.

Negative Controls mean that your business can not do certain things unless formally approved by investors. These are also known as protective provisions, such as future fundraising, change in shareholding structure, taking debt, merger & acquisition decisions, etc., and are covered as veto rights under the Reserved Matters of the Shareholder's Agreement.

> Read and negotiate hard on the Negative Controls to retain maximum control. What you cannot negotiate to remove, insist on getting a threshold in. For example, if a change in related party transaction would require investor approval, you can negotiate that increase in related party transactions only above Rs. 50 Lakhs per annum requires such approval.

An investor may appoint a Board Observer who has the right to attend the board meetings of the company. They do not have voting rights but can let their opinions be known.

Investors often take the right to appoint a Board Observer but rarely do so. Instead of spending time during negotiation on removing the Board Observer, talk to other founders that the investor has invested in and ask them whether they really appoint a Board Observer.

You need to understand the motive of your investors well and take an appropriate call on the items that you need to spend more time on during negotiations.

2.2	**Pre-emptive Rights**	The Investors shall have a pro rata right to participate in any future issue of shares by the Company to any third party and to retain their shareholding on a fully diluted basis in the Company on the same terms and conditions (including price) as offered to such third party. Circumstances where pre-emptive rights will not be applicable will be detailed in the Definitive Documentation.

Assume that an investor holds a certain stake in your company at the present. In the future, when you will issue more shares to other investors, the present-day investors will get the first right to put in money and retain their shareholding on a fully diluted basis.

2.3	**Anti-Dilution Protection**	If at any time after Closing, the Company issues to any third party, equity shares or instruments convertible to equity shares, at a price per share that is lower than the price paid for the Equity Shares (or their conversion price), then the Investors shall be entitled to antidilution protection on a broad based weighted average basis. In such an event, the Company shall be bound to, and the Promoters shall be bound to cooperate with the Investors and the Company such that, the Company forthwith takes all necessary steps to issue additional equity shares to the Investors. Circumstances where anti-dilution protection will not be applicable will be detailed in the Definitive Documentation.

If a startup performs poorly due to any reason, there's a chance that it gets devalued in future investment rounds. The investors coming on the cap table get shares at a price lower than that of earlier investors. To protect themselves against any such loss in the future, **an investor gets the right to buy more shares in the company at a lower price to increase their stake.**

There are two kinds of antidilution: full ratchet antidilution and weighted average antidilution.

Full ratchet anti-dilution provisions are used by early-stage investors to protect their interests in case of a downward valuation by a bigger investor at a later stage. If, say, an investor invests at Rs 10 per share in a startup, but later, another investor puts in money at Rs 5 per share, that means the startup's valuation has halved to accommodate the new investor. In such a case, the previous investor's shares would now also be valued at the new price, doubling the equity previously held by the investor, without any new money invested.

In the **weighted average anti-dilution**, the number of shares issued at the reduced price is taken into consideration in the repricing of the previous round, and not just the new price flatly. If the number of new shares issued at the reduced price is very low, the older investors don't get any significant advantage because of the low weightage of the new price. Hence, **the weighted average anti-dilution is more friendly to startup founders than ratchet-based anti-dilution**.

2.4	**Promoters' Lock In**	The Promoters shall not be entitled to transfer to any person, the shares held by them in the Company, directly or indirectly, for a period of [3 (three)] years from the date of Closing ("Lock-in Period"). The Promoters may however transfer their shares to any person during the Lock-in Period subject to the prior written approval of the Investors and right of first refusal or tag along right as set forth in this Clause 2.

Promoters' Lock-in is an economic term and is similar to the concept of ESOPs. Employees get the shares of the company, or exercise their ESOPs, gradually as they continue working with the company depending on the vesting schedule set.

Investors put a lock-in clause on founders to restrict their access to their shares if they stop contributing to the growth of their company. Similar to the employees, founders receive their shares at the end of each year that they spend with the company or any other defined period. This is also known as reverse vesting. Usually, the period is taken as 3 to 4 years if investment happens in the early stages.

> If you have spent a considerable time, say 3 years, already building the company, you can negotiate shorter reverse vesting of, say, 1 or 2 years on account of this time invested.

2.5	**Vesting of Promoters' Shares**	25% of the shares held by each Promoter shall be deemed to have vested on the date hereof, and the remaining 75% of the shares held by each Promoter ("Unvested Shares") will be restricted over a 4-year period starting from the date of Closing ("Vesting Period"). Upon the completion of the first year, the Unvested Shares will be vested in equal instalments, every [3 (three)] months, over the next [3 (three)] years and shall cease to be part of the Unvested Shares. It is hereby clarified that the first quarterly vesting shall occur at the end of the 15th (fifteenth) month. In the event of termination of any of the Promoters' employment with the Company any time during the Vesting Period, only the shares that remain part of the Unvested Shares shall be transferred to the Company and in the event such transfer to the Company is not feasible (by reason of restrictions under applicable law or otherwise), such Unvested Shares shall be disposed of in a manner determined by the Board and the Investors. [LV Note: The manner of disposal of the Unvested Shares can be customised based on the understanding between the Parties.]

This clause gives the details on how the shares of the founders will be vested from year to year. When an investor comes on board, they make the founders earn their shares through the reverse vesting clauses, as stated in the previous section.

But what happens if the investors fire the founder and replace them with another CEO? If it happens at the end of 2 years of a 4-year reverse vesting period, the founder will hold only 50% of their actual shares, as only 2/4 of their shareholding would have been vested. However, if the founder has the **accelerated vesting** clause put in the Shareholder's Agreement, it will ensure that if they are terminated without cause (i.e., for reasons other than fraud), their unvested shares will immediately stand vested.

It must be noted that a founder may not want accelerated vesting for all of their top management, because it, in a way, incentivizes getting fired without cause and still getting to earn their entire shareholding through accelerated vesting.

2.6	**Promoters' and Non-Selling Investors' Right of First Offer**	In the event any of the Investors ("Selling Investor") intends to sell all or part of their shareholding ("ROFO Shares") in the Company to a third party ("Third Party Buyer"), then such Selling Investor shall first offer to sell the same to the Promoters and in the event: (a) the Promoters refuse to purchase the same; or (b) such Selling Investor obtains an offer from any Investor other than the Selling Investor ("Non-Selling Investor") for purchase of the ROFO Shares at a price higher than the price at which the same was offered to be purchased by the Promoters ("Offer Price"), then such Selling Investor shall sell the ROFO Shares to such Non-Selling Investor, provided that the price of the ROFO Shares shall not be lower than the Offer Price. The Promoters and the Non-Selling Investors shall each have the right to purchase the ROFO Shares in proportion of their respective shareholding in the Company at the Offer Price (or higher). In the event: (a) none of the Non-Selling Investors agree to purchase the ROFO Shares; or (b) the Selling Investor obtains an offer from a Third Party Buyer for purchase of the ROFO Shares at a price higher than the Offer Price, then such Selling Investor shall sell such ROFO Shares to such Third Party Buyer, provided that the price of the ROFO Shares shall not be lower than the Offer Price.

Every investor, at some point, wants to earn their profits and take an exit. For whatever reason, if an investor wants an exit and starts finding suitors in the market to sell their shares, a negative sentiment against the startup may develop in the ecosystem. It sends a signal that things are probably not well so the investor wants out.

A founder wishes to avoid this scenario. **ROFO ensures that if an investor wants to sell their shares, they must approach the founders first.**

If the investor has asked for a higher price, the founder may not be able to afford to buy all their shares. But they can agree to a purchase by a different investor that they bring in because a higher price also means a higher valuation and hence, a positive signal to the market.

In case the price is lower, the founder can take some time and either purchase the shares on their own or manage the transaction internally with the help of other investors of the company. If the deal occurs within a startup, the news can be controlled with no damage to perception.

A founder should always ask for ROFO rights in the Term Sheet.

2.7	**Investors' Right of First Re-fusal**	Subject to the Promoter's lock-in as set forth in Clause 2.4 of this Term Sheet, in the event any of the Promoters or any other shareholders other than the Investors ("Selling Shareholder") intends to sell all or part of their shareholding ("ROFR Shares") in the Company to any person, then such Selling Shareholder(s) shall first offer the ROFR Shares, to all the Investors ("Non-Selling Shareholders") at the same price as they have offered to such person. The Non-Selling Shareholders, at their sole discretion, shall have the right to purchase the ROFR Shares in proportion to their inter se shareholding in the Company.

Now if a founder wants to sell their shares of the company, ROFR ensures that the first offer to purchase the shares needs to be made to the existing investors of the startup. Only when the investors refuse to purchase the shares, the founders can sell their stake to third-party investors.

Their refusal, however, develops a perception among the other investors that the shares may be overvalued.

ROFR is usually a measure that investors take to dissuade external investors from buying the shares of the founders.

2.8	**Tag-Along Right**	Subject to the Promoter's lock-in as set for in Clause 2.4 of this Term Sheet, in the event any of the Promoters, or the other shareholders other than the Investors decide to sell their shareholding in the Company or a portion of it to any person ("Buyer"), and the Investors do not exercise their right of first refusal as referred to under Clause 2.7 of this Term Sheet, then the Investors shall have the right (but not the obligation) to require the Promoters or the other shareholders as the case may be, to ensure that the Buyer purchases the pro-rata Equity Shares on the same terms and simultaneously with the shares of the Promoters and the other shareholders. The Promoters and/or the other shareholders shall not sell any of their shares to the Buyer unless the Buyer purchases the Equity Shares. It is hereby clarified that any transfer of shares by any of the Investors shall not be subject to any tag along rights. The procedure governing exercise of tag-along right will be detailed in the Definitive Documentation.

These rights allow an investor or shareholder (including the founders) to tag along with another bigger shareholder, who may be negotiating a deal of sale of his shares in the company. This means that the new buyer of shares may have to purchase shares of not just the shareholder negotiating the deal, but of every other shareholder who has tag-along rights.

If the founder seeks an exit from the startup, it becomes especially mandatory for them to get their investors an exit as well. **Tag-along rights are a control term that investors impose over founders to restrict their capacity of selling shares of the startup.**

2.9	ESOP	The Company shall implement an Employee Stock Option Plan ("ESOP") constituting at least [•]% and not exceeding [•] % of the post-issue share capital of the Company on a fully diluted basis, with approval of the Investor Director, the quantum of which will be decided in the Definitive Documentation. The ESOP will be used for attracting and retaining talent in the Company.

ESOPs are stock options given to employees to award them for their efforts in building the startup. Similar to the advisor equity, the investor will ask the founders to set aside an ESOP pool before they enter the cap table. This means that the investor will not be diluted but only the founders will be diluted by the equity set aside for ESOPs. Hence, it is an economic term and **you will have to negotiate that the ESOP pool is implemented post the issues of the investor's shares.**

Investors may also ask a founder to set aside a standard 10% or 20% of the equity as an unissued ESOP pool. Unless the founders clearly see the need to set aside a large ESOP pool, they will have to negotiate and justify a smaller pool to reduce their dilution.

A few points that founders, depending on their situation, can use to negotiate:

- If all key people are already a part of the founding team, there's no need of setting aside a large ESOP pool
- Number of potential hires may be low
- Number of key personnel required may be low

There can be many other pointers, but it's imperative to have sound reasoning to build your case for a lower ESOP pool. At no point, should it appear that your individual wants are above the company's priorities.

2.10	**Affirmative Voting Rights**	The Company and its shareholders shall not be permitted to take any decisions on certain matters without such matters having first received the approval of the Investor Director at a Board meeting. The customary affirmative rights will be listed in the Definitive Documentation. The Investors will have the right to vote pro-rata to their shareholding (on an as if converted basis) in all shareholder meetings.

The voting rights are based on the powers the investors hold through seats on the Board of Directors' table. It details the instances when the founders need the approval of the investors to move forward with decisions and when they do not.

2.11	**Liquidation Preference**	Subject to applicable law, the holders of Equity Shares shall have preference over other equity shareholders ("Liquidation Preference") to distribution from the Company or from other third parties, as the case may be, upon the occurrence of a liquidation event (as described in the Definitive Documentation) and shall be entitled to receive in preference to the holders of other equity shares, an amount which is equal to either: (a) the pro-rata share of the Investor's shareholding on as if converted basis plus all declared but unpaid dividends; or (b) the Investment Amount plus all declared but unpaid dividends, whichever is higher. Transactions constituting liquidation event shall be detailed in the Definitive Documentation.

Liquidation preference occurs in two manners: Participating and Non-participating. In Chapter 12, Fundraising Instruments & Mechanics, we saw how founders are at a disadvantage when participating preference shares are issued to investors.

Negotiate for investors to receive non-participating shares, or at least get scenarios built in to ensure that as a founder, you are not at a complete disadvantage while still covering investors' apprehensions.

2.12	**Information Rights**	As long as the Investors hold any shares in the Company, the Investors shall receive from the Company (i) quarterly (un-audited) financial statements within [30 (thirty)] calendar days from the end of the preceding quarter, (ii) annual (audited) financial statements within [60 (sixty)] calendar days following the closure of the preceding financial year, (iii) operating / business plan within [30 (thirty)] calendar days prior to the commencement of the following yoar and (iv) any other operational and financial information as per the requirement of the Investors.

When an investor puts money into a startup, it is natural that they want to stay informed on the progress of the business. They include this clause in the Term Sheet that stating the information they seek and at what frequency.

A founder should try to negotiate and minimize the frequency of this information sharing. It takes effort to prepare such reports and it shouldn't lead them to keep a dedicated resource just for this purpose.

2.13	**Exit Mechanism**	1. The Company and the Promoters shall make all reasonable endeavors to provide exit to the Investors by way of: (a) an initial public offering of the Company at a mutually agreed minimum valuation within 5 (five) years from the date of Closing; or (b) strategic sale of the Equity Shares at the price acceptable to the Investors within 6 (six) years from the date of Closing provided the Company and the Promoters fail to facilitate an exit under Clause 2.13(1)(a) above. 2. Drag Along Option: In the event the Company and the Promoters fail to provide an exit to the Investors in accordance with Clause 2.13(1) above, the Investors shall have the unilateral right to sell their Investor Instruments (including shares) to any third party and the right to drag along the Promoters requiring the Promoters to sell whole of part of their shares, if required by such third party, to enable exit by the Investors. Detailed provisions with respect to the exit rights of the Investors shall be incorporated under the Definitive Documentation.

The founder is duty-bound to provide a successful and profitable exit to their investors. This exit usually takes place as an IPO, strategic sale, or drag-along option.

An IPO is the liquidation event when a company goes public and lists on the stock markets. A strategic sale may take place in the form of an acquisition by a larger business.

Drag along options are a control term that the investors hold. If investors feel that the founders are driving the company's value down or there is not much growth potential anymore, the investors can find a prospective buyer for their shares and get them to buy the entire company. This can be done when they have the right to drag along every other shareholder to compulsorily sell to the prospective buyer at the terms negotiated.

2.14	**Free Transfer-ability**	Subject to Clause 2.6 and provided that the Investors do not sell the Company's securities held by them to any competitor of the Company, the securities held by the Investors in the Company shall be freely transferable at any point of time, subject to applicable law. The term 'competitor' shall be defined in the Definitive Documentation.

This clause builds on the ROFO rights and states that the investors are allowed to sell their shares based on the terms and conditions that have been stated in the Term Sheet.

3.0 Documentation and Incidental Matters

3.1	**Definitive Documen-tation**	The parties shall enter into a Share Subscription and Shareholders' Agreement ("SSSHA") for the furtherance of the said Proposed Transaction and to inter alia incorporate the rights and obligations of the Investors and the other shareholders of the Company, within [90 (ninety)] days from the date of signing of this Term Sheet, which date may be mutually extended by the Parties. The SSSHA, the restated articles of association of the Company and any other documents incidental to the Proposed Transaction shall be collectively referred to as "Definitive Documentation".

After the Term Sheet has been negotiated and signed by the investors and the founders, the definitive documents (Shareholder's Agreement, Share Subscription Agreement, etc.) are drafted to make the deal final. The definitive documents are elaborate, detailed documents that state all the terms and conditions of the transaction with no ambiguity.

3.2	**Conditions Precedent to Closing**	1. A complete legal and financial due diligence of the Company to be completed to the satisfaction of the Investors. 2. Obtaining of all regulatory permissions, approvals or consents required in relation to the Investors' acquisition of the Equity Shares. 3. Execution of the Definitive Documentation in form and substance in accordance with the agreed terms as enshrined in this Term Sheet, together with any other agreements and documents that may be deemed necessary by the Parties. 4. Execution of an employment agreement between the Company and the Promoters in form and substance agreeable to the Investors. 5. Amendment of the Company's articles and memorandum of association and any existing shareholders agreement to permit the issuance of the Equity Shares and all associated rights of this Proposed Transaction and as provided for in the Definitive Documentation. 6. No material adverse change shall have occurred in the business, financial condition, results of operations, or prospects of the Company and its subsidiaries. 7. Any other conditions precedent that may be deemed necessary by the Investor(s) pursuant to the due diligence conducted on the Company or otherwise.

Conditions Precedent (CP) refer to the tasks that must be completed before the promised amount gets transferred or the deal documents are signed. This may include things such as approval from existing shareholders or regulatory approval on some pending non-compliance.

Some term sheets also have a clause on Conditions Subsequent (CS) to closing. They refer to the tasks that a startup must complete after receiving the funds and signing deal documents, such as informing relevant government authorities about the deal through necessary statutory filing, issuing share certificates, etc.

3.3	**Standstill Provisions**	During the period between the Effective Date and the date of execution of the Definitive Documentation / or the date of termination of this Term Sheet, whichever is earlier, the Company shall not, without the Investor's consent: a) enter into any commitment or transaction for acquisition of property, business or any other asset, or do anything which is not contemplated by this Term Sheet and which would have a material adverse effect on the business of the Company and the Proposed Transaction, save and except in the ordinary course of business; b) conduct the business of the Company otherwise than in the ordinary course; c) enter into any commitment, transaction, arrangement or agreement with related parties (as defined under the Companies Act, 2013); d) incur any substantial indebtedness; e) appoint or relieve from the services of the Company any senior employee; or f) make any change in the share capital of the Company.

This clause is another protective step that investors take in their interest. After a Term Sheet has been signed, it may take 2-3 months to conduct the due diligence processes and draft the Shareholder's Agreement. During this period, the startup cannot make any material change that may drastically impact or change the business.

3.4	Representations and Warranties	The Company represents to the Investors that the Proposed Transaction: (a) is in accordance with applicable law, including but not limited to, Indian foreign exchange regulations; and (b) shall not result in the Company violating any terms in respect of existing corporate or statutory approvals.

An important aspect of any contractual agreement is the right representation of data and information. You need to ensure that the startup is compliant with the rules and regulations of the law, the tax returns have been filed, and that every such detail is in its right place. **Even if there's a small conflict or non-compliance, inform the investor and prevent any unnecessary consequences.**

3.5	Statutory Approvals	The parties understand and agree that each party shall be responsible for obtaining the statutory approvals required for completion of their respective commitments of the Proposed Transaction described herein. The parties agree that they shall, where necessary, provide no objection letters and any other correspondence that may be necessary for the other party to obtain statutory approvals.

This clause follows the previous one and states that the startup should have all the necessary permissions and approvals to conduct business in the country.

3.6	Events of Default	The Definitive Documentation will set out customary events of default and consequences. The events of default shall include breach of any provisions of the Definitive Documentation by a party.

The definitive documents list the details of the events of default if there is a breach of provision and the consequences that will follow.

4.0 General

4.1	**Expenses**	All costs and expenses which constitute the basic and requisite transactional expenses in respect of the transaction contemplated herein (including consultancy/advisory fees, due diligence, stamp duty or other statutory charges) ("Basic Expenses") shall be borne by the Company. Any expense in addition to the Basic Expenses initiated by an Investor shall be borne by such Investor.

It has become an industry standard that the startup has to pay all the professional charges incurred in the process of raising funds, both on their and the investors' sides.

You can negotiate to put a cap on the lawyer's fees. Lawyers usually charge on an hourly basis, and without constraints, they may take longer to draft the agreements leading to higher costs.

4.2	**Confidentiality**	Each party hereto shall keep all information about the Proposed Transaction (including the terms of this Term Sheet and the discussions between the parties) confidential and shall not disclose the same to any third party without the prior written approval of the other parties. Standard exceptions to confidentiality obligations (including disclosure of information mandated under applicable law) shall apply. Any disclosure to a party's representatives, employees, agents or assigns shall be strictly on a need-to-know basis.

Investors include this clause of confidentiality to prevent the founders from Term Sheet shopping. So when you negotiate with other investors for a deal, you must be careful about the information you disclose. This clause is binding and the investors can take legal action if you disclose details about their offer externally.

4.3	**Exclusivity**	The Company and the Promoters agree that following [60 (sixty)] days from the execution of this Term Sheet, neither the Promoters nor the Company, either by themselves or through any other person, shall approach or participate in any discussions or negotiations or solicit, discuss and/or encourage any financing for the Company by any other person in any manner and will not provide any information relating to the Company to any other potential investor and will clearly indicate to such other potential investors that the Company and the Promoters are bound by this Clause 4.3.

This clause is another protective measure investors take to dissuade founders from negotiating deals with other investors. It states that the Term Sheet and the offer of investment are exclusive and the founder cannot discuss the details with any other potential investor.

4.4	**Termination**	This Term Sheet shall terminate [90 (ninety)] days from its execution unless mutually extended by the parties or mutually cancelled by the parties. It shall automatically stand terminated upon replacement by the Definitive Documentation.

A Term Sheet stands valid for a certain number of days, usually 90. Unless this duration is mutually extended by both the parties, the offer will stand cancelled after the period is over. The Term Sheet is automatically terminated and replaced by the Definitive Documents upon their signing.

4.5	Amendment	The parties may amend the terms of this Term Sheet by mutual consent in writing.

The Amendment clause is self-explanatory and states that the terms of the Term Sheet can be changed by getting mutual consent from the investors and the founders.

4.6	Governing Law and Jurisdiction	This Term Sheet shall be governed by the laws of India. Any disputes arising out of or in connection with the validity, interpretation or implementation of this Term Sheet or the Definitive Documentation shall be subject to the exclusive jurisdiction of the courts of [•].

The Term Sheet is governed by the laws of India.

A founder must ensure that the jurisdiction is set as the State in which the company is registered. If set in investor's State, then if things go wrong and you face a legal suit, you will have to spend additional time and money travelling to that location.

Classifying Term Sheet Clauses

Every founder should prepare to negotiate the clauses of the Term Sheet and place them in the startup's favour as much as possible. A thinking framework to proceed with this preparation is to divide the clauses into three categories as follows.

1. **Non-negotiable:** These are those clauses or terms that you consider non-negotiable. If these are not fulfilled, then you'll strongly consider backing out from the association.
2. **Negotiable:** These are those clauses that you will try and make more favourable for yourself but are ready to compromise to some extent. Having a priority order of the clauses more crit-

ical to you would help with better planning.

3. **Leverage:** Always have a set of clauses that you can use as leverage to negotiate for better terms elsewhere. These may be otherwise acceptable to you in their current form, but the investors may not be sure of that. So you can use this gap in knowledge to negotiate better terms on the non-negotiable and negotiable clauses.

BATNA and the Need for Multiple Investors

BATNA stands for Best Alternative To a Negotiated Agreement and refers to the bargaining power you gain when there are multiple investors interested in your startup. As the founder, it's likely that you are in discussions with multiple investors and it's possible that more than one ends up being interested to fund you. This is, of course, assuming that you stay within the professional constraints of confidentiality.

When you have multiple interested parties, it allows you to compare the offers made. When an offer is in hand, the BATNA is simply the best alternative to it, and it gives you more bargaining power to negotiate with either of these investors.

This was evident in the episodes of Shark Tank India. A founder was in a less powerful position when they would start a pitch because they were still seeking investment with no offers in hand. If at the end of the pitch two or more sharks became interested, the tables would turn. The sharks would now offer better deals just to grab the opportunity. The startup founders now had a choice to accept the best deal from the shark they preferred. In the show, BATNA for the founder was visible to everyone. Under regular circumstances, only the founders are aware of it.

However, you must always stay within the confines of professionalism and not go overboard with Term Sheet shopping. The investor community is tight-knit and knowledge about your negotiations with multiple investors may spread quickly. You should also take care to not disclose the details of any Term Sheet. The confidentiality clause of the Term Sheet is binding and you may get into legal trouble.

Lead Investors & Syndicates

Fundraising rounds usually involve multiple investors. In fact, in some cases, many angel investors under an angel syndicate agree to fund a startup they find promising. Getting signatures of every such individual can be a tedious process and lead to unnecessary delays. To avoid this, one person representing the Syndicate signs on behalf of all such investors. These investors give consent to be represented by this individual and it reduces the friction in the process.

Also, when multiple investors and VCs are involved, the fundraising round is led by one lead investor putting in the maximum amount, in most cases. This investor, usually a well-known VC, leads the efforts on behalf of all investors to execute and conclude the fundraising. Lawyers, negotiations, due diligence, and all the other tasks that accompany fundraising are usually undertaken by this investor. Founders usually interact with them for matters directly pertaining to the process. This, again, helps make the process efficient.

16. Fundraising Paperwork & Compliance

This chapter covers the paperwork and compliances needed outside the Term Sheet to complete the fundraising process. Let's go through them one by one.

What is the purpose of Memorandum & Articles of Association?

Memorandum of Association (MOA) and Articles of Association (AOA) are the two charter documents which define the terms based on which a company will be managed and business will be conducted.

The MOA contains clauses on the name of the company, its state of registration, main and other objectives, its capital, etc. It details out all the basic information of the company.

The AOA defines the rules & regulations and the rights and obligations that govern different functions of the company.

- Board of Directors - meetings they need to attend, decision-making powers, who gets appointed as the Chairman and the powers they have, and similar details are listed out for people holding a board seat.

- Shareholders - meetings they need to attend, decision-making powers, voting rights across different categories of shareholders (equity, preference, and any other) and similar details are listed out for shareholders.
- Borrowings - who can borrow, when, who from, approvals needed, limits, etc. are clearly elaborated.
- Rights and powers of persons holding different positions in the company are mentioned.
- Rights & restrictions on the transfer of shares are elaborated

Similar details are furnished for different positions and activities in the company.

It is mandatory for the clauses of the Shareholders' Agreement (SHA) to be incorporated in and made part of the AOA.

What are Definitive Agreements - SSHA, SSA, SHA, SPA

Who is the owner of a company? Instinctively, it's the founders that come to mind first. As correct as that is, the founders become partial owners after an investment round. When investors put in money and obtain shares of the company, they become shareholders which basically gives them partial ownership. Later, when employees exercise their ESOPs and convert them to shares, they also become shareholders of the company.

The Shareholder's Agreement (SHA) formally represents the understanding between all the shareholders of the company. It details the rights of the different shareholders, their decision-making powers, the dividends they may receive, and other details pertaining to sale and purchase of shares. In every subsequent fundraising round, the SHA needs to be modified to accommodate the new investors and update any terms necessary.

There are 3 types of definitive agreements one must be aware of:

1. Share Purchase Agreement (SPA)
2. Share Subscription Agreement (SSA)
3. Shareholder's Agreement (SHA)

Share Purchase Agreement (SPA)

Whenever an individual or organization purchases the existing shares of the company from the founders or a shareholder, a Share Purchase Agreement needs to be drafted. The main scenarios when an SPA comes into the picture are:

1. When a VC firm purchases the shares of angels or other existing investors
2. At the time of acquisition of the startup by a bigger entity

This agreement comprises the details of the share purchase transaction between the buyer and the seller. The Share Purchase Agreement acts as the official record of all such transactions.

Share Subscription Agreement (SSA)

The Share Subscription Agreement (SSA) is drafted to document the transaction details of any particular investment. It officially assigns a valuation to the company and consequently, the subscription price for the investor and the ownership stake in the company. It also mentions the number and type of shares they receive, the dates on which the investment payments are made, and all other terms that define the investment.

Shareholder's Agreement (SHA)

The Shareholder's Agreement (SHA) lays down the terms and conditions for all the shareholders of a company to ensure that the overall interests of the company do not get compromised. It consists of the terms of engagement between the shareholders, their rights and controlling powers, their dividend payments, etc.

Usually, a Shareholder's Agreement is valid only when it has been signed by every shareholder of the company. But if multiple angel investors from a syndicate have invested, then they usually select a syndicate lead to sign on everyone's behalf.

> Using a Roll Up Vehicle (RUV) while Raising an Angel Round
> Some problems with raising an Angel Round with a lot of individual investors are chasing them for signatures, asking them to wire funds committed, and of course, having so many people on your cap table as shareholders. AngelList India has a feature called Roll Up Vehicle (RUV) through which the process is automated, the entire amount collected by AngelList on its platform by doing all investors' KYC, setting up a separate entity, and then wiring the amount into your company as a single cheque and single entry on your cap table. It's basically a different name for a Special Purpose Vehicle (SPV). AngelList charges 2% of the amount invested from each of the investors for carrying out this activity and no carry (share of profits from their investment in the startup if it scales).

During the early stages of a startup, in the first or second round of investments, the SSA and the SHA are combined into one and called the **Share Subscription and Shareholder's Agreement (SSHA)**.

When there has been no investment in a startup, the founders are the only shareholders. Hence, **a shareholder agreement drafted between the co-founders is basically the Co-founders' Agreement (CFA)**. This document is signed by the co-founders and includes the clauses on:

1. Ownership in Equity
2. Decision Making and Board Seat
3. Roles & Responsibilities
4. Ownership of Intellectual Property
5. Dilution in case of future fund-raise
6. Exit clauses
7. Vesting of shares
8. Dispute resolution
9. Non-compete

10. Restrictions on transfer of shares
11. Remuneration

You can refer to Annexure 16.1 for a sample Co-founders' Agreement.

Steps to Create an SHA

1. The founders and the investors agree on the valuation of the start-up which is mentioned in the term sheet. The founders now need Valuation Certificates for the same.

   There are three different laws under which the valuation certificates may be required:

   i) The Income Tax Act, 1961

   Under this act, a valuation certificate is required from a merchant banker.

   However, if your startup has been registered on the Startup India website and filled a declaration in For 2, then you are exempted from taking this certificate.

   ii) The Companies Act, 2013

   Under this act, a valuation certificate is required from a Registered Valuer.

   iii) The Foreign Exchange Management Act

   When a foreign investor wants to invest in your startup, you have to take a valuation certificate either from a Registered Valuer or a Chartered Accountant.

   You will also have to file the form FC-GPR with the RBI if you do end up raising from a foreign investor.

2. Now that the valuation has been defined, the next step is to define the number and category of shares that will be allotted to the incoming investors of the startup.
3. Next, the Memorandum of Association is amended to change the value of authorized capital and account for the new shares that will be allotted to the investors. To bring this change into effect,

the startup has to hold a board meeting to pass a board resolution for the amendment. Then an extraordinary general meeting is held and a shareholder's resolution is passed. These resolutions are simply approvals of the amendments made in the MOA.

4. The resolutions are filed with the Registrar of Companies (ROC) on the website of the Ministry of Corporate Affairs (MCA) in two different forms. A copy of the resolution and the modified MOA is filed in form MGT-14, whereas the details on the increase in the authorized capital are filed in form SH7.
5. The term sheet can now be converted to a shareholder's agreement. Depending on the complexity of the terms, the skill of the lawyer, their time commitment, etc., lawyers can take 2-3 weeks to prepare the agreement. In case your investor is a veteran of the field, they may have templates ready. Then this process takes even lesser time and may complete in a single week itself.
6. Another round of negotiations takes place on the terms of the freshly-drafted shareholder's agreement. Representatives (lawyers, CAs, etc.) of both parties discuss the elaborated details and finalise the agreement.
7. Again, the founders hold a board meeting and an extraordinary general meeting of all the shareholders to pass a resolution that approves the finalized agreements.
8. After the approval, the terms of the SHA are incorporated into the Articles of Association. Another round of meetings is held to approve the amendments to the AOA.
9. After getting all the approvals, the copies of the resolutions and a copy of the amended AOA is filed in form MGT-14 on the website of the Ministry of Corporate Affairs.
10. You now need to open a separate bank account. The investment will be sent into this account by your investors. However, the startup cannot put the money to use until the allotment of shares is complete.
11. The allotment of shares is carried out in a board meeting by the

Board of Directors.

12. Once the startup has allotted shares to its investors, it files a form PAS3 with the Ministry of Corporate Affairs.
13. The Ministry of Corporate Affairs will now send written approval to the PAS3 form and the last filed MGT-14 form. Now you can transfer the funds to your primary bank account and start using them.
14. Issue share certificates to all your investors.
15. Finally, get share certificates stamped from the local stamp duty office.

Who should make the Definitive Agreements?

As a founder, if you're tasked with getting all the definitive agreements prepared, the knee-jerk response would probably be that of reluctance. "Why add another chore to this already laborious list?" If a marquee investor is involved in the fundraising process, chances are they would get the drafts prepared by their lawyers and send across for your thorough study. If only smaller investors are involved, you may be asked to get it done entirely. While it may appear onerous, and it often is, getting these agreements prepared yourself has advantages that may outweigh the costs.

When you have to prepare them yourself, you obviously need a lawyer who specializes in drafting such agreements. This involves additional costs for you, but it also gives you the control to draft the terms at your convenience first. You can then anchor the agreement to your needs, and negotiations, if any, must be initiated by the other party. Although theoretically, it doesn't signify any change whether the investor prepares the draft or you, but psychologically, it's always better to set the terms and defend them than fight against the tide to effect changes.

If the VCs insist on getting the drafts prepared, you must first negotiate for a cap on the lawyer fees to ensure it doesn't burn your pocket. Secondly, you must still hire a legal consultant, a specialist with startups and fundraising, to study the terms and negotiate on your behalf. Despite the best of your efforts individually, you'll probably not see things from the perspective of an expert. They can help identify loopholes you miss, protect you from possible pitfalls built into the Term Sheet, and possibly negotiate better terms. Hiring one would obviously involve an extra cost, but it may save you significantly more in the long run.

In 2021, I had a client who was raising a small amount through a convertible note from an incubator fund. They had been admitted as a part of a cohort and every startup had been offered similar terms on the funding amount, valuation cap, and other control clauses. They had prepared the definitive agreements and my job was to vet the entire document.

At first, I was baffled by the enormity of the document. For a meagre amount in the first round, I had expected to see a 20-25 page doc at best, but they had prepared a painfully detailed 100-page epic, which was more suited to a Series B stage fundraise and beyond. Secondly, there were a number of clauses that I found unnecessary and the incubator's lawyer agreed to eliminate or modify them. But he put his foot down on others and refused to change them because all startups in the cohort had been offered the same terms and they couldn't make exceptions for one. These were edge cases which potentially allowed the incubator to take full control of the company, and I found them unwarranted at such an early stage.

My job then was to educate the founder on the possibilities, and allow them to decide if they still wanted to proceed with the terms. Another thing we did was inquire from startups who had participated in previous such cohorts and check how they were treated. They agreed that those terms were built into their agreements too but were never triggered, and the feedback was positive overall. The decision then came down to the trust these founders had in the incubator and also the necessity of the amount and benefits this incubator would offer. Either way, my involvement helped them take a decision from a position of awareness and not ignorance.

Had the agreements been made by us at the first place, the ball would have been in their court to initiate changes and manage negotiations. So when taking a decision to hire your own lawyer, check the cost trade-offs on both immediate and long-term basis. A VC doing it by themselves may be cheaper, but still, ensure that the terms are corroborated by an experienced professional before signing.

Conditions Precedent (CP) and Conditions Subsequent (CS)

Conditions Precedent (CP) refers to the items that need to be completed by the startup before the Term Sheet gets signed. The Clause 3.2 of the Term Sheet shared in the previous chapter lists 7 requirements that need to be fulfilled by the startup before the document can become valid.

Similar to CP, there would be conditions that can't possibly be completed before the Term Sheet gets signed, but would still need to be fulfilled at some stage to finally enable the investors to lawfully transfer the promised amount. These are known as Conditions Subsequent (CS). There would be certain compliances, for example, that may be needed to be completed within, say, 60 days of the Term Sheet signing. The nature of such compliances may be sequential and couldn't possibly be done before the signing, so putting those as part of CS makes the founders obligated to fulfill those in a certain timeframe.

There may be some conditions mentioned under CP which may potentially create bottlenecks in the progress. Founders can negotiate and move such items from CP to CS to ensure faster movement. Most conditions otherwise can only be put under either CP or CS given their requirements.

Most conditions otherwise can only be put under either CP or CS given their requirements.

Transactions Costs of a Fundraising Round

The cost involved in drafting a Shareholder's Agreement varies based on the funding round, size of the investment, investment instrument, etc.

When a startup raises money in the form of a convertible note, the professional charges and lawyer's fees may amount to at most Rs. 50,000.

If an investment of Rs. 2-3 crores occur in a valued round in the form of CCPS or CCDs, the total cost may approximately amount to Rs. 2-3 lakhs.

When a marquee VC comes on board, a "standard" term of the Term Sheet requires the startup to bear the legal fees for the VC's lawyer as well as their lawyer. As discussed in the last chapter, it would be better if you could negotiate a cap on this fees to keep this expense under control.

As a thumb rule, you can expect the total cost of the fundraising process to be around 3-4% of the transaction size, especially if there's an investment banker involved too.

Steps to Complete a Funding Round

These are the steps I refer to for closing funding rounds with my clients. You can use them to keep track of your progress and pending items.

Step. No.	Particulars
1	Send notice to convene Board Meeting
2	Convene Board Meeting for meeting • Appt of Merchant Banker & Registered Valuer for Valuation Report
3	Draft & Execute Term Sheet
4	Send notice to convene Board Meeting

Step. No.	Particulars
5	Convene Board Meeting for the following: • Consider the valuation report as received. • Fix day, date, venue and time of extraordinary general meeting • Deciding the list of allottees (not exceeding more than 50 at a time and 200 aggregate in the financial year excluding the qualified institutional buyer) • Finalisation of draft PAS-4 • Finalisation of notice for extraordinary general meeting along with the explanatory statement as required in the law. • Decide the offer period • Increase/Re-classification in Authorised Capital of the company subject to the approval of shareholders.
6	Draft & Execute Share Subscription & Shareholder Agreement
7	Open a separate bank account in a scheduled bank to receive money.
8	Convene extraordinary general meeting
9	File MGT-14 and then the private placement offer letter i.e. PAS-4 cum application shall be dispatched to the proposed allottees with the following attachments: • Certified true copy of the Special resolution • Explanatory statement
10	Dispatch private placement offer letter cum application to the proposed allottees within thirty days, either in writing or in electronic mode.
11	Proposed Allottees shall subscribe to the shares in the private placement offer letter cum application along with the subscription money paid either by cheque or demand draft or other banking channel and not by cash.
12	The money as received shall be deposited in a separate bank account as opened in accordance with point no. 2
13	Convene Board Meeting for • the allotment of shares within 60 days of receipt of money. • Restatement of Amended AOA as per SHA • Fix day, date, venue and time of extraordinary general meeting • Finalisation of notice for extraordinary general meeting along with the explanatory statement as required in the law.

Step. No.	Particulars
14	File PAS-3 within fifteen days of allotment of shares with the following attachments: • List of allottees • Certified true copy of the special resolution along with explanatory statement • Valuation Report • Copy of contract in case the shares are being issued for consideration other cash. • Complete record of private placement offers and acceptances in Form PAS-5
15	Issuance of share certificates to the allottees within 2 months of allotment
16	Payment of stamp duty on issuance of share certificates as per the prevailing relevant state law.
17	Updation of Statutory Registers
18	Convene extraordinary general meeting
19	File MGT-14 with the following attachments: • Amended AOA • Certified true copy of the special resolution • Explanatory statement

RBI & Income Tax Implications

We touched upon these pointers in the first point under the section 'Steps to Create an SHA' in this chapter. Basically, if you raise funds from an investor based outside India, you are required to mandatorily obtain a valuation certificate from a CA, even if it's an unvalued round. You also need to file Form FC-GPR with the RBI.

If you're a startup registered with the Startup India website and have filed a declaration in Form 2 on the Income Tax website, then you're not required to get a merchant banker's certificate of valuation after fundraising.

However, if you're operating as a regular business and are not registered on Startup India, you'll be mandatorily required to get a merchant banker's certificate of valuation if there's any transfer of shares between people or entities.

17. Due Diligence

Securing a term sheet or any confirmation from an investor is, at best, a principle agreement to put money in. It finally goes through only after investors thoroughly study the company and corroborate the claims made by the founders while pitching. This process is also known as *due diligence.* It is necessary for all types of investing activities at the organizational level - startup funding, private equity investments, mergers & acquisitions, strategic investments, and IPOs.

In this chapter, let's understand the different types of due diligence investors do before actually transferring the amount promised, and how founders can make the entire process efficient.

Types of Due Diligence - Financial (FDD), Legal (LDD), Technical (TDD)

Today, there are three types of due diligence undertaken by all investors regardless of the nature of the business - financial, legal, and technical. There can be more if the situation or the business necessitates, which we have discussed later, but these three are permanent features. Let's understand each of them briefly.

Financial Due Diligence (FDD)

All matters pertaining to commercial and financial aspects of the business are done under FDD. The goal is to verify the numbers claimed by founders in their discussions and pitch deck, and check if there are any that don't fully satisfy their claims.

For example, in many startups that sell products online, Revenue and Sales are used interchangeably. Normally, investors would consider Revenue as the money that actually hits the startup's account when the sale is made. In many cases, the amount would be the same as the value of Sales done. But when sold through a third-party platform, like any e-commerce website, there may be some immediate transactional costs that get deducted in the amount that the startup receives. If this value is significantly lower than what has been claimed as 'Revenue', then it may get called out.

Sometimes, the quality of revenue generated is also analyzed. Revenue through sales done on own website is viewed more favourably by investors compared to those generated from a third-party platform like Amazon. It indicates a higher control of the business and low vulnerability to any tactical ploys by Amazon.

Similarly, revenue obtained after offering heavy discounts or by incurring high marketing spend ranks lower than the revenue obtained through organic word-of-mouth publicity. It signifies the merit of your product to sell on its own and denotes novelty and quality.

The values claimed as DAU and MAU are subject to a similar rigour if those are crucial for your business. Basically, all the metrics critical to the health of your startup and which contributed to the valuation offered would be studied thoroughly.

The FDD checklist has been added as Annexure 17.1 for your

reference.

Legal Due Diligence (LDD)

LDD mainly pertains to the legal and compliance-related aspects of the business. It is done to ensure that all the government-mandated requirements for your company are in place. It also checks whether the necessary agreements pertaining to vendors, customers, employees, or any contractors have been done appropriately.

The LDD checklist has been added as Annexure 17.2 for your reference.

Technical Due Diligence (TDD)

TDD is where investors analyze and assess all the technology-related aspects of the business. The technical infrastructure is studied to ensure there are no gaps in security or capability to execute at scale. The codebase is inspected for its effectiveness in delivering a smooth user experience[1].

The priority areas of this process vary by stage[2]. At the seed stage, the due diligence checks mainly for the ability to release a competent product and its ability to handle moderate scale. In Series A, B, and C, the ability to develop and grow the product rapidly is assessed. At Series C, D, and beyond, when the product is in a more matured state, its ability to expand and handle heavy volumes is checked. At all stages, the security and data privacy aspects are also inspected for any possible gaps.

Managing the Due Diligence Process - best practices

The due diligence process often takes time and delays the arrival of money in the account. Founders must do everything on their part to ensure easy compliance and quicker execution. Some of the best practices I advise startups to adopt have been listed below.

- Keep two pre-scheduled meetings daily - at the start and the end of the business day - with internal stakeholders responsible to share information with investors or auditors. If not done, DD will never be concluded fast as it's not a core business activity.

- Build a comprehensive data room on Google Drive or OneDrive for easy access to data.
- Don't provide editing rights of the data room to more than 1 or 2 persons. It helps maintain the clarity and sanctity of data.
- Keep a checklist and share it among all stakeholders to keep track and visibility of the progress.
- Completion status of DD-related activities should be colour coded such that the pending activities or blockers never miss attention.

Due Diligence Checklist

All types of due diligence have separate items that need to be checked off to conclude them. Broadly, the template may look like what I've shared here in the given table. It's taken from the FDD checklist I use.

S.No.	Information Request List	Target Date	Owner	Remarks
A	GENERAL INFORMATION			
1	Business Presentation	1/9/22	CFO	
2	Description of the following			
	a. Description / details on the following (if not covered in as much detail as part of Business Presentation mentioned above):	3/9/22	CEO	
	b. Revenue Streams (past, current and future revenue streams, include description of all revenue streams to be captured)	5/9/22	COO	
	c. Areas of Focus – Target Customer types (include segmentation undertaken based on size, needs or other criteria)	7/9/22	CEO	

The left-most column is self-explanatory. The second column mentions a due diligence deliverable for the company. Target Date is when you aim to get this completed. Owner refers to the internal stakeholder responsible for preparing and providing that deliverable.

The different colours under the Target Date column can signify the completion status.

I have shared the entire checklist for FDD and LDD in Annexures 17.1 and 17.2 respectively. They will give you an idea about what's needed to conclude these two types of due diligence. If you have obtained or are close to obtaining a term sheet, you can refer to them and commence relevant activities quickly to avoid delay.

Other areas of Due Diligence

Apart from FDD, LDD, and TDD, there may be other types of due diligence needed depending on the nature and maturity of a company. Typically, the larger and more complex the company, the more elaborate the due diligence. Some of the different types of due diligence are given below:

- **Data & Privacy**: The social media giants are often under fire for allegedly not having adequate data and privacy measures for their users. For companies that hold sensitive customer information, e.g. Fintech startups, this could be separate due diligence altogether to ensure the robustness of their processes.
- **User:** Elon Musk, in July 2022, backed out of his $44 Bn deal to acquire Twitter primarily on the grounds that the social media giant had a much higher portion of 'fake users'. While the claims are not yet substantiated publicly as of writing and Twitter denies the numbers quoted by Musk, a high fake user proportion reduces the capability of the company to generate revenues since the number of people actually using the product is low. Companies that rely heavily on their user base to generate revenues and command valuation may be subjected to separate due diligence for this.
- **Environment, Social, and Governance (ESG)**: Some large, listed companies also do ESG reporting as a part of their

policy to ensure better governance and promote sustainable practices. When these organizations acquire smaller companies, they do an ESG due diligence to identify any gaps with their standards. Certain investors may also choose to do something similar for the startups they invest in.

Similarly, there can be other due diligence practices undertaken depending on the preference of the investor or the necessity of the business.

What happens if the DD goes bad?

In 2022, we saw a few high-profile cases of alleged startup frauds and illegal practices being played out in the media. Elizabeth Holmes, founder of now-defunct healthtech company Theranos, was found guilty of defrauding investors with faulty and exaggerated claims of the ability of their devices[3]. In May 2022, Ankiti Bose, founder of Zilingo, was ousted from the company on grounds of financial irregularities.

Theranos and Zilingo are the worst-case outcomes of due diligence gone bad. Often, frauds are well-guarded for a period by their shrewd operators and when they do come to light, they have acquired gigantic proportions by then. Theranos was such an example, and Zilingo to a possibly lesser extent.

The objective of due diligence is basically to verify the claims made by founders about the business performance and to check if all compliances are in place. As long as there's nothing obviously astray, startups get through the process unscathed, especially the early-stage ones when investors tend to be more lenient on account of limited data.

However, on the founders' part, they must always strive to be honest and transparent with their business's performance and not hope for certain things to stay undiscovered. If there indeed are things that need hiding, they need to be sorted before approaching investors or should be called out upfront. When they do get discovered, it leads to broken trust and a bad name. Antics to drive up valuation or secure funding never work in the larger scheme of things.

When the claimed performance metrics don't match the actuals in due diligence, it can lead to either a revised valuation or even withdrawal of the investor from the deal. Valuation is given on the basis of the numbers claimed, and if they are found to be adrift, then the valuation needs revision. In cases where the difference is more serious and deliberate, it indicates disregard and dishonesty on the founders' part, and investors could withdraw from the deal. Remember that a signed term sheet won't get you the money and the promised valuation if the numbers claimed are inaccurate.

18. Compliance Basics that a Founder Must Know

This chapter covers the basic compliance needs that every founder must be aware of. I've seen many founders discover about certain compliance needs only when they get a notice from a government authority. This helps you be prepared better and avoid any unnecessary troubles.

Goods & Services Tax (GST)

The Goods and Service Tax is typically divided into the Central GST (CGST), State GST (SGST), and Integrated GST (IGST). When you make a sale within the state, you will split the 18% of GST into the CGST and SGST at 9% each. For an interstate sale, when you sell outside the state, the total GST amount of 18% is added in the IGST column.

There are certain exceptions to the rules though. Your accountant will help you figure out the GST you need to pay.

Details of a GST invoice

The GST that you collect from a customer during a month needs to be deposited by the 20th of the subsequent month to the GST department in an online return called the GSTR 3B.

The GST invoice has the words "Tax Invoice" as the heading and mentions the details, among others, on:

1. Name of the company
2. Registered Address
3. Contact details (Phone Number, Email, Website)
4. Invoice Number
5. Invoice Date
6. Receiver's Name
7. Receiver's Address
8. Receiver's GST number
9. Description of Goods or Services
10. HSN or SAC Code of the goods or services
11. Your signature
12. GST Rate (as per CGST, SGST or IGST)
13. Amount

HSN stands for Harmonized System of Nomenclature and applies to goods. SAC stands for Service Accounting Code and applies to services. These are codes that define a certain good or service and are used for identification purposes.

Must-dos after getting GST registration

Getting a GST registration is great, but not enough. There are compliances to be done to avoid paying a heavy penalty to the government at any time.

1. It is mandatory to have a board on the main gate of your registered office that displays the name of your company and its GST number.

2. It is mandatory to display the GST registration certificate at a prominent location within your office premises.
3. The Aadhaar profile of the signatories mentioned on the GST certificate should be linked to the GST portal.
4. You may register your company with your home address, considering it permanent. When you open an office in a co-working space or an independent location, you need to get this place incorporated as an additional place of business on the GST certificate.
5. You can open multiple offices in the same state as long as all those offices are listed as additional places of business on the GST registration certificate.

If you open an office in a different state, you will require another GST number and will have to file separately for that state. This happens because GST is both a state and a central subject.

Tax Deduction at Source (TDS)

If you have been working as an employee, you must be used to the tax deducted from your salary by your employers. When one starts the entrepreneurial journey and becomes a business owner, it becomes their responsibility to deduct taxes for different people in different instances and pay them to the government.

TDS for salary

Tax deducted on salaries paid to the business's employees falls under Section 192 of the Income Tax Act. An employer has to take the following steps to ensure tax deduction from the salary of their employees:

1. Estimate the annual salary of the employee, depending on whether they continue to work with you.
2. Take a declaration from the employee on their tax-savings investments of the year.

3. With the help of your accounting team, calculate the tax liability of the employee for the year based on their slab rate.
4. Divide the annual tax liability by 12 and deduct the resultant amount from your employee's salary each month.

Usually, companies ask their employees for information on their tax-saving investments in April. Then they will ask for all the proofs sometime in January of next year. If there is a mismatch between the two, there will be a different tax liability when then needs to be paid by the employee.

As an example, suppose your annual salary is 15 Lakhs per annum (LPA). At the beginning of the financial year, you claimed that through the year, you'd invest or spend on different things which would essentially bring down your taxable income to 12LPA. For a 12LPA taxable income, following the old tax slab, the total annual tax liability comes out to be Rs. 1,72,500. (Old income tax slab based on annual taxable income: 5% for 2.5L-5L; 20% for 5L-10L; 30% for >10L)

But in January, when you were asked to submit the proofs of your expenditures and investments which contribute to the reduction in taxable income, it was found that the actual tax saving investments were less and the taxable income would actually be 13L. That would mean an extra Rs. 30K would be paid in taxes from what was calculated initially. So for the months of January, February and March, an extra 10K is deducted by the company from the in-hand salary that was being paid originally to comply with the tax requirements.

The TDS return for salary is filed in Form 24Q.

TDS for Payments other than Salary

This form of TDS is deducted from payments made to vendors. Vendors can be divided into two categories: professional services and contracted manpower.

Accounting, tech, legal, etc. services fall under the umbrella of professional services. The section of TDS that applies in this scenario is section 194 (J or C) of the Income Tax Act.

The TDS rate is 10% for professional services. Assume that your CA gives you an invoice of Rs. 1 lakh for their services and charges 18% GST on it. The total bill would amount to Rs. 1.18 lakhs. You will, however, deduct TDS on the base value of Rs. 1 lakh only. Essentially you pay the CA Rs. 1.08 lakhs and deposit Rs. 10,000 as TDS to the government.

Contracted manpower usually refers to part-time or contracted employees. As an example, if you pay an agency to fumigate your office premises, the cost would not count as a professional expense but an expense under contracted manpower. Assume that the cost for the fumigation turned out to be Rs. 1.18 lakhs inclusive of a GST of 18%. When an individual performs any such service, the TDS rate is 1%, whereas, for every other entity like a partnership, company, etc., the TDS rate is 2%. Considering that the fumigation services were performed by a company, you will essentially pay them Rs. 1.16 lakhs and deposit Rs. 2000 as TDS to the government.

The TDS return for payments other than salary is filed in Form 26Q.

TCS (Tax Collection at Source)

TCS usually applies to e-commerce businesses or companies that make large purchases like the purchase of scrap, raw materials, etc. It is usually filed in a separate return.

TDS on payments to foreign vendors

TDS deducted on payments made to foreign vendors have to be filed in a separate return.

Timeline of TDS filing

TDS returns are filed four times a year, i.e. every quarter.

Quarter	Last date of TDS filing
April - June	31st July
July - September	31st October
October - December	31st January
January - March	31st May

Details of a TDS return

The TDS return mentions the details, among others, on:

1. The name of the vendor
2. The date they provided the service on
3. Invoice Date
4. Amount of Payment made
5. Amount of TDS Deducted
6. Percentage of TDS Deducted
7. PAN Number of the vendor

Companies often deposit cumulative challans for the TDS deducted for vendors. You must ensure that you state the PAN of the vendors correctly so that the government knows who to give credit to for the tax that you have deducted.

It is the business's responsibility to deposit the TDS with the government by the 7th of the subsequent month on the website of the Income Tax Department.

Acknowledgements

None of the thoughts in this book are my own. It is a compilation of my learnings coupled with my experience of using these concepts in my work as a CFO and Advisor with startups.

This book is dedicated to all the brilliant first-principle thinkers who have unknowingly contributed to this book - Sean Ellis, Brad Feld, Alejandro Cremades, Andrew Chen, Jim Collins, Shane Parrish, Rizvan Virk, Kunal Shah, Avnish Bajaj, and all my teachers that I've been fortunate enough to learn from. I'm merely standing on the shoulders of giants.

Speaking of Giants and Gods, no amount of gratitude to my parents would be enough - for their blessings, for their values, the upbringing, the education, the resources, for inculcating in me the thirst for learning and reading, for guiding me in my career, in my personal life - for absolutely everything and beyond, right next to God Almighty. It is their good karma the benefit of which God has bestowed on me by making me an instrument for any work that I call my own.

I'm grateful to my wife, Aditi, for being my partner in crime and virtue alike. She has been a patient sounding board and a hard critic for quality. Like with everything else in life, she deftly handled the things I'm terrible at and ensured I maintained a balance between facts and art. She also gets all the credit for branding my internet persona. Whatever little people know of me through social media, she's the brain behind it.

My sister, Kashika, helps me execute the concepts presented in the book with clients I work with. She generously does the dirty groundwork while I lead the more comfortable office meetings. Many of the insights I developed were largely a consequence of the heavy lifting done by her. She doesn't always get the credit she deserves, but this won't be one of those occasions.

Thanks to the folks at Wyzr - Yashraj, Amlan, and Ankita- for agreeing to take up this ambitious project. They brainstormed for hours with me on the content and structure, painstakingly wrote parts of the book, strung together all my disparate thoughts into this work of toil, and edited it well enough to compete with the best books in this area. This would not have been possible without them, not one bit.

Finally, thanks to my ever-curious audience on social media for constantly pushing me to learn more, and to you, the reader, for showing faith in me by picking this book up.

Annexure

6. Setting Yourself Up - Co-founders & Advisors

6.1 FAST Agreement (Founder Advisor Standard Template) - https://fi.co/fast

13. Reaching out to Investors

13.1 Angel networks, VC firms, Accelerators, and Incubators active in India (non-exhaustive, indicative list)

1. Angel Networks in India
2. Ah! Ventures: https://www.ahventures.in/
3. AngelList: https://www.angellist.com/
4. Bengaluru Angels: http://www.thebengaluruangels.com/
5. BITS Spark: https://bitsspark.org/
6. Calcutta Angels Network: https://www.linkedin.com/company/calcutta-angelsnetwork/about/
7. Chandigarh Angels: https://chandigarhangelsnetwork.com/
8. Chennai Angels: https://www.thechennaiangels.com/
9. CIO Angel Network (CAN): http://www.cioangelnetwork.com/
10. Delhi Angels: https://delhiangels.org/
11. Encubay: https://www.encubay.com/
12. Excubator: https://excubator.org/#/home
13. Faad Network Private Limited: https://www.faad.in/

14. Harvard Angels: https://www.hbsangels.com/
15. Hyderabad Angels: https://hyderabadangels.in/
16. Indian Angel Network: https://www.indianangelnetwork.com/
17. JITO Angel Network: https://www.jitojiif.com/jito-angel-network/index.html
18. Lead Angels Network: https://www.leadangels.in/
19. LetsVenture: https://letsventure.com/
20. Mumbai Angels Network: https://www.mumbaiangels.com/
21. Nativelead: https://nativelead.org/
22. Seeders: https://www.seeders.in/
23. Stanford Angels: http://stanfordangels.co.in/
24. Startup Angels Network: https://startupangelsnetwork.com/
25. Venture Catalysts: https://venturecatalysts.in/
26. We Founder Circle: https://www.wefoundercircle.com/
27. Z Nation Lab: https://znationlab.com/

Venture Capital firms in India

1. 100X.VC: https://www.100x.vc/
2. 2am VC: https://www.2amvc.com/
3. 3one4 Capital: https://www.3one4capital.com/
4. Aarin Capital: https://aarincapital.com/
5. Aavishkaar Capital: https://aavishkaarcapital.in/
6. Accel Partners: http://www.accel.com/
7. Alpha Wave Global: https://www.alphawaveglobal.com/
8. Ankur Capital Fund: https://www.ankurcapital.com/
9. Antler: https://www.antler.co/
10. Ascent Capital: https://ascentcapital.in/
11. Axilor Ventures: https://www.axilor.com/
12. Axon Partners Group: https://www.axonpartnersgroup.com/
13. Basil Partners: https://basilpartners.com/
14. Battery Ventures: https://www.battery.com/

15. Bertelsmann India Investments (BII): https://www.biifund.com/
16. Bessemer Venture Partners: https://www.bvp.com/india-home
17. Blume Ventures: https://blume.vc/
18. Canaan Partners: https://www.canaan.com/
19. Catamaran Ventures: http://www.catamaranventures.com/
20. Chiraetae Ventures (previously IDG Ventures India): https://www.chiratae.com/
21. Dholakia Ventures: https://www.dholakiaventures.com/
22. DSG Consumer Partners: https://dsgcp.com/
23. Eight Roads Ventures: https://eightroads.com/en/
24. Elevation Capital (previously SAIF Partners): https://elevationcapital.com/
25. Fidelity Growth Partners India: https://india.fidelity.com/
26. Forum Synergies: http://forumsynergies.com/
27. General Atlantic: https://www.generalatlantic.com/
28. GrowX Ventures: http://www.growxventures.com/
29. Helion Ventures Partners: http://www.helionvc.com/
30. Ideaspring Capital: https://ideaspringcap.com/
31. Incubate Fund India: https://www.incubatefund.in/about-us/
32. India Quotient: https://www.indiaquotient.in/
33. Inflection Point Ventures: http://www.inflectpoint.com/
34. Inflexor Ventures: https://www.inflexor.vc/
35. Infuse Ventures: http://www.infuseventures.in/#
36. Intel Capital: https://www.intelcapital.com/
37. Inventus Capital Partners: https://www.inventuscap.com/
38. IvyCap Ventures: https://ivycapventures.com/
39. Jungle Ventures: https://www.jungle.vc/
40. Kae Capital: https://kae-capital.com/
41. Kalaari Capital: https://www.kalaari.com/?tp=1
42. Khosla Ventures: https://www.khoslaventures.com/
43. Kisho Capital: https://kishocapital.com/

44. Lightbox: https://lightbox.vc/
45. Lightspeed Venture Partners: https://lsvp.com/
46. Lok Capital: https://www.lokcapital.com/
47. Magic Fund: https://www.magic.fund/
48. Mahindra Partners: https://www.mahindrapartners.com/
49. Matrix Partners: https://www.matrixpartners.in/
50. Mayfield Fund: https://www.mayfield.com/
51. Naspers: https://www.naspers.com/
52. New Enterprise Associates: https://www.nea.com/
53. Nexus Venture Partners: https://nexusvp.com/
54. Nirvana Venture Advisors: http://www.nirvanaventures.in/
55. Norwest Venture Partners: https://www.nvp.com/
56. Omidyar Network India: https://www.omidyarnetwork.in/
57. Omnivore Partners: https://www.omnivore.vc/
58. Orios Venture Partners: https://www.oriosvp.com/
59. Parampara: https://paramparas.com/index.html
60. Pentathlon Ventures: https://pentathlon.vc/
61. PointOne Capital: https://pointone.capital/
62. Prime Venture Partners: https://primevp.in/
63. Qualcomm Ventures: https://www.qualcommventures.com/
64. Saama Capital: https://www.linkedin.com/company/saama-capital/
65. Sequoia Capital India: https://www.sequoiacap.com/india/
66. SIDBI Venture Capital Limited (SVCL): https://www.sidbiventure.co.in/
67. Social Alpha: https://www.socialalpha.org/
68. SoftBank Group: https://group.softbank/
69. StartupXseed Ventures: https://startupxseed.in/
70. Steadview Capital: https://www.steadview.com/
71. Stellaris Venture Partners: https://www.stellarisvp.com/
72. Tiger Global: https://www.tigerglobal.com/

73. Titan Capital: https://www.titancapital.vc/
74. Trifecta Capital: https://trifectacapital.in/
75. Unicorn India Ventures: http://www.unicornivc.com/
76. Unilazer Ventures: https://www.linkedin.com/company/unilazer-ventures-privatelimited/about/
77. Unitus Ventures: https://unitus.vc/
78. Ventureast: https://www.ventureast.net/
79. Warburg Pincus: https://warburgpincus.com/
80. YourNest: https://yournest.in/
81. Zodius Capital: https://zodius.com/

Accelerators

1. 500 startups: https://500.co/
2. 9Unicorns: https://www.9unicorns.in/
3. AIM Smart City Accelerator: http://www.aimsmartcity.com/
4. Amplifi: https://www.amplifi.asia/
5. Aspire Labs: https://www.aspirelabs.com/
6. Aurum Ventures: https://www.aurumventures.in/index.html
7. Brigade Real Estate Accelerator Program (REAP): https://www.brigadereap.com
8. BW Accelerate: http://bwaccelerate.businessworld.in/
9. Cisco Launchpad: https://launchpad.cisco.com/#~stickynav=2
10. cKinetics Accelerator: https://www.ckinetics.com/innovation-capitals/#accelerator
11. Cybersecurity Accelerator Program: https://www.indiaaccelerator.co/accelerator/cyber-security/
12. DevX Accel: https://www.devx.work/accel/
13. Edison Accelerator: https://startups.gehc.co/
14. Forge Accelerator: https://www.forgeforward.in/
15. GHV Accelerator: https://www.ghvaccelerator.com/
16. Ginserv: https://www.ginserv.in/
17. GSF: https://gsfindia.com/index.html

18. HealthStart: https://healthstart.co.in/
19. Huddle: https://huddle.work/
20. Humane Entrepreneurship Program: https://humaneentrepreneurs.org/
21. India Accelerator: https://www.indiaaccelerator.co/
22. Jaarvis Accelerator: https://jaarvisaccelerator.com/
23. JioGenNext: https://www.jiogennext.com/
24. Maruti Suzuki MAIL: https://www.marutisuzukimail.com/
25. Marwari Catalysts: http://www.marwaricatalysts.com/
26. NetApp Excellerator: https://startup.netapp.in/
27. PadUp Ventures: https://www.padup.in/
28. PVC Partners Accelerateam: http://pvcpartners.com/
29. Rebalance: http://therebalance.com/
30. SIGMA: https://zinnov.com/sigma-accelerator/
31. Sparknext: http://www.sparknext.com/
32. Starfleet: https://aeternitystarfleet.com/
33. Startup 360: https://www.startup360.in/
34. Startup Accelerator Chamber of Commerce: http://www.saccindia.org/india/
35. Startup Accelerator India: https://www.startupacceleratorindia.in/
36. Startup Oasis: https://www.startupoasis.in/
37. Supply Chain Labs: https://supplychainlabs.in/
38. Target Accelerator: https://targetaccelerators.com/
39. TechStars: https://www.techstars.com/accelerators
40. The GAIN: https://thegain.in/
41. TLabs Accelerator Program: http://www.tlabs.in/
42. UIncept: https://www.uincept.com/
43. Xelerate: https://www.srix.in/Xelerate/index.php
44. YCombinator: https://www.ycombinator.com/

Incubators

1. 10,000 Startups: https://10000startups.com/
2. 3i Zone: https://3izone.com
3. 91Springboard: https://www.91springboard.com/
4. AIC NMIMS: https://aic.nmims.edu/investor-connect-program/
5. Amity Innovation Incubator: https://www.amity.edu/aii/
6. Arise: http://ztmbpd.iari.res.in/?q=content/arise
7. BetOnIndia Technology: https://betonindia.in/
8. BITS Pilani Technology Business Incubator: https://www.bitspilani.ac.in/pilani/technologybusiness/TechnologyBusinessIncubator
9. CIE at IIIT Hyderabad: https://cie.iiit.ac.in/
10. CIIE- IIM Ahmedabad: https://ciie.co/#page1
11. Cisco thingQbator: https://thingqbator.nasscomfoundation.org/#
12. Create: https://www.icreate.org.in/
13. DERBI Foundation: https://derbifoundation.com/
14. Electropreneur Park: https://electropreneurpark.in/
15. IIM Calcutta Innovation Park: https://iimcip.org/
16. IIT Mandi Catalyst: https://www.iitmandicatalyst.in/
17. IITM Incubation Cell: http://www.incubation.iitm.ac.in/home
18. ISB DLabs: https://www.isbdlabs.org/en.html
19. JSS Step: https://www.jssstepnoida.org/
20. LIVE - IIM Kozhikode: https://www.iimklive.org/
21. MN iHub: https://mn-ihub.com/
22. NutriHub: https://nutrihub-tbi-iimr.org/
23. Purple Ventures: https://www.purpleventures.co.in/
24. Rainmatter: https://rainmatter.com/
25. Riidl: https://www.riidl.org/
26. SIIC - IIT Kanpur: http://www.siicincubator.com/
27. SINE - IIT Bombay: https://www.sineiitb.org/

28. Social Alpha: https://www.socialalpha.org/
29. Sonoma Management Partners: http://www.smpequity.com/index.html
30. SR Innovation: https://www.srix.in/index.php
31. Startup Karnataka: https://startup.karnataka.gov.in/
32. TBI - Amrita Vishwa Vidyapeetham: https://www.amritatbi.com/
33. TIDES - IIT Roorkee: http://tides.iitr.ac.in/
34. TotalStart: http://www.totalstart.org/
35. TurningIdeas: https://turningideas.com/
36. Venture Center: https://mobile.venturecenter.co.in/
37. Venture Studio - Ahmedabad University: https://ahduni.edu.in/academics/schoolscentres/venturestudio/
38. Villgro: https://villgro.org/
39. VIT Technology Business Incubator: https://www.linkedin.com/in/vit-technologybusiness-incubator-2a17b4200/
40. We Hub: https://wehub.telangana.gov.in/
41. Xelpmoc: https://www.xelpmoc.in/startup

16. Fundraising Paperwork & Compliance

16.1 The Co-Founders' Agreement (prepared by University of Pennsylvania) https://tinyurl.com/co-founder-agreement

16.2 Vendor Agreement https://www.pandadoc.com/vendor-agreement-template

16.3 Customer Agreement https://www.pandadoc.com/service-contract-template/

16.4 Employment Agreement https://tinyurl.com/employment-agr This format of the Employment Agreement is also available on the Startup India and LetsVenture websites.

17. Due Diligence

17.1 Financial Due Diligence

S. No:	Information Request List
A	**GENERAL INFORMATION**
1	Business Presentation
2	Description / details on the following (if not covered in as much detail as part of Business Presentation mentioned above):
	a. Detailed description of the business model of the Company including business verticals of the past and present and verticals that the Company plans to cater to in the near future post investment.
	b. Revenue Streams (past, current and future revenue streams, include description of all revenue streams to be captured)
	c. Areas of Focus – Target Customer types (include segmentation undertaken based on size, needs or other criteria)
	d. Detailed description of the product offerings provided, including breakup of margin % earned on each product offered
	e. provide a list of all existing and under development products and services & its versions, along-with timelines.
	f. List of large / key customers (cumulatively accounting for at least 50% of current revenues) and their product usage patterns (over the past 12 months). If the Company is consumer / user based company, please provide details of user data (e.g. DAU, MAU, No of registered users, CAC, user churn etc)
	g. List of Key Vendors and Partners and a brief on transactions with these parties
	h. List of Competitors in India and globally
	i. Description or copy of company's purchasing policy, credit policy
	j. All surveys and market research reports, done by the company (For E.g. Weblinks of articles and press releases etc)
	k. Key areas that the Company faces challenges in when running and growing the business and the action plan to address these.
B	**BASIC REGISTRATION/OTHER SPECIFIC DOCUMENTS**
1	Certificate of Incorporation, MOA and AOA.

2	Copy of PAN, TAN, Registration CertificatesofVAT, Service Tax, GST, Excise, PF, ESIC, PT, Shop and Establishments for all premises used, IEC code, and any other registration certificate as applicable to the company
3	Descriptive list of all significant acquisitions, restructurings, reorganizations, spin-offs and other transactions (intercompany or otherwise) not in the ordinary course of business which have occurred in the Company history.
4	Copies of any letter rulings, non-privileged tax opinions obtained for all such transactions.
C	**FINANCIAL STATEMENTS/REPORTS & MIS INFORMATION**
1	Signed Audited Financial statements along with, annexures, notes to accounts, trial balance, audit reports, CARO report, cash flow statements and any other report that forms part of the annual financial statements for Target Company for the Historical Period (from Inception till last financial year for which audit has been completed).
	Unaudited financials for that part of the Historical period where audit is not complete.
2	Accounting Data for the Historical Period that matches the audited and unaudited financials as provided above. (Tally Backup / Quickbooks login / Xero.com Login or any other accounting software used for the historical period)
3	Internal Audit Reports (if any)
4	Management letters issued by the auditors during the historical period
5	Transfer Pricing - Provide copy of Form 3CEB filed, Transfer Pricing Study Report, Inter-Company agreeements, Arms Length Pricing workings, if any.
6	MIS prepared, key KPI's for the Historical Period. (Customer Acquisition cost, Life Time Value, Productwise bifurcation, No of bookings and customers, Average cost etc). Where for any reason MIS and financial accounting data do not match, please provide reconciliation statements.
D	**PROFIT AND LOSS ACCOUNT**
D1	**Revenues**
1	Detailed monthly revenue trend of the Historical Period for each revenue line along with key drivers of revenue.
2	a . Commercial contracts / agreements that are linked to revenue (one time or recurring).
	b. Qualitative and quantitative revenue data which should include but need not be limited to areas such as:
	Revenue breakup based on contract length
	One time revenue and recurring revenue
	Repeat customer revenue and new customer revenue

	Geographical split
	Domestic Vs International
	c.Provide Sample invoice raised and major contracts by the company on various parties, provide different bills having different components/ services which are provided by the company. Note on the process of billing and computation of commission income on a sample basis
3	Details of customer benefit policies impacting the revenue of the Company, i.e. special discounts, any other terms / conditions
D2	**Employee Cost & Other Related Details**
	a. Salary register containing details of all salaries paid for employees in the historical period. The salary register should have all details like salary breakup in components (Basic, DA, Allowances), PT, TDS, Reimbursements amongst others. The details should match with the accounting records of the Company.
	Please provide sample copies of appointment letter, employment agreements, non - compete agreement, details of bonus, incentives,performance matrixfor sample employees
	b. Details list of Employees who were/are invloved in the product development and provide copies of Confidential Information & Invention Assignment Agreements entered with them.
	c. Copies of Employee Innovation & Proprietary Information Assignment Agreements, if any.
	d. Details of contract labour (payment, aggregate workers, compliance to any law, deployment). (if,any)
	e. Details of compensation and ESOPs to the promoters and key management team.
	f. Salary advance policy if any
	g.Org chart indicating breakdown of employees by key departments/teams
	h. Indication ofdepartments/teams where additional employees will be hired in the coming few months, and the nature of talent being hired
D3	**Rent**
	a. Details of offices along with rent / lease agreements, purpose of office i.e. Registered Office / Corporate Office / Branch / Sales Office
	b. Details of operating leases and finance leases entered into by the entity in the historical period with details of leased property, area, lease rentals, lease period and lease escalation and termination clauses.
D4	**Professional fees**
	a. A List of law firms, accounting firms, consulting firms and similar professionals or experts engaged by the company detailing service availed and amount paid for it along with contracts where executed

	b. Invoices for the sample cases
D5	**Marketing / Business promotion Expenses**
	a. Monthly trend in marketing costs along with description on how marketing costs are helping in acquisition of customers
	b. Breakdown of sales expenditure (between customer acquisition & customer support) on a monthly basis, for the last 12 months
	c. Breakdown of customer onboarding costs incurred on a monthly basis, for the last 12 months
	d. Marketing expense budget of the company. Also to provide budget v/s actuals for the same.
D6	**Technology cost & IPR documents**
	Details of technology costs incurred by the company during the historical period, including
	a. Cost of equipment, servers, service contracts etc.
	b. Cost of building up of App and website / domain
	c. Cost of web storage space / online tools used
	d. Details on Intellectual Property developed by the Company /Founders/Key Employees and documents pertaining to registration of Intellectual Property
D7	**Other expenses**
	a. Details of customer compensations / claims paid and disputed during the historical period, if any; include all instances of rebates/discounts given due to product downtime or support issues.
	b. Discount policy of the company for bulk orders
	c. Details of exceptional, prior period or non-recurring items of income and expenditure.
	d. Invoices for the sample cases
	e. Any other agreements with vendors (i.e. payment gateways, marketing agencies, bankers, investors, etc)
E	**BALANCE SHEET**
E1	**Fixed assets**
	a. Fixed asset register as on 31st march [PY] and till date
	b. Listing of assets (property and equipment) acquired on lease and lease agreements. Note on lease accounting.
	c. Details of charges or lien created against any fixed assets through guarantees or loan arrangements.

	d. Details of any intangible assets(also inhouse development expenses) and any expenses capitalized during the historical period
E2	**Receivables and advances**
	a. Details of Debtors/advances given, ageing of accounts and expected realisation and details internal system follow up. Confirmations for over and above Rs.1lakhs
	b. Details of Advances/ Deposits given, Description/ Nature of the advances given for.
	c. Details of Bad debts or provision for bad debts
	d. Details of credit period given to debtors
E3	**Cash and bank**
	a. Details of all the bank accounts, bank statements (in PDF only/ authorized by bank) till date. Bank loan statements and sanction letters, if any
	b. Details of Bank overdraft/ Term loans and Term deposits in tabulated form having date of deposit and maturity, interest etc.
	c. Monthly bank reconcilation statement for all the banks.
	d. Credit card statement and credit policy
	e. Details of any type of prepaid (e.g. Happay)/corporate credit cards, issued to employees.
E4	**Current liabilities and provisions**
	a. Details of Creditors/advances taken, ageing of accounts and expected realisation and details internal system follow up.Confirmations for over and above Rs.1lakhs
	b. Details of Deposit received from Customers/ parties. Nature of the same.
	c. Details of leave pay and retirement benefit accruals.(provide actuary report for gratuity,if any)
	d. Any other payables or Outstanding govt. dues
E5	**Borrowings and debts**
	a. Schedule of borrowings (secured and unsecured) segregated into short term and long term debt indicating lender, limit, drawdown to date, repayment terms, interest rates, security etc. Details of default in repayment of loans and interest, if any.
	b. Copies of loan agreements / santion letters
	c. Repayment schedules, as currently applicable for each of the loan account indicating principal and interest details.

	d. Computation of provision for interest as for outstanding loans as at [.]
	e. Purpose for which loan is taken and utilized.
E6	**Investments**
	a. Details of Investment other than Term deposits/any other liquid funds,made by company
	b. Balance confirmations statements for the above.
	c.Reconciliation of amount appearing in balance confirmation with books of accounts in terms of amounts recognisedas income and asset (ledgerwise) .
E7	**Related party transactions**
	a. A list of related and affiliated entities, specifying the extent and nature of the relationship with such entities and their management.
	b. Provide details of transactions with each related party during the financial year
	c. Details of any exposures on account of related parties like guarantees, asset security etc, if any.
	d. Details of past dues ofrelated party written offby thecompany,if any.
E8	**Shareholding of the Company /Sister Concerns/ etc & Shareholders Agreements (including related documents).**
	a. Details of shareholding at the time of inception, current shareholding pattern and post investment shareholding
	b. Investment Agreements executed by the Company since inception, Share Purchase Agreements, Valuation Report, FCGPR & FCTRS filed, if any.
	c. List of Sister concerns /holding and subsidiaries along with ROC Master data
	d. ESOP policy/ trust, and list of ESOPs given to employees granting date, vesting period in tabulated form
F	**TAXES**
F1	**Direct Taxes**
	a. Computation for PY and current Year, income tax returns & acknowledgements and notices received from income tax depts, if any
	b. 26AS form for the past three years
	c. Details of TDS deducted and paid. (i) Acknowledgments copies of TDS returns, (ii) challans (iii) workings for all the quarters, (iv) reconcilaition with the books of accounts and (v) notices recieved from the dept., if any
	d. Deferred tax workings , MAT workings, Amt workings for the previous audited financial year, if any
	e. Tax Audit reports for period of review

	f. 15CA/ CB forms for non domestic transactions
	g. Equalization levy (payment fo 6% taxes on advertisement above Rs. 1,00,000 in non domestic transactions)
	Details of parties and amount paid, workings and challans
	h.Annual returns/ SFT's filed by company.
F2	**Indirect Taxes**
	a. VAT
	Details of (i) vat workings, (ii) vat returns, (iii) challans (iv) reconciliation with books of accounts and (v) notices received from dept, if any
	b. Service tax
	Details of (i) Service tax workings, (ii) Service tax returns, (iii) challans (iv) reconciliation with books of accounts and (v) notices received from dept, if any
	c. Goods and Service Tax (GST)
	Details of (i) GST workings, (ii) GST returns, (iii) challans (iv) reconciliation with books of accounts and (v) notices received from dept, if any
F3	**Labour Law Compliances**
	a. ESIC (applicable on if more than 10 employees and having wages less than Rs. 21,000/-)
	Details of (i) ESIC workings, (ii) ESICregisters and returns, (iii) challans (iv) reconciliation with books of accounts and (v) notices received from dept, if any
	b. PF (applicable if20 or more employees drawing salary less than Rs. 15,000)
	Details of (i) PFworkings, (ii) PFregisters and returns, (iii) challans (iv) reconciliation with books of accounts and (v) notices received from dept, if any
	c. PT (applicable for all the employees inclusing director and company- state wise applicability)
	Details of (i) PT workings, (ii) PT registers and returns, (iii) challans (iv) reconciliation with books of accounts and (v) notices received from dept, if any
	d. Payment of Bonus Act (applicable if20 or more employees drawing salary less than Rs. 21,000)
	Details of (i) Bonus workings, (ii) Bonus registers, forms and returns, (iii) Any exemption enjoyed by the Company and (v) notices received from dept, if any

17.2 Legal Due Diligence

S. No:	Information Request List
A	GENERAL INFORMATION
1	The Company's certificate of incorporation, including any amendments.
2	Business location (s) :- Details regarding registered office, principal office, branch office(s), other office(s), factories, etc. (Form INC-22):
	a) Address and mailing address, if any
	b) Contact No.
	c) Contact email id.
	d) Website
3	List of all the products and services manufactured/distributed/offered by the Company.
4	A copy of the letter head of the Company.
5	A copy of latest captalisation table of the Company.
7	Name and address of the company secretary of the Company, if any. If there is no company secretary as on date, then the person performing the functions of the company secretary.
8	Name and address of the statutory auditors (and internal auditors) of the Company. (e-form ADT-1)
9	Copies of the up to date Memorandum of Association and Articles of Association of the Company.
10	A certified copy of the statutory registers maintained under the Companies Act, 2013 or other similar corporate documents of the overseas subsidiaries of the Company, if any.
11	All agreements, memoranda, and any other documents pertaining to any bankruptcy or reorganization proceedings with which the Company has been involved.
12	Information pertaining to all related party transaction with details as regarding:
	a) Quantum of the transaction;
	b) Pricing and justification of arm's length pricing;
	c) Shareholders/ affiliates of the related parties;
	d) Business of related parties.
	e) Nature of the service provided or nature of transactions undertaken
	f) Necessary copies of the resolutions
13	All filings made with the Registrar of Companies from incorporation along with their challans.
14	List of all authorization and power of attorney with all Directors.
15	A statement whether any shares of the Company are held beneficially.

B	SHARE CAPITAL & MANAGEMENT
B1	SHARE CAPITAL
1	A statement indicating the authorized, issued, subscribed and paid up share capital, classes of shares of the Company including modifications therein since incorporation, and details of securities issued for consideration other than cash along with copies of the resolutions.
2	Copies of documents (if any) or information regarding verbal agreements/understanding of any agreement or commitment to create, issue or transfer shares/ conversion of loan into equity. Shareholders / share subscription/ share purchase agreements.
3	A schedule of the holders of the Company's stock options, including the number of options held by each holder and description of terms of options, including any agreement thereof.
4	All agreements relating to any liens or encumbrances on shares of the Company's capital stock.
5	Any agreement, contract, commitment or other arrangement that may affect the Company's ability to issue new shares, bonds or other securities.
6	In respect of each series of preference shares, the names of and the number of shares held by each preference shareholder, category of preference shares (i.e. cumulative / non-cumulative, convertible / non-convertible).
7	Details of shares encumbered, creation of charges, liens and pledged by the promoters and related party shareholder entities and copies of agreements relating thereto.
8	Details of all convertible / non-convertible / partially convertible debentures as on the last record date.
9	Details of all transactions between the Company and its founders and directors (including all persons in whom founders and directors are interested) and supporting documents relating thereto, if any.
10	Details of dividends declared and paid by the Company since incorporation.
11	Details of any security interest created on or underlying any Company's shares or debentures.
12	In case of an acquisition of shares, copies of the share certificates and in the event the shares are in demat form, copies of the demat account statement. Please also provide us with copies of the board and shareholder resolutions in relation to all share allotments (rights issues or private placements), all RoC filings in relation to all share allotments and copies of all share transfer forms received by the Company along with copies of the board resolutions approving all such transfers.
13	Audited financial statements of the Company since incorporation (including notes to accounts), including all documents relating to any prior, pending or threatened audit, investigation or inspection of the Company or its respective officers or directors involving the operations of the Company.

14	Unaudited financial statements for the current financial year with notes to accounts.
B2	**DIRECTORS & ADMINISTRATION**
1	Minutes or other records of all meetings or actions of the board of directors, any board committees and general meeting (AGM/EGM) of the Company or subsidiary since incorporation including notice of holding the meeting along with detailed agenda and shorter consent letters from directors/ shareholders, if any.
2	A list of directors (identifying the chairman, managing director, independent directors and whether they are executive/non-executive) of the Company other directorships and business interests, annual remuneration, percentage of shareholding in the Company or any associated Company(ies), date of appointment and the date of retirement, if applicable. (Form DIR-12, MR-1 and Form MBP-1 along with notice of declaration in Form DIR-8 under Section 184 (1) of the Companies Act, 2013).
3	A complete list of copies of any personal guarantees, indemnifications furnished by the directors on behalf of the Company and vice versa.
4	A complete list of directors of the Company having any service agreement(s) with the Company. Please provide copies of the service agreements. In the absence of any service agreements please provide complete details of the terms and conditions applicable to their employment, including remuneration and other emoluments payable to them, if any. Please provide us with copies of the resolutions passed by the Company approving the terms and conditions of engagement of each of the directors.
5	A list of loans along with copies of loan agreements, if any, granted to any of the directors by the Company, including all loan, shareholder and repurchase agreements made for the benefit of any officer, shareholder or employee of the Company. A list of loans and advances along with copies of underlying agreements, if any, granted to the Company by any of its directors.
C	**PERSONNEL**
1	Copies of the standard appointment letters issued in respect of each category of employees and all employment agreements with employees.
2	Employee handbook or similar documents describing the Company's policies and practices.
3	Employee benefit plans and arrangements, including bonus plans, retirement plans, pension plans, deferred compensation plans, profit sharing plans, employee stock option plans and management incentive agreements.
4	Details of consultants hired by the Company, and copies of the relevant consultancy agreements.

5	Full details of all confidentiality agreements entered into between the Company and its directors and employees, together with copies of such agreements.
6	Please provide us with a copy of the standing orders of the Company, if any.
7	List of all employees, detailing date of hire, annual compensation and incentive compensation potential, and specifically identifying key employees.
D	**ASSETS**
D1	**IMMOVABLE PROPERTY**
1	A list of all immovable/ real property owned, leased, occupied and/or used by the Company, indicating against each property the manner in which it is held by the Company (i.e. ownership/ freehold, lease, license or otherwise) and the purpose for which it is used by the Company along with complete copies of all title deeds and other instruments under which the Company owns, leases, occupies and/or uses such immovable/ real properties. Please also provide copies of documentary evidence of registration of the title deeds in relation to each of the real/ immovable property owned, leased, occupied and/or used by the Company, with the relevant Sub-Registrar of Assurances.
2	Complete particulars of all mortgages and/ or other charges on each real/ immovable property owned, leased, occupied and/or used by the Company, and copies of all agreements/ instruments evidencing or relating to the creation and/ or satisfaction of each such mortgage and/ or other charge, along with any forms files in relation thereto.
3	Copies of all agreements executed by the Company for use of its key premises, factories, storage facilities and other locations.
4	Please confirm that all necessary licenses and consents relating to the use and occupation by the Company of each of the real/ immovable property owned, leased, occupied and/or used by it, have been obtained and are in full force. Please provide copies of the same.
D2	**MOVABLE PROPERTY**
1	Complete particulars of all charges on the movable property owned, leased and/ or used by the Company, and copies of all agreements/ instruments evidencing or relating to the creation and/ or satisfaction of each such charge, including related e-forms (CHG 1 and CHG 4).
2	Copies of all agreements and instruments under or pursuant to which any movable property is owned, leased and/ or used by the Company, including any lease agreements, lease financing arrangements, etc.
D3	**INTELLECTUAL PROPERTY**

1	List of all registered and unregistered (including applications in process) intellectual property rights, including all trademarks, service marks, trade names, copyrights and other system and intangible rights owned or which belong to the Company. Please provide documents in support of registration of intellectual property rights in case they are registered. Details and copies of applications filed abroad regarding such intellectual property right ownership, license or other usage, if any.
2	Details of domain names owned / used by the Company and their registration, if any.
3	Any licenses or other agreements with respect to the proprietary rights of the Company or third parties, except for licenses or agreements pertaining to "off-the-shelf" or standard products of third parties including software used by the Company
4	A list of any employees or consultants who have not signed proprietary information and invention agreements, including a list of any periods of time when employees or consultants performed services for the Company while not bound by such agreements.
5	Details of any litigation in relation to intellectual property being used by the Company. Also, a statement indicating where there are any third party intellectual property rights which might be infringed by the operations of the Company. If yes, complete details thereof.
E	**LOANS AND BORROWINGS**
1	Documents and agreements evidencing borrowings or available borrowings, whether secured or unsecured, or other financing arrangements, including loan and credit agreements, promissory notes lines of credit, financial leasing and other financing arrangements of the Company and any guarantees of any of the above.
2	A statement of the outstanding loans (including secured and unsecured), debt instruments, debentures (including secured and unsecured), rates of interest, affirmative and negative covenants in the loan agreements and conditions.
3	Any borrowings from the shareholders/Directors. If yes, please provide details?
4	Any guarantees of third-party obligations, related to the Company or otherwise.
5	Details of any encumbrances, charges, liens and pledges created on the shares held by the founders.
F	**REGULATORY COMPLIANCES**

1	Statutory registers maintained by the Company under all applicable labour laws and enactments, together with a complete list of the same. The address where the statutory registers, records and books of the Company are kept. Please also confirm that the Company maintains all the statutory registers required to be by it under various applicable labour laws and enactments, including under local state legislations.
2	Copies of the registration certificates obtained by the Company under the Employees' Provident Fund and Miscellaneous Provisions Act, 1952, Employees State Insurance Act, 1948, Contract Labour (Regulation and Abolition) Act, 1970, and other labour related legislation as applicable.
3	Please provide us with a copy of the sexual harassment policy adopted by the Company under the Sexual Harassment of Women at Workplace (Prevention, Prohibition and Redressal) Act, 2013. Please confirm if the Company has set up a committee under the said act.
4	Please share the details of reasonable security measures adopted by the Company for the purpose of safeguarding the sensitive and personal data and information being collected from the service providers through its website as per Information Technology Act, 2000 read with Information Technology (Reasonable Security Practices and Procedures and Sensitive Personal Data or Information) Rules, 2011.Also, Please share the executed copy of information security policy and programme as adopted, if any.
5	A statement confirming that all filings (periodic or otherwise) have been made with all regulatory authorities within the specified timelines. Please provide details of any non-compliances/ defaults reported in this regard. Please also provide us with copies of all approvals obtained and all filings made with the RBI (if applicable), including in respect of any foreign investments received by the Company and/ or any overseas investments made by the Company.
G	**OPERATIONS**
1	Agreements or contracts material to the business of the Company, including contracts with key clients.
2	Agreements with major or critical suppliers, collaborators or subcontractors.
H	**INSURANCE**
1	A schedule of all insurance coverage procured by the Company for its employees, directors, contractors or its assets (including intellectual property rights) and business, together with copies of all such policies.
I	**LITIGATION**

1	Particulars of and supporting documentation pertaining to the following nature of litigation or disputes to which the Company or any of its directors are a party:
	(a) Infringement of intellectual property rights and any commercial dispute
	(b) Dispute by the Company or against the Company and any of its officers, directors, employees, consultants, clients, customers and any other stakeholders
J	**MISCELLEANOUS**
1	A schedule of all payments made by the Company to Indian or foreign governments or officials of Indian or foreign governments or any vendor for availaing the Services
2	Copies of all other registrations, license, approvals and permits obtained by the Company during the course of its business.

Sources

Preface

Avnish Bajaj, "Character traits important for founders and investors to possess", Matrix Partners: https://www.matrixpartners.in/matrixmoments/character-traits-important-for-founders-and-investors-to-possess

1. Taking the Idea to MVP through a GTM

1. companiesmarketcap.com, "Market capitalization of Fitbit (FIT)": https://companiesmarketcap.com/fitbit/marketcap/
2. Kunal Shah, Tech Sparks 2016 event by YourStory - https://www.youtube.com/watch?v=76eNxRSyOyE
3. Andrew Chen, The Cold Start Problem
4. Andrew Chen, The Cold Start Problem
5. Kunal Shah, The Knowledge Project with Shane Parrish - https://www.youtube.com/watch?v=nl1PIagzgUo&t=4631s
6. Kunal Shah, The Knowledge Project with Shane Parrish - https://www.youtube.com/watch?v=nl1PIagzgUo&t=4631s
7. The Economic Times, Nov 24, 2018 - "940 dams, barrages built on Ganga restricting its flow: Environmentalists" : https://economictimes.indiatimes.com/news/politics-and-nation/940-dams-barrages-built-on-ganga-restricting-its-flow-environmentalists/articleshow/66784449.cms
8. Bharat Goenka, on podcast 'The Indian Dream' titled "Building Tally with Bharat Goenka": https://open.spotify.com/epi-

sode/1FqfCpaG8ewFg61VisxHhE?si=nSLAxxIxQtOCZ4NAm-0Wk2g&nd=1

2. Product Market Fit

1. Marc Andreesen, quoted from Andrew Chen's blog titled "When has a consumer startup hit product-market fit?": https://andrewchen.com/zero-to-productmarket-fit-presentation/
2. Marc Andreessen, quoted by Michael Seibel on Y Combinator's blog titled "The real product market fit": https://www.ycombinator.com/library/5z-the-real-product-market-fit
3. Andrew Chen - https://andrewchen.com/zero-to-productmarket-fit-presentation/
4. Anu Hariharan, on Y Combinator's session titled "Nine Business Models and the Metrics Investors Want (SUS 2019)": https://www.ycombinator.com/library/8E-nine-business-models-and-the-metrics-investors-want-sus-2019
5. Startuptalky, "The Success Story of FirstCry, the Largest Online Store for Baby and Kid Products!" - https://startuptalky.com/firstcry-success-story/#firstcry_HowwasFirstCryStarted
6. Startuptalky, https://startuptalky.com/ashok-soota-story/#:~:text="Entrepreneurship Simplified. "-,Ashok Soota- Professional Life,million run-rate in 1999
7. MindTree, "Mindtree Reports Strong Q4 And Full Year Performance In FY22": https://www.mindtree.com/about/news/mindtree-reports-strong-q4-and-full-year-performance-fy22

3. Getting Your First Users/Customers

1. thehardcopy.co, "Marching to a Different Beat" - https://thehardcopy.co/marching-to-a-different-beat/

5. Understanding Financial Ratios and Accounting Statements

1. Zerodha, "Understanding the P&L Statement (Part 1)" on Zerodha Varsity: https://zerodha.com/varsity/chapter/understanding-pl-statement-part1/
2. Wings of Fire, SRCC: https://www.quora.com/What-are-the-new-format-and-old-format-of-balance-sheet

6. Setting Yourself Up - Co-founders & Advisors

1. Ali Tamaseb, "Land of the super founders - a data driven approach to uncover the secrets of billion dollar startups" on Medium: https://alitamaseb.medium.com/land-of-the-super-founders-a-data-driven-approach-to-uncover-the-secrets-of-billion-dollar-a69ebe3f0f45
2. Haje Jan Kamps, "Breaking a myth: Data shows you don't actually need a co-founder" on Techcrunch: https://techcrunch.com/2016/08/26/co-founders-optional/
3. Rizwan Virk, Startup Myths and Models - What You Won't Learn in Business School

7. Understanding Employee Stock Options (ESOPs)

1. Business Today, "Meesho's MeeSOPs: Employees can convert 25% of salary to ESOPs": https://www.businesstoday.in/entrepreneurship/news/story/meeshos-meesops-employees-can-convert-25-of-salary-to-esops-315049-2021-12-10

8. Sources of Finance

1. Livemint, "Aditya Birla Fashion to acquire 51% stake in designer brand Sabyasachi": https://www.livemint.com/companies/news/aditya-birla-fashion-to-acquire-51-in-designer-brand-sabyasachi-11611759486851.html

9. Valuations - What is your startup really worth?

1. Indiatimes.com, "Google-backed Neobank Open Becomes 100th Unicorn Of India, 14th Startup To Join Unicorn Club This Year": https://www.indiatimes.com/worth/news/neobank-open-becomes-100th-unicorn-of-india-568547.html
2. Aswath Damodaran, "User and Subscriber Economics/Value: A User-Based Valuation of Uber" on YouTube: https://www.youtube.com/watch?v=hA3Dgx4ovGM&t=435s
3. Alexander Jarvis, "How do you value your social media startup with investors?": https://www.alexanderjarvis.com/value-social-media-startup-investors/
4. Inc42, "Indian Tech Startup Funding Report 2021": https://inc42.com/reports/indian-tech-startup-funding-report-2021/
5. Moneycontrol, "Zomato IPO listing | Food delivery giant makes

a stellar debut with nearly 66% premium, at Rs 125.85": https://www.moneycontrol.com/news/business/ipo/zomato-ipo-listing-food-delivery-giant-crosses-rs-1-lakh-crore-m-cap-after-stellar-debut-with-nearly-53-premium-7210471.html

6. Moneycontrol, "CarTrade IPO shares debut at Rs 1,600, a 1.1% discount to issue price": https://www.moneycontrol.com/news/business/ipo/cartradc-ipo-shares-debut-at-rs-1600-a-1-1-discount-to-issue-price-7363151.html
7. Business Standard, "Nykaa lists at 79% premium to issue price; market cap crosses Rs 1 trillion": https://www.business-standard.com/article/markets/nykaa-lists-at-79-premium-over-issue-price-market-cap-cross-rs-1-trillion-121111000260_1.html
8. Economic Times, "PayTM shares hit lower circuit on debut after biggest Indian IPO": https://economictimes.indiatimes.com/tech/startups/paytm-shares-plunge-13-61-below-ipo-price-on-listing-market-cap-at-rs-1-20-lakh-crore/articleshow/87772234.cms
9. Economic Times, "Cred funding: Cred raises $80 million funding led by GIC at $6.4 billion valuation": https://economictimes.indiatimes.com/tech/funding/cred-raises-80-million-funding-led-by-gic-at-6-4-billion-valuation/articleshow/92111072.cms

10. Creating a Pitch Deck

1. Sequoia Capital, as available on slideshare.net: https://www.slideshare.net/PitchDeckCoach/sequoia-capital-pitchdecktemplate
2. Accel Partner, as available on slideshare.net: https://www.slideshare.net/prayanks/accel-partners-india-sample-pitch-deck
3. Piktochart, credit to the respective companies who made the pitch decks: https://piktochart.com/blog/startup-pitch-decks-what-you-can-learn/
4. Karan Bajaj, "How to Write a Successful Startup Pitch Deck: 12 Slides that Matter (+Top 5 Indian Venture Capitalists to pitch)": https://www.karanbajaj.com/how-to-write-a-successful-startup-pitch-deck-12-slides-that-matter/
5. Copy.ai, pitch deck shared on vip.graphics: https://vip.graphics/copy-ai-pitch-deck/

6. Competition table - https://www.dreamit.com/journal/pitch-deck-competition-slide
7. SET India, Shark Tank India: https://www.youtube.com/watch?v=vqcLhrteu6M
8. Andy Raskin, "Want a better pitch. Watch this." on Medium: https://medium.com/firm-narrative/want-a-better-pitch-watch-this-328b95c2fd0b

12. Fundraising Instruments & Mechanics

1. The Economic Times, "Altf coworking to introduce consumer stock options for clients": https://economictimes.indiatimes.com/tech/tech-bytes/altf-coworking-to-introduce-consumer-stock-options-for-clients/articleshow/85652309.cms?from=mdr

13. Reaching out to Investors

1. Wikipedia, "Shark Tank India (season 1)": https://en.wikipedia.org/wiki/Shark_Tank_India_(season_1)
2. Allie Janoch, "How I Turned A Cold Email Into A $2.5M Seed Round" on Medium: https://medium.com/@alliehoch-janoch/how-i-turned-a-cold-email-into-a-2-5m-seed-round-c33bd80f5590
3. Alexander Jarvis, "Writing a cold email template for venture capital investors": https://www.alexanderjarvis.com/writing-a-cold-email-template-for-venture-capital-investors/
4. Karan Bajaj, "How to raise startup funding with no product": https://www.karanbajaj.com/how-to-raise-startup-funding-with-no-product/
5. Brian Chesky, "& Rejections" on Medium: https://medium.com/@bchesky/7-rejections-7d894cbaa084

15. Understanding & Negotiating a Term Sheet

1. LetsVenture, as available on Startup India website: https://www.startupindia.gov.in/content/dam/invest-india/Templates/public/Tools_templates/internal_templates/Lets_Venture/TERM_SHEET_EQUITY.pdf

17. Due Diligene

1. TMS, "Technical Due Diligence: Make No Mistakes – Follow

These 9 Key Elements": https://tms-outsource.com/blog/posts/technical-due-diligence/

2. Sergey Kubrak, "Technical Due Diligence: Meaning, Process and Checklist": https://djangostars.com/blog/tech-due-diligence/
3. The Economic Times, "US jury finds Theranos founder Elizabeth Holmes guilty in fraud trial": https://economictimes.indiatimes.com/tech/tech-bytes/us-jury-finds-theranos-founder-elizabeth-holmes-guilty-in-fraud-trial/articleshow/88678829.cms

About the Author

Sarthak Ahuja has over a decade of experience in startup advisory. He is a Chartered Accountant and a Gold Medalist from the Indian School of Business.

As an investment banker, he's worked with companies in SaaS, e-Commerce, and D2C, in industries such as FinTech, EdTech, Gaming, Healthcare, and F&B, among others. He's also an Executive Coach and a faculty of M&A at top-tier business schools in India.

He creates educational content for the founder community on his social media platforms with a combined following of over 1.8 million as of March 2024.

He has also authored *Founder's Office*, a collection of 150+ impactful lessons for entrepreneurs and business leaders.

You can follow him on LinkedIn and on his Instagram handle @casarthakahuja.

Also by Sarthak Ahuja:

Explore Books by WYZR